FIRST
WHITE FROST

FIRST
WHITE FROST

Native Americans and United Methodism

Homer Noley

ABINGDON
Nashville Tennessee

FIRST WHITE FROST

Copyright © 1991 by Abingdon Press

All rights reserved.

This book is printed on recycled acid-free paper.

Library of Congress Cataloging-in-Publication Data

Noley, Homer, 1932-
    First white frost : Native Americans and United Methodism / Homer
Noley.
        p.   cm.
    Includes bibliographical references and index.
    ISBN 0-687-13051-4 (alk. paper)
        1. Indians of North America—Missions.   2. United Methodist Church
(U.S.)—Missions—History.   3. Indians of North America—History.
4. Indians of North America—Social conditions.   I. Title.
E98.M6N65   1991
266'.76'08997—dc20   91-10312
                                                                          CIP

Excerpts from *History of Methodist Missions*, vols. 1 and 2, by Wade Crawford Barclay, copy-
right © 1949 and 1950 by the Board of Missions and Church Extension of the Methodist
Church, reprinted by permission of the Board of Global Ministries of The United
Methodist Church.

Excerpts from *Documents of United States Indian Policy*, by Francis P. Prucha, © 1975,
reprinted by permission of University of Nebraska Press.

Excerpts from *Indian Removal: The Emigration of the Five Civilized Tribes*, by Grant
Froeman, new edition copyright © 1953, 1972 by the University of Oklahoma Press.
Reprinted by permission.

Excerpts from *The Sand Creek Massacre*, by Stan Hoig, copyright © 1961 by the University of Oklahoma Press, reprinted by permission.

Excerpts from "Indian Missionary, Projects Supported or Aided by the Board of Home
Missions and Church Extension of the Methodist Episcopal Church," 1931, report of the
Board of Home Missions, reprinted by permission of the Board of Global Ministries of The
United Methodist Church.

MANUFACTURED IN THE UNITED STATES OF AMERICA

To my daughters
Lisa, Kimberly, and Miki

P R E F A C E

Historical events that are alienated from their original social and political contexts are often incomprehensible and stimulate questions such as "Why didn't they do this?" or "Why did they do that?" This book is an attempt to see Methodist missions to Native Americans within the milieu of immigrant-Native relations and the broader contexts within which they developed—or at least were attempted.

I wish to thank the General Commission on Archives staff in Madison, New Jersey, for initiating the project and for committing adequate resources in terms of both funds and personnel to help bring this project to its completion.

Also I wish to thank the editorial committee for entrusting me with the task of researching and preparing this book.

I am grateful to the archivists of the Annual Conferences for their help. Several of them took the time to assemble and mail to me packets of material for my use. In addition, local church leaders who have sent materials to me have been very helpful.

I wish to thank Sherry Cook for typing the final draft of the manuscript, for carefully checking my reference notes for accuracy, and for getting this book on its way to the publishers.

I also express my gratitude as a pastor to my two churches for their patience and encouragement: the Grace Memorial United Methodist Church in Independence, Kansas, and the United Methodist Church in Sycamore, Kansas.

Homer Noley
Independence, Kansas

Nitakechi, leader of the Choctaw Southern District, one of the most traditional of the Choctaw leaders, had the sad task of leading the people of his district on the forced march from Mississippi to Indian Territory. He said that three thousand Choctaw men, women, and children "would be ready to start 'the first white frost of October.' "

ACKNOWLEDGMENTS

One of the principal needs of The United Methodist Church has been to recover and make known the history of its racial/ethnic membership.

During the fall, 1984, and winter, 1985, the General Commission on Archives and History of The United Methodist Church sponsored a series of four two-day consultations which brought together historians and leaders from United Methodism's Native American, Asian American, Black, and Hispanic communities. Each of these consultations reviewed and assessed what had been done regarding the history of its constituency and what needed to be done to recover its story. This volume, one of a series of four, is the result. We are confident that it makes a significant contribution to our denomination's history.

The General Commission on Archives and History is grateful to the General Conference, and especially to the General Council on Ministries, for the financial support which has made this and the other volumes possible. We also express our appreciation to the authors and editors whose expert labors now broaden our knowledge of the history of the church and to the United Methodist Publishing House without whose cooperation there

would be no series. A special word of appreciation goes to Rebecca
Marnhout who skillfully copy edited all four volumes.

Present and former members of the General Commission's staff,
Carolyn DeSwarte Gifford, Susan M. Eltscher, and C. Jarrett Gray,
Jr. have made important contributions to this project.

> Major J. Jones, *Chairperson* (*1980-1988*),
> Ethnic Heritage and History Committee
> Charles Yrigoyen, Jr., *General Secretary,*
> General Commission on Archives and History

Native American History Consultation Members

> Josephine W. Migler
> JoAnn Eslinger
> Harry D. Folsom, Secretary
> Russell George
> Linda Johnson, Chairperson
> Pam Lineberger
> Homer Noley

Consultants

> Marvin Abrams
> David R. Adair
> Ben Bushy Head
> Simeon F. Cummings
> Thom White Wolf Fassett
> Robert Pinezaddleby
> Becky Thompson

CONTENTS

THOSE MANLIKE CREATURES IN THE AMERICAS

It is perhaps a small matter of justice that in our times a valid American history, whether secular or ecclesiastical, is impossible without some reflection on the original possessor and cultivator of the continent—the American Indian.

Historians, in a more enlightened contemporary stance, seek a more comprehensive narrative of the events that brought the peoples of this continent to the place where they are. Reginald Horsely comments, "No general American history conference is complete without its 'Indian' session, and even journals short of space have been willing to devote entire issues to Native American subjects."[1] He cites problems in the writing of Native American history that seem obvious enough except in their specific dimension. The problems relate to the credentials of those doing the writing and the integrity of the material.

The basic tools of understanding are held by three people: the Native American scholar, the anthropologist, and the historian. While it may be possible to find a Native American historian or a Native American anthropologist or even a Native American anthropologist who writes history, it is not guaranteed that these conjunctions will result in the production of a satisfactory Native American history. Robert Berkhofer, who has made some important contributions on the subject, says, "American Indian history must move from being primarily a record of white-Indian relations to become the story of Indians in the United States (or North America) over time."[2] He also sees the need for a joint approach to Native American history on the part of Native Americans, anthropologists, and historians.

Cooperation between the historian and the anthropologist is essential, Berkhofer claims, if the goal is to be achieved. Vine Deloria, who doesn't claim to be a historian but whose writings continue to be respected by those seeking usable materials on the subject, implies that the gaps of history may be intriguingly fertile ground for understanding the incomprehensible events in American history:

> Thus, instead of introducing another social science division into the articulation of history, we should really be honest and recognize that, despite all the majesty, power, and sadness that it invokes in us, the story of Chief Joseph has already been done. But what about James J. Hill, his railroad and the Sioux wars? Nothing. That is the failure of contemporary historians. They want popularity and not the truth.[3]

Understanding those incomprehensible events should lead to appropriate reforms in federal policy toward Native peoples.

In addition to the problem of cultural and political selectivity in the development of historical records is the problem of what we might call the disciplinary cradle—the schools that produce the historian and the anthropologist. It is not certain that a Native American trained in white schools employing white instructors and methods will produce results much different, if at all, from those of white persons in the same field. The criteria for fact finding and the methods employed by anthropologists and historians must be tested and reformed. History may be primarily documentary, but it shouldn't be seen as only documentary. Oral tradition has been an important means of preserving evidence of societal presence for many centuries. It should be given a little more weight today. Neither anthropology nor history rests on principles or methods that are absolute, as mathematics does. The choice of a point of reference too often becomes merely the judgment of the scientist or historian. Thus whether a people are civilized or not civilized (as it is thought to be understood today) depends on the judgment call of the person or group making the first diagnosis. Events that follow that judgment are justified by the diagnosis.

Our purpose here will be to discuss the work of Methodism among Native American peoples within the contemporary historical and social context of the people affected. While it is being affirmed more and more that the overall mission of the church among Native Americans has not succeeded, it must be noted that there were successful missions in the various fields of service, and also spectacular failures. A second look at these missionary activities in their historical and social settings may help us understand why some failed and others succeeded, for whatever purpose we need such understanding.

This is not a promotional work, so there will be no attempt to euphemize events in history that affected Native American–immigrant relations. Attempts by historians to do this have generally led to one side or the other's being the heavy; most frequently it has been the American Indian. Readers are encouraged to continue reading even if their nervous system is straining to vent itself of anger or grief. It is better to get as much understanding as one can achieve with limited information.

It is popular among contemporary writers of American history to say that the Indians of North America had no written records to tell their viewpoint of history. In a good many cases, records were available but in an unfamiliar medium. In 1820 a Delaware pictograph known as Walum Olum was "obtained" by a Kentucky physician, which when translated in 1822, first into Delaware and then into English, proved to be a history of the world from creation to the time of European arrival. This quotation is from the last of six songs: "The Walumolum was made by Lekhibit (the writer) to record our glory. Shall I write another to record our fall? No! Our foes have taken care of that; but I speak what they know not or conceal."[4]

An interesting discussion has been going on for some time, presumably led by anthropologists and archaeologists, on the subject of the origin of Native American peoples. Unfortunately, today's public schools teach one of the theories as if it were fact, namely, the Bering Strait land bridge theory. It is a theory not supported by adequate evidence, but it is held by those who need convenient answers to their questions. The truth is nobody knows the origins of the Native tribes on this continent.

Perhaps a more basic discussion on the same subject occurred following Columbus's accidental landing in the Caribbean. In his reports and the reports of others, human beings were seen in the New Land. Columbus wasn't disturbed, because he thought he had landed in India. But after it was concluded that this was in fact a new continent (new to Europeans, that is), a new problem arose—a theological problem.

> In March 1493, the Catholic Church was presented with an unforeseen problem. . . . The difficulty now confronting the prelates was that [Columbus] had returned with passengers, Amerindians, who had all the appearances of being human beings. But how could their existence be accounted for? The biblical account of Creation described three continents, each occupied by the seed of the three sons of Noah who survived the Flood, Shem, Ham and Japheth.[5]

Forced to take a position because of "mounting evidence of man-like creatures inhabiting the Americas,"[6] the Catholic Church in the person of Pope Giuliano della Rovere (Julius II) issued a declaration in 1512 that the Native people were human beings, descended from Adam and Eve and the Babylonians. So the Native people, by declaration of the church, were human and therefore eligible for salvation.

The discussion persisted for several centuries and even into the present age. The discussion, however, has been conducted without Native American participation. The passive disinterest in the inquiry into Native Americans' origins serves to enhance the absurdity of the quest. Only Voltaire, according to Barry Fell, "considered that the American Indian had arisen de nova in America, by whatever mechanism had similarly caused human beings to appear upon the face of the earth in other continents."[7] Native Americans can feel relief, knowing that there is at least one European who does not wish that they (Native Americans) had come to this continent from some other place.

Perhaps Voltaire had no scientific basis for his belief, but he had just as much empirical data to go on as anyone else in his time. Consider that the scientists who promote the Bering Strait land bridge theory suggest that the crossing by Native American ancestors generally occurred about thirty-five thousand years ago; some sources say as much as seventy-five thousand years ago.[8] Put another way, these scientists, at least, concede that Native peoples populated this continent as early as 33,000 B.C. That means Native Americans were present on this continent before the existence on earth of the Sumerian civilization (3000 B.C.) and the advent of the major religions: Judaism (1800 B.C.), Hinduism (1500 B.C.), Shintoism (600 B.C.), Confucianism (551 B.C.), Buddhism (600 B.C.), Christianity (A.D. 26) and Islam (A.D. 622)[9]—and so goes the discussion.

Native civilizations on the American continent ranged (as they did in every other continent) from the village community to the large, city-oriented community. Civilizations on this continent developed without contact with civilizations on other continents, so their contributions to humanity are uniquely their own. They are remarkable contributions when you consider that among them are included 48 percent of the world's table vegetables and the Mayan calendar, which is more accurate than the presently used Gregorian calendar. "They developed a hieroglyphic writing, and invented the zero and place system."[10] Their inventions included bronze; stone buildings and pyramids (employing no mortar); intricate textiles of cotton, llama, and alpaca wool; paved roads; and the suspension bridge.[11] They also invented rubber processing, terrace systems that allowed for farming at high altitudes, and highly developed religious systems.

The great centers of Native American civilization in South America were those of the Andean, Mayan, and Mexican peoples. In North America civilizations rose and then declined, as they did among other peoples on other continents. The pyramid and mound builders had strictly organized city-state systems. Cahokia was a thriving city of thirty thousand citizens during the first and second centuries A.D. The earthen pyramid in Cahokia, Illinois, near St. Louis, Missouri, is the largest (base dimension) in the world, comprising sixteen acres. The peoples of North American tribes were primarily agrarian. They raised large fields of corn and other crops, often, especially in the Southeast, producing a surplus that could be used for trading with other tribes.

The tribes were generally small in number, ranging from a few hundred to perhaps a quarter of a million persons. The total population estimate of one million at the time of Columbus's arrival has been discarded by recent writers (although it is still taught in public schools). It is now said that the actual Native American population at the time of Columbus was ten to twelve million in North America.[12]

Tribal existence was spiritually based and featured a family-oriented social system. Tribal history and social and spiritual teachings were based on the oral tradition. Many tribes had intricate social structures that bore most of the features present in smaller tribes. The Haida and Tlingit systems, for example, included the nuclear family (immediate), the extended family, and the sublineage, lineage, clan, and, of course, tribal groups. Within their societal system the various aspects of tribal life were regulated (e.g., marriage, tribal industry, warfare, trade with other tribes, etc.).[13]

The Europeans' arrival on the American shores was a painful and unfortunate event for Native American civilizations, especially those in their beginning stages. Progress and development in South America abruptly stopped. Cultural treasures were destroyed by the Spaniards, except for the previous metals, gold, and silver that were stolen by the invaders. Mayan literature was destroyed by Spanish priests, who regarded Mayan script as pagan writing. Fortunately, three books of the Mayan people (codices on the subjects of the horoscope, astronomy, and ritual formula) have survived to provide evidence of Mayan cultural development. In North America, agriculture was the principal occupation of tribal peoples. For example, in the Southwest certain tribes were still experimenting with corn cross-breeding when the European arrived, at which time the experiments abruptly stopped.

The Native and the European Encounter

The charters allowing for exploration and colonization issued by Spain and England usually prohibited seizure of lands inhabited by Christian peoples.[14] They also instructed the exploring party to propagate the gospel to the "heathen" peoples with whom they came into contact.

Twenty-six years after the Mayflower dropped anchor far off course (necessitating a hastily drawn up self-authorization called the Mayflower Compact), John Elliot, a Congregationalist, became the first Protestant missionary of note to work among the Native tribes, launching his ministry in 1646. His work would still be considered unique even in comparison to today's efforts.

He came to New England in 1631, when the coastal tribes were still recovering from a devastating epidemic that decimated them in 1616. In spite of their own suffering, when the immigrants landed, the tribal people welcomed them and aided them, ensuring their survival during that first harsh winter.

The Native People and the Puritans

In spite of the efforts of the some writers to depict these and all tribes of North America as unsettled hunters and wanderers, it must be recognized that these tribes maintained settled communities and cultivated large fields of grain and vegetables. They had developed methods of processing grain and other foods so they could be stored for winter use. It was from their storehouses that they aided the Mayflower immigrants. But instead of being grateful to the Wampanoag people, a Puritan reflecting on the event a few years later said, "[The plague] was a wonderful preparation the Lord Jesus Christ by His providence for His people abode [sic] in the Western worlds."[15]

According to reports, the plague (smallpox), brought to these tribes by an English slaver, Captain Hunt, killed about two-thirds of the Wampanoag people and about 90 percent of the Massachusett tribe. The Mayflower community seized the well-cleared Wampanoag cornfields from the defenseless people. Still, Massasoit, head sachem of the Wampanoags, "formed a friendship with the Plymouth settlers which he honored as long as he had life."[16]

Massasoit's goodwill gesture, during which he brought gifts of food to the colonists for a thanksgiving feast, is well known. He died, in 1661, and tensions immediately began to develop. The

Puritans attempted to control the Native tribes by imposing "trespassing" laws, under which many Indian people were charged and jailed. Sabbath laws were imposed that prohibited all Indian activity on the sabbath. Death was the penalty for blasphemy, which was said to include refusal to accept "the colonist's religion."[17]

When Europeans first appeared on the eastern shores, Native American people saw them only as another people with whom they could trade; thus they did not resist their landing, they welcomed them.

The story of Squanto, Samoset, Massasoit, and the Pilgrims is well known, but the story is usually so fragmented that its proper sequence is confused. The following is a reconstruction of the tale commonly told.

Squanto, it is said, was captured and sold into slavery in Spain before the epidemic, in 1616–17. He later came to be a resident in an English home, where he learned to speak English. He ultimately made his way back to his homeland after the epidemic and found most of his people destroyed by the plague; the remainder were trying to recover and reestablish normal tribal life.

It was while he was helping his own people nurse themselves back to normal tribal life that Samoset reported that refugees from the ship, whom they had been observing for months, were camped on the old Wampanoag village site that the tribe had abandoned in an attempt to escape the plague. He also reported that they were dying from another malady, unknown to the Indians before the coming of the white man—starvation.

Massasoit, being told of the situation, took a delegation, which included Samoset and Squanto. They established friendships with the pilgrims, and over the next several months, Squanto arranged for food to be prepared by the women of the tribe and to be taken to the starving band of Europeans. For at least a year the sole source of food for the Pilgrims was the friendly people of Massasoit.

Massasoit and the leader of the small band of Europeans, about fifty in number, pledged peace between their peoples. Squanto became a teacher and interpreter for the Pilgrims. He taught them to plant the "three sisters"—corn, beans, and squash—as well as pumpkins and other vegetables. He taught them how to cook in the manner of the Indian people and also how to prepare food for storage for the winter months. The friendship was affirmed in a thanksgiving feast shared by Indians and Pilgrims. It was during this feast that the Indian people introduced popcorn to the amazed Europeans.

Even earlier than the Mayflower incident was the establishing of the Jamestown Colony in 1607. The two groups of immigrants had one thing in common besides their national origin: Both the Mayflower people and the Jamestown people would have starved if it had not been for the generosity of the coastal tribes. The women of the tribes baked bread and prepared other foods that were taken in large quantities to the strangers on their shores.

Both Massasoit's people and Powhattan's people came to regret that they had not been more cautious in their greeting of the newcomers. They saw their homelands being seized, and ultimately even the large fields of grains, which the tribes were willing to share with the whites anyway, were seized. Under such circumstances, establishing a Christian mission to the Indians that had love and justice as its basic tenets might seem an extraordinary undertaking.

John Elliot's primary assignment was as pastor to the church at Roxbury, among the immigrants. He proposed to his church that he establish a mission among the coastal tribes. His congregation agreed and became a sort of sponsoring agency for the work. The views of John Elliot seemed far in advance of his time. He learned the language of the tribes he ministered to and insisted on training leaders from among the tribal people to do the work of evangelism among their own people. Elliot had a clear view of his purposes. In a report dated 1670 he said:

> And while I live, my purpose is (by the grace of Christ assisting) to make it one of my chief cares and labors to teach them some of the liberal arts and sciences, and the way how to analyze, and lay out into particulars both the works and word of God; and how to communicate knowledge to others methodically and skillfully, and especially the Method of the Divinity.[18]

He saw his role as being an evangelist, organizer, teacher, and trainer, but evangelism effected by the church would be done by the Native congregation and indigenous leaders.

John Elliot began his work in 1646, just twenty-six years after the Mayflower landing. Previous to 1646 he learned the language of the Massachusett Indians by taking into his home a Native American who had been captured during the Pequot war. The unnamed Indian lived in Elliot's home and "accompanied him on his visits to the Indians in the neighborhood."[19] According to Sweet's account,[20] when Elliot preached his first sermon to the Massachusett Indians in their own language, it impressed not only the Indians but also the Puritan ministers. The Massachusetts Assembly passed an act ordering that the ministers should elect annually two clergy to act as missionaries to the Indians. With this additional help, Elliot's work developed rapidly. By the time of the tragic war of 1675, he had organized fourteen towns of "praying Indians," with a total membership of four thousand Native American Christians. Each town was under the leadership of indigenous officers. A school was located in each town to provide academic and vocational training.

Another concern was reflected in the response of one of Elliot's colleagues, a Mr. Mahew. When asked by the Indians to be the pastor of Martha's Vineyard, he declined, saying that it would be of greater advantage for him to remain in a position to be "their friend, and do them good, to save them from the hands of such as would bereave them of their lands."[21]

The Puritans were feverishly seizing Indian lands without giving compensation. Apparently the mission was able to use its influence to prevent seizure of some lands. Unfortunately, it must be noted that the Mahew family took possession of Martha's Vineyard in spite of the presence of more than two thousand Native peoples already living on the island. Because of continual theft of the tribal lands by the Puritans and the attempt on their part to impose oppressive laws on the tribal peoples, relations between the Native coastal inhabitants and the Puritan immigrants headed toward total collapse.

The Pequot Nation perhaps didn't realize the key position they held in their part of the world, which was the southern coastlands of what is now called Connecticut. The Pequots occupied a place on the coast (at present-day Mystic) that placed them in a position to trade with both the Dutch to the west and south and the English to the northeast. Growing tired of being cheated by the English, they cut off trade with them and declared that henceforth they would trade exclusively with the Dutch.

In the meantime the Pequot/Mohican Confederation was undergoing internal conflict that erupted into armed conflict between the tribes. The English immigrants, frightened by the forcefulness of the Pequots, took advantage of the internal conflict. Alleging that the Pequots had killed certain English traders accused of cheating the Indians, the English immigrants attacked the unsuspecting Pequots early in the morning on May 26, 1637, while the people were still sleeping. Unprepared for all-out war, the Pequot people were overcome. This was an event that continues to stand as a symbol of the spiritually discredited Puritan leadership. Over four hundred Pequot men, women, and children were burned alive in the palisaded village. Cotton Mather described the burning people as a "sweet sacrifice" to God.

Captain John Underhill, a participant in the atrocity against the Pequots, states in his eyewitness account that the immigrant soldiers approached the village, which was enclosed inside a palisade wall or fence. After making openings in the palisade, they attempted an assault on the people by entering their homes. The assault failed, and Underhill explained: "Seeing the fort was too hot for us, we devised a way how we might save ourselves and prejudice them." [22]

It was then that they decided to torch the Pequot homes. The soldiers surrounded the Pequot village as the fire raged within the walls. Men, women, and children were being burned alive. Pequot men, unwilling to leave their families in the burning inferno, tried courageously to carry the fight to the English soldiers from within the flames. Captain Underhill, amazed at their heroic efforts, wrote, "Many courageous fellows were unwilling to come out, and fought most desperately through the palisades, so as they were scorched and burnt with the very flame, and were deprived of their arms, in regard the fire burnt their bowstrings; and so perished valiantly." [23]

These warriors deserved mercy, he said, if only there was the chance to bestow it. Many of the fighting Pequots were able to move their old men, women, and children to the openings in the palisades, where they ran to seek safety. They were met by soldiers with drawn swords. Underhill writes, "Down fell men, women and children."

Underhill, seeking to justify the outrage, used Holy Scripture in a remarkably twisted interpretation: "Scripture declareth women and children must perish with their parents. . . . We had sufficient light from the word of God for our proceedings." [24]

Massasoit, who established and maintained peace with the Pilgrims and retained his personal friendship with the Puritan immigrants, died in 1661. His son Alexander (Wamsutta), who along with his young brother, Philip, accepted English names along with their real names, assumed leadership of the tribe and immediately came under pressure to resist white encroachment. He was strong and outspoken in his resistance. When he was ordered by the Puritans to appear before them to attest his "loyalty," he refused. He was arrested and subjected to severe questioning. He died from the Puritans' brutal treatment.

Metacom (known to the whites as Philip) assumed tribal leadership in 1662 and began a long-term preparation to consolidate his leadership. The preparation included collecting firearms, establishing forges deep in the forest for repair and reconditioning weapons, and seeking alliances with neighboring tribes.

During this tension-filled period of history, from 1646 to 1675, John Elliot did his mission work. In 1675 an all-out campaign against the immigrants erupted, and Metacom led a force of twenty-one thousand against the whites, who by this time numbered forty thousand. In a speech Metacom stated the reason for the declaration of war:

> Brother, you see this vast country before us, which the Great Spirit gave to our fathers and us; you see the buffalo and deer that now are our support. Brothers you see these little ones, our wives and children who are looking to us for food and raiment; and you now see the foe before you, that they have grown insolent and bold; that all our ancient customs are disregarded; the treaties made by our fathers and us are broken and all of us insulted; our Council fires disregarded, and all of the ancient customs of our fathers; our brothers murdered before our eyes, and their spirits cry to us for revenge. Brothers, these people from the unknown world

will cut down our graves, spoil our hunting and planting grounds, and drive us and our children from the graves of our fathers, and our Council fires, and enslave our women and children.[25]

By the time of Metacom's move against the immigrants, the Plymouth "colony" was not much of a factor, having been overshadowed by the Massachusetts Bay Company and four other companies. Metacom's forces saw early success by eliminating twelve immigrant towns and exacting a toll of one thousand European lives before the tide turned. The large number of fighting forces available to the immigrant companies made it impossible for Metacom's forces to wage an extended campaign.

Metacom's statement of the causes for war was correct, and his warnings also were affirmed. Indian survivors, including Metacom's wife and son, were sold into slavery. In spite of vigorous work by John Elliot and other Puritan ministers, the mission never achieved the force it once had. Elliot's death in 1690 closed the bittersweet era of mission and human conflict. The Plymouth Colony failed, and in 1691 its adherents became a part of the Massachusetts Bay Company, which had also lost its charter (1684) and had come under direct control of the king.

In summary, it may be said that until the war of 1675, Elliot's missionary work was successful in the context of his stated goals. He led the organization of fourteen towns of "praying Indians," with a total membership of four thousand Native Christians. His towns were based on an interpretation of the Old Testament. They were self-sustaining plantations developed by the Indian citizens. The rulers and teachers of each town were Native Americans. The spread of Christian teachings to neighboring tribes was effected by the Native Christians themselves. All ministry was done in the tribal language.

On the other hand, from a Native American viewpoint, it may be said that there were certain failures in the mission plan that placed the Indian towns in precarious positions and that eventually doomed them forever. In general, there was no political or spiritual bridge from the Indian Christian towns to the established tribes. In addition, the Christian Indian towns too closely resembled the immigrant towns, thus making them alien to both traditional Indian tribes and immigrant Europeans. Predictably, when the war of 1675 broke out, they were caught in the cross-fire. Many Indian town residents joined Metacom's forces, but most tried to protect the towns from destruction.

Natick, one of the Indian Christian towns, still exists today. After the war white immigrants forced the Indian residents out of Natick, seizing their large cultivated agricultural fields. Today it is a small city in Massachusetts of some 31,057. Natick was the mission headquarters, and it was here that the Bible was printed in the tribal languages. Another Indian town, Wamesit, also taken over by immigrants, is located near the present city of Lowell, Massachusetts. Wamesit (as it is called today) lies near the junction of Interstate 495 and Highway 38 and has a population of 2,700. Other surviving towns are not apparent in sources consulted by this writer.

From the death of Elliot until well into the eighteenth century, there was apparently little interest in Indian missions. In fact, religion itself was minimally practiced. In 1701 the Society for the Propagation of the Gospel in Foreign Parts was organized in England because of the concern for the Native people and blacks (the latter being enslaved). The society also expressed concern for the white population, whom they described "as destitute of a source of religion as the Natives themselves."[26]

The spiritual darkness that cloaked the Eastern Seaboard at the turn of the eighteenth century offered no balm for the pain of human conflict. The clutching hands of immigrant greed forced Indian families from homes they had inhabited for centuries. Their large farms were taken over by European immigrants, who were not just interested in any land—they wanted the cleared and cultivated fields of the Indian residents. The wise council of William Crenshaw, preaching to a group of immigrating English people before they boarded their ship, was eloquent but futile: "A Christian may take nothing from a Heathen against his will, but in fair and lawful bargain."[27]

Suffering occurred among the immigrants too, since they were unfamiliar with what they called "the wilderness." Many of them starved, while perhaps being surrounded by food in the form of wild fruits, berries, and other natural foods. In addition, social elements that troubled the pioneer immigrants were introduced in their midst. As early as 1620 England began to colonize Virginia with convicts, and slaves were purchased by several Virginia planters.[28]

With the death of Powhattan, Indian resistance to white encroachment on Indian lands was no longer restrained. New encroachments were attacked and the immigrants driven off lands they had squatted on. Unsuccessful expeditions were sent against the Indian people, and resistance continued. While the Massachusetts Companies were moving into the shadows, the specter of things to come was materializing in other parts of the Eastern Seaboard. The Virginia Company ended in 1624 under charges from England that it failed to meet the terms of its charter, which included propagation of the Christian religion and yielding material profit to England through trade. William W. Sweet cites personal reasons and the king's dislike of Virginia's leadership as the real reason.[29]

The same author says that the arrival of the royal governor John Harvey in 1630 resulted in "much suffering" for the church: "Up to this time the ministers who had come out to Virginia were generally men of character and sincerely devoted to the advancement of true religion, but from this period forward the type of ministers in the colony changed for the worse." [30] But if things looked dark for the immigrants in the Indian land, it was also dark in England, as Sweet says: "But it must be born in mind that during the same period religion was at a low ebb in England, as well as in the Colonies, and the established Church had settled into a deathlike stupor, from which no power seemed to be able to arouse it." [31] In spite of the spiritual gloom, some developments of lasting positive value for the immigrants did occur. For example, William and Mary College was established, with one of its objectives being "that the Christian faith may be propagated amongst the Western Indians to the glory of Almighty God." [32]

The Great Awakening of the early eighteenth century ushered in a new interest in Indian missions. In 1734 the Reverend John Sargent established a mission among the Housatannuck Indians in western Massachusetts near Stockbridge. Sargent reported 182 baptisms, and there were more than fifty children enrolled in a school developed in cooperation with Sargent by a Mr. Hollis, a Baptist clergyman.[33] It is the presence of Jonathan Edwards as pastor of that same church among the Housatannuck Indians that creates some interest.

Jonathan Edwards, along with George Whitefield, was responsible for igniting the Great Awakening. He graduated from Yale University (founded 1701) at the age of seventeen and later became an assistant pastor at Northampton, Massachusetts. Following the death of the pastor, Edwards became the senior pastor. In opposition to the "half-way covenant," a sort of formal and technical church membership concept, he declared that only persons who had had an intense personal experience would be eligible for the Lord's Supper. He was dismissed as pastor, and from 1751 to 1757 he served as a missionary to the Housatannuck (Stockbridge) Indians at Stockbridge. His ministry to the Indian people was judged as "satisfactory" but not significant by most sources. It would seem that his real reason for accepting the assignment was to use the time to write his major work, *Freedom of the Will* (1754).

However, Edwards fostered a theological concept in which the Indian people figured as supporting actors, as it were. In a work entitled *The History of the Work of Redemption* (1739), he set forth the thesis that all signs indicated that the last days were at hand and that "America was indeed the Promised Land."[34] He cited three occurrences that, for him, confirmed his thesis:

1. The Reformation occurring close to the time of the European discovery of America.
2. The propagation of the gospel among the heathens (Native tribes). "America" was the last continent and the Natives of "America" were in the uttermost parts of the earth and all men in the western hemisphere had to be evangelized.
3. The American revival (the Great Awakening).[35]

Edwards pointed out that "America" was the only continent that did not have the "church of God" in it and was therefore wholly possessed of Satan until the coming of Europeans.[36] While such contentions are not likely to be taken seriously today and in fact seem almost childish, they formed the deadly philosophy that provided the justification for the frenzied encroachment on Indian lands, the destruction of human life and societies, and the impoverishment and degradation of Native people that would take place for five hundred years. Yet there is no appearance of any intent on the part of Jonathan Edwards that his theological and philosophical proposals were to provide the literary foundation for injustices against the Native people.

It was Edwards's contact with a young convert of the Great Awakening, David Brainerd, that gave him an opportunity to make an important contribution to the cause of Indian missions. Brainerd was a graduate of Yale who, after being licensed to preach, had accepted an assignment as a missionary among Indians near Stockbridge (where the Housatannuck Mission was located). Through Brainerd's influence that mission was consolidated with the mission at Stockbridge. After being ordained by the Presbyterian Church in 1744, he opened his work among Native Americans in Jew Jersey; he eventually extended his work to the Susquehannah. He grew close to Edwards, to whose daughter he was engaged. Unfortunately, however, he contracted tuberculosis, from which he died in 1747 in the home of Jonathan Edwards. But despite the brevity of his career (three years), his contributions provided the inspiration for a renewal of efforts at missionizing Native American peoples. Brainerd's total dedication to his ministry to Native peoples in New Jersey and along the Susquehannah was apparent in his toleration of the pain and personal suffering that accompanied his efforts at evangelization of Native peoples. This devotion inspired a host of missionaries after his death. Jonathan Edwards published a biography of Brainerd along with Brainerd's diary; this publication became one of the most important contributions to Indian missions in the early eighteenth century.

After the peak of the Great Awakening, the Presbyterians began work among the Six Nations in relation to the Society in Scotland for Propagating Christian Knowledge. They also established work in Long Island.[37]

The Moravians were perhaps the most influential religious group to appear in Europe and what is now called the United States. Their early contacts with Martin Luther through Jan Augusta brought about a cordial relationship between the two movements of Protestant Reformation and Moravian Missionary. Their missionary zeal was well known through their missions among the Moravian Diaspora in Europe, which brought about a resurgence of their church and also uplifted the Protestant church. In the colonies their primary emphasis and "mission" was to the Native tribes of North America. They spent their initial days in the Oglethorpe Colony. Finding their religious practices incompatible with the rigid English church, they removed to New York and then to Pennsylvania, founding Bethlehem, which came to be their permanent headquarters. Another center was established in 1758 in Winston-Salem, North Carolina.

The Moravians began their work among the Indians in New York in 1740, and there a series of tragedies began that exemplifies the frenzied land grabbing and injustices of immigrants against Indian people.

Christian Henry Rauch, the first moravian missionary in America, headquartered at Shekomiko, a "Mohegan town" where the Moravians baptized their first Christian converts from among the Indians and admitted them into the church.[38] Driven out of the region by European immigrants, they moved to the forks of the Delaware and established a mission settlement for their converts called Tents of Grace about thirty miles from Bethlehem. The Indian congregation grew in size to around five hundred.

According to Sweet, the French and Indian War "brought terrible suffering to the Moravian missionaries and their Indian converts."[39] On November 24, 1755, the Tents of Grace settlement of Moravian Indian Christians was attacked by white "settlers." However, the missionaries spirited their Indian converts out of the Indian town before the assault began. One Moravian leader, Bishop Nitschman, was shot, and ten missionaries were burned to death by white bigots. The Indian converts found refuge in Bethlehem among other Moravian Christians. Another town, Wechquetank, established by Indian converts to the Moravian faith and their missionaries, was destroyed by Scotch-Irish "settlers." Once again, the missionaries suffered. The Indian converts this time found refuge in Philadelphia, where the English government provided protection for them.

The Moravian Indian converts, along with their missionaries, then traveled for five weeks to the lands of Susquehannah and again established a Christian Indian town, this time called Tents of Peace. David Zeisberger became a prominent Moravian missionary there. This town became prosperous and for several years existed with some success. However, another kind of resistance was eventually encountered. The Native American tribal people, who saw the Christian Indian town as too closely resembling white towns, brought pressure against the Christian Indian residents. The final move for these unfortunate Moravian converts was west, where they founded "a group of villages in what is now Ohio" along the Tuscarawas River in 1770.[40] This time they were able to live in relative peace for a period of time.

In contrast to explicit and implicit advocacy of murderous treatment of Native American Christians and their missionaries stood another attitude toward mission among "Negroes, Indians and the underprivileged, as well for the privileged few."[41] "Hopkinsianism," as it was popularly called, bore the influence of Jonathan Edwards. Samuel Hopkins (1721–1803) actually lived in the home of Edwards while he was studying theology with Edwards.[42] Hopkins reflected "a new social consciousness and broad humanitarianism."[43] Sin was considered by Hopkins to be self-love; the way to overcome self-love was through disinterested benevolence and complete submission to God's will. This benevolence was to be extended to all people. A part of Samuel Hopkins's theological system was a doctrine of general atonement; that is, Christ died for all, not just for the privileged few and not just for Europeans. Hopkins breathed life into the missionary movement and is credited with helping to plant antislavery sentiments among the Congregationalists.

Another missionary movement that has been noted in some church histories is that of the Quakers. It is commonly said of William Penn (1644–1718), the dominant personality among the Quakers, that "fair treatment was accorded the Indians" by Penn and the Quakers. That remark exemplifies the unusual logic of the colonial mind. It is difficult to see how Penn could accord fair treatment to the Indians while at the same time negotiating a charter from King Charles II so he could possess the land belonging to the Indian people. The claim that Penn purchased land from the Indians is misleading since it involved only small parcels of land, certainly not the whole of Pennsylvania.

Nevertheless, the Quakers, apart from their own land seizure from the Indians, carried on a mission that won converts from among the dispossessed Indian peoples. But the Quakers were also subject to persecution, and attempts to colonize Christian Indians resulted in disaster. In 1763, following the French and Indian War, the Quaker village of Conestoga was attacked by white bounty hunters from Paxton. In spite of efforts by Quaker missionaries and white Quaker residents of Lancaster to protect Indian Christians, the "Paxton Boys" broke into the compound and brutally massacred Christian Indian men, women, and children.

THE PROGENY OF SHEM

The Methodist connection to historic missions among Native Americans was through John Wesley. In October 1735 Wesley and his brother Charles were passengers on a ship bound for the colony of James Oglethorpe in Georgia. John Wesley had accepted an invitation by Oglethorpe to be a missionary to the English immigrants and also to the Native peoples with whom the colonists had come into contact.

On board that same ship were twenty-six Moravians who were going to America for a similar purpose. Wesley was impressed by the deep faith of the Moravians; during a violent storm at sea, he was amazed that while panic swept through the other passengers, the Moravians remained calm. They sang hymns and worshiped as the sea crashed about them, smashing parts of the ship. In answer to Wesley's query about the storm at sea, "Were you not afraid?" they replied, "I thank God, no."[1] What sort of people could have such faith that even the threat of death could not make them afraid?

These were the Moravians, led by a spiritual leader who would ultimately die attempting to save the lives of Native American converts in Pennsylvania: Bishop Nitschmann. Nitschmann was shot to death at Tents of Grace in November 1755 by European immigrants.

Wesley's experience in the Oglethorpe Colony left him depressed and unsure of his spiritual condition. His brief visitation among Georgia's Creek tribespeople was unsuccessful in planting a seed of ministry among the Native people. Although apparently the colonists had already established somewhat of a foothold among the Creeks—according to Josephy,[2] some colonial traders had married Creek women, and these men usually made their homes in the Creek villages—the mission of Wesley to the Native people of Georgia would nevertheless have to wait for another day and other means of ministry to see its completion. John Wesley returned to England in 1738, and at Aldersgate Street in London found the peace and deliverance that he sought.

In 1739 on New year's Day Wesley founded the Fetterlane Society, and he later developed evangelistic work in an old foundry in London.[3] The Foundry became the center of Methodism in London. Although Methodism had its beginnings in England in 1739, the first Methodist missionaries (to white colonists) did not arrive in America until 1769, in the persons of Richard Boardman and Joseph Pilmoor. From 1769 to 1784 Methodist churches in the colonies were governed and supplied by English Methodism. Ministers appointed to serve white Methodist churches in America were technically missionaries; thus when one speaks of Methodist missions or missionaries between 1739 and 1784, one is not necessarily referring to Indian missions.

The southeastern section of what is now called the United States was the cradle of Native American Methodism in the South. The region was heavily populated by Native American tribes who were living in settled communities, farming the land, and carrying on commerce among themselves and distant tribes. Several families of tribes were identified, including the Muskogean, Iroquoian, Caddoan, Siouan, and Coahuiltecan. Within these family groupings are the major (larger) tribes of the Southeast: the Choctaws, Chickasaws, Seminoles, and Creeks of the Muskogean group. The Cherokee tribe (Iroquoian), added to those four, makes up the five predominant tribes in the region, commonly known to whites as the Five Civilized Tribes. Other important tribes were the Lumbees, Hichitis, Yamasees, Apalachees, Alabamas, Mobiles, Houmas, Timicuas, Tunicas, Chitimachas, Calusas, Atakapas, Caddos, Kichais, Wacos, Tawakonis, Biloxis, Quapaws, Yuchis, and Tonkawas.[4]

These tribes were established in permanent communities and had close-knit societies. Tribal economy was based on agriculture; large farms were maintained to supply the community with food and also to provide a surplus to use as a trading commodity to secure goods from other tribes. Only by historical reflection does anyone describe any part of tribal activity as "religious," because what is described by white historians and anthropologists as "religion" was an integral feature of tribal life. There was no distinction between the sacred and the profane in the life-style of the tribal citizen, since all of life and its pursuits was based on a recognition of the relationship of the created world and the Creator.

The Spirit of the Creator pervaded everything, giving conscious significance to everything composing the tribal citizen's environment. The ethical relationships of tribal citizens among themselves were based on this consciousness. Being outside of this relationship was, for the individual, a condition of banishment, which was far more painful than personal incarceration. Territorial rights were observed by tribes living adjacent to one another, and disputes were settled peaceably to preserve the balance of power. Disputes that flared into violence were quickly extinguished, to keep lines of communication open for trade and other international traffic.

The physical plants of tribal communities included domestic dwellings, a large central structure where council meetings were held, storehouses for grain and other foods stored for winter use, and recreational areas where the popular stick-ball game was played and ceremonial and recreational (folk) dancing was performed. Food prepared by the women of the tribe included various kinds of bread derived from corn (cornbread, shuck-bread, etc.); vegetable dishes of various kinds (including what contemporary people call goulash), such as baked squash and pumpkin; and meat (deer, fowl, and fish), which was roasted, boiled, or fried. *Ton-fulla* (hominy and meat), *sofky* (the Creek version of the former), and hickory nut hominy were a few favorites. Daily tribal life was well ordered, and the appropriate division of labor was recognized and guided people in their daily lives.

Politically the tribes were organized into districts and towns, and matters affecting the whole tribe were discussed in a council meeting composed of the headmen of each district and/or town. It was not unusual for a council leader to leave the council meet-

ing to seek advice and comments from his constituents before
voting on matters affecting the tribal citizens he represented. This
practice irritated white colonists, who were accustomed to having
a single ruler over all the people.

The eighteenth century was a period of decisive struggle
between Spain, France, and England over their territorial claims
in this part of the continent. The role of the five predominant
tribes in the Southeast (and other influential tribes) in that struggle has generally not been mentioned in public school textbooks.
The English presence was primarily east of the Appalachian Mountains, while the French presence was mainly west of the Appalachian Mountains, from the Ohio Valley and Canada to the north to
New Orleans to the south. The Spanish were in Florida, Mexico,
and South America. At issue during the eighteenth century was
the ownership of the Ohio Valley and Florida. The Oglethorpe
Colony was established to prevent the northward expansion of the
Spanish, who claimed Florida. James Oglethorpe, also known as
General Oglethorpe, was the strategist for this operation.

During the time of John Wesley's sojourn in the Oglethorpe
Colony (1735), the English were already trying to persuade the
Creeks to join them in various expeditions against the enemies of
the colonies. The Creeks maintained a policy of neutrality in most
cases. Brim, an astute and shrewd headman of the Creeks, preferred to preserve a balance in his relationship with the three
European nations, to preserve trade with them all. In fact, most
of the major tribes of the Southeast had become dependent on
trade with these foreign nations, almost to the exclusion of trade
relationships with other tribes. Guns and ammunition, farm implements, and various kinds of dry goods and hardware were needed and available from trade.

The Cherokees were from time to time allied with the English,
but for a similar reason—to pursue the trade relationship with the
English. The Choctaws at this point in history were engaged in
trade with the French and would have occasion to align themselves
with the French when that relationship was threatened. In almost
every instance, tribal self-interest seemed to be reflected in the
relationship of individual tribes to European nations.[5]

The European nations sought to exploit the tribes and on occasion found themselves being exploited in turn. An English lead-

er in the Carolinas complained in 1717, "The last time they (the Cherokees) were here (in Charleston) they insulted us to the last degree . . . and indeed by their demands (with which we were forced to comply) made us their tributaries."[6]

The Creeks had emissaries negotiating with both the French and the English, as well as with other major tribes. The tribal leaders purposed to manage the conflict involving the three European nations for whatever benefits might thereby accrue to them. It was recognized by both tribal leaders and European leaders that good working relations with the Native tribes, especially the Iroquois Confederacy and the major southeastern tribes, were essential to the prosecution of a European war on American soil. According to an account of early conflicts between the English and the French, these two European armies couldn't even negotiate the terrain to make contact with each other, much less engage in field combat, which was their intention.

Between 1689 and 1713 the English made three attempts to attack French strongholds. Because of weather, disease, and inadequate transportation systems, they were unable to find the French. The strongholds targeted were Port Royal, Nova Scotia, and Quebec. Guerilla fighting under the training and leadership of tribal military leaders was essential to a war effort on Indian land. Most sources dealing with this period state simply that the English (French, etc.) "enlisted" the aid of major tribes. Actually they negotiated for assistance of the tribes. The various tribal governments made independent decisions when called upon by the English or the other European nations to engage in war. They often refused the requests. In 1692 the Iroquois were asked by the English to wage war against the French. The Iroquois stung them with a speech, the essence of which is contained in the following quote:

> You sett us on dayly to fight & destroy your enemies & bid us goe on with courage, but wee see not that you doe anything to it yourselfs—neither doe wee see any great strength you have to oppose them if the enemy should breake out upon you the war must also be hottly pursued on your sides, what is it that our neighbors of N: England and the rest of the English that are in covenant with us doe. They all stay att home & sett us on to doe the work.[7]

The tribal headmen knew that it was possible for them to be used as pawns by the three European nations, and most, like the Iroquois, regularly declared their independence from the European colonies in their decision-making powers. The tribal leaders also knew that as long as the three European nations were warring against one another, they could use the situation to their advantage by bargaining for better trade relationships in exchange for their alliance, if they were not otherwise hurt by the alliance. Also, as the Iroquois speech indicates, the tribal leaders saw that the European nations were vulnerable as long as their energies were being consumed in warring against one another.

In 1715 the Yamasees, enraged over the seizing of Yamasee women and children by white colonists in Charleston for the slave trade, spearheaded an intertribal alliance that came close to putting the English out of business in America. Close to annihilation, the Carolinians pleaded with the Cherokees not to join the alliance against them. At the same time, emissaries from the Creeks sought to bring the Cherokees into the Yamasee war as a part of the intertribal alliance. Failing to win the Cherokees, the Yamasees and the alliance drove the settlers out of the outlying territories and destroyed ninety of one hundred trading outposts, but stopped short of completing the operation by not storming Charleston. The vulnerability was seen but not capitalized on.

This period of history, during which the major tribes could play European nations against one another for the tribes' advantage, was coming to an end. The Seven Years' War (1756–63) was a struggle between France and England over the Ohio Valley. Its conclusion left the British with squatter's rights and, at least in their own minds, the ownership of lands to as far west as the Mississippi River. It left the Iroquoian Confederacy and other major tribes in that region without a bargaining chip. Spain had forfeited "rights" in Louisiana and Florida, and France lost its foothold. The only European contender for Indian land was England.

However, it was not long before the greed of the English colonials and England brought about another inter-European conflict, but this time it was brother against brother. Following the Seven Years' War, England declared a line of demarcation between the colonies and tribal lands, ostensibly to prevent further violent contact between white immigrants and tribes in the Ohio Valley.

This enraged the immigrants because they thought that their victory over France gave them license to seize lands in the Ohio Valley regardless of the Native tribes living there.

The legendary Ottawa war leader Pontiac rose suddenly to power when Native peoples reacted to punitive laws devised by Indian-hater General Jeffrey Amherst to control the tribal people, who had formerly traded and cooperated with the French. Pontiac and his forces laid siege to Detroit, while others of his forces eliminated British trading posts wherever they were established. The siege on Detroit lasted from May 1763 to October 1763 and was an event regarded even today as an outstanding military achievement. Ultimately, it was broken because the French did not, as expected, return to aid their old allies. Also, the tribes involved grew weary of the long siege and began to withdraw.

From this point on, the immigrant colonists and the English government were on a collision course. The southeastern tribes played the bargaining game one more time as both British and immigrant colonists sought to either win them into a military alliance or secure a pledge of neutrality. The major tribes remained neutral because they could see no advantage for them, regardless of which side should win.

The gospel as a light to the nations was more like a flash of lightning in a distant sky during this period. Samuel Sewell, a Puritan leader, lit the sky once. Sewell was a Harvard graduate and a chief justice of the superior court (1718–28). He was one of the special commissioners selected to preside over the Salem witchcraft cases (1692) in which nineteen persons were condemned to death.[8] He was the only one of the judges to recant publicly when the witch trials were officially disavowed in 1697. He was a commissioner of the Society for the Propagation of the Gospel in New England, and a letter he wrote set forth his ideas of a practical humanitarianism as applied to white and Indian relations. In regard to evangelism among Native American tribes, he echoed John Elliot's conviction of the need for Native leadership:

> I have met with an observation of some grave divines, that ordinarily when God intends good to a nation, he is pleased to make use of some of themselves to be instrumental in conveying of that good unto them. Now God has furnished several of the Indians

with considerable abilities for the work of ministry and teaching school. And therefore I am apt to believe that if the Indians so qualified were more taken notice of in suitable rewards, it would conduce very much to the propagation of the Gospel among them.[9]

He saw that success of Native leaders as ministers would influence others to work to fit themselves for leadership. Sewell formulated a simple but important principle when commenting on the social and political aspects of planting the gospel among Native tribes:

> I think it requisite that convenient tracts of land should be set out to them [the Indians]; and that by plain and natural boundaries, as much or nary be—as lakes, rivers, mountains, rocks—upon which for any Englishman to encroach should be accounted a crime. Except this be done, I fear their own jealousies, and the French friars, will persuade them that the English, as they increase and think they want more room, will never leave till they have crowded them quite out of all their lands. And it will be a vain attempt for us to offer Heaven to them if they take up prejudice against us, as if we did grudge them a living upon their own earth.[10]

The immigrant colonists were more inclined to take land belonging to the tribes than to secure it for their use, so it is likely that this counsel fell on deaf ears. Nevertheless, it was a flash of the gospel light in the darkness of the eighteenth century. It is a principle worth remembering, that "it will be . . . vain . . . for us to offer Heaven . . . if we grudge them a living upon their own earth."

A number of things began to converge in the early part of the eighteenth century that seemed to set the stage for coming generations. In 1732 James Oglethorpe founded the last colony as an English buffer against Spanish expansion. Also, another tribal people, the Lumbees, are noted as beginning to make their mark in history, to be revealed many generations into the future. Edward H. Spicer notes that "the first records that clearly cite the Lumbees are land grants to individuals beginning in 1732."[11] The Lumbee people were working in community, developing a portion of North Carolina, where the fullness of their achievements would symbolize Native American adaptability and the practical effects of the will to survive.

In the north the Housatannuck mission was initiated by the Reverend John Sargent in 1734. It is from this mission that we trace the personalities and work that found expression throughout the eighteenth century for missions among the Native American people.

In his journal John Wesley tells of being asked to support Indian schools in America:

> Sat. 8 (1767) At the request of Mr. Whitaker of New England, I preached and afterward made a collection for the Indian schools in America. A large sum of money is now collected, but will money convert heathen? Find preachers of David Brainerd's spirit, and nothing can stand before them; but without this what will gold and silver do?[12]

From the time he himself came to the colonies, hoping to work among Native Americans, Wesley apparently never forgot and continually urged his workers in the colonies to consider work among the Native tribes.

Given the political intrigues that spanned most of the eighteenth century, involving the major tribes of the Southeast and the North, especially the Iroquoian League in the North, the integrity of missionaries and their mission was in doubt. The biblical dictum "You cannot serve God and Mammon" (Matt. 6:24) was set aside as missionaries, on the one hand, offered a religion of love and eternal life, and colonists, on the other hand, were forming militia to kill tribal people or drive them from their homes in order to take their lands and crops. The moral persuasions of John Hopkins, John Woolman, William Penn, and now Wesley fell on ears dulled with greed. Wesley wrote to Asbury in 1787 and declared his concerns:

> One thing has often given me concern. . . . the progeny of Shem (the Indians) seem to be quite forgotten. How few of these have seen the light of the glory of God since the English first settled among them! And now scarce one in fifty among whom we settled, perhaps scarce one in an hundred of them are left alive! Does it not seem as if God had designed all the Indian natives not for refor-

mation but for destruction? Undoubtedly with man it is impossible to help them. But is it too hard for God? Pray ye likewise the Lord of the Harvest and he will send out more laborers into his Harvest.[13]

Of all the prophetic voices of the eighteenth century, including Hopkins, Woolman, and Penn, only Wesley expressed horror at the genocide that was taking place.

Methodists in the colonies generally had a difficult time almost from the beginning, but problems for both lay persons and clergy among the Methodists intensified during the Revolutionary War. Wesley never favored the break-up between the colonies and England. He lashed out at colonial leadership and the degradation of the quality of life in the American colonies. Sweet characterizes his criticism as follows: "In America, he [Wesley] says there has been a huge outcry for liberty, but the Americans have destroyed liberty, for a clergyman cannot even pray for the King in America; nor is there any civil liberty; indeed "wherever these brawlers for liberty govern, there is the vilest slavery."[14]

Wesley's instruction to his clergymen in the American colonies was to remain neutral. Persecution of Methodists followed as they fell under suspicion of being disloyal. Asbury left Maryland because Maryland required the clergy to take oaths to take up arms if called upon. He was unwilling to take an oath and went to Delaware. While in Delaware he stayed in the home of Judge White, an Anglican. Sweet relates the following incident:

> In April, 1778, a patrol came to the house of Judge White, seized the Judge on a charge of being a Methodist, and although he was finally freed, he was detained five weeks. This occurrence led Asbury to leave Judge White's house and after traveling on back roads far into the night he finally found shelter. Once, due to alarming rumors, he took refuge in a swamp until sunset.[15]

By 1778 all of the missionaries sent by Wesley had fled to England, with the exception of Asbury. In a dialogue with George Shadford, Asbury declared, "My convictions are as clear and strong as ever that it is my duty to remain." When Shadford said that for his part his work was done, Asbury replied, "One of us must be wrong."[16]

Shadford gave no further information as to what he perceived his work to be, but Asbury had firsthand experience with the condition of life in the colonies and saw that the church was only minimally at work among the people. The popular concept of the white colonist as a person of high moral quality, innocent and serene, who only wished for a place to work for a living and to worship as he or she pleased, is pure fantasy. White colonists were not all Christians, as the spirits of white eighteenth-century missionaries would be glad to rise up and confirm.

> Of the hundred and one immigrants aboard the Mayflower, only 12 belonged to the first New England church. Not more than one out of five of the Massachusetts Bay Colonists during the early years were members of a church. In 1760 only one New Englander out of eight was a church member. The ratio in the middle colonies was one to fifteen, and in the South about one in twenty. The church historian William Warren Sweet said of the early days of this country that "there came to be more unchurched people in America, in proportion to the population, than was to be found in any country in Christendom." In 1800 only an estimated 7 percent of the population were church members.[17]

Asbury wrote in his journal that he frequently traveled with armed guards, ostensibly to protect him against "Indians,"[18] but the circuit riders were more frequently assaulted by white highwaymen than by "lurking" Indians. Peter Cartwright, who was no friend to Indians, gave this description of a white settlement in Kentucky in 1793:

> Logan County, when my father moved to it, was called "Rogues' Harbor." Here, many refugees, from almost all parts of the union, fled to escape justice or punishment; for although there was law, yet it could not be executed, and it was a desperate state of society. Murderers, horse thieves, highway robbers, and counterfeiters fled here until they dominated and actually formed a majority.[19]

Historians consistently tell lurid tales of "Indians" attacking the homes of innocent settlers on the frontier. The settlers were anything but innocent. If they were on the so-called frontier, they were on Indian land with the intent of staying there by force. The settlers deliberately moved onto lands that were being used and under cultivation by tribes who had lived there for centuries. The intent of the settlers was from the beginning to wrest the land from the Native people, without compensation or negotiation: "A basic cause for lack of religious development was the pioneer's brute struggle for existence against the harsh elements and savage Indians, with limited, primitive equipment. He was preoccupied with the fundamental necessity of keeping body and soul together on this earth, rather than preparing his soul for the next world."[20]

Even Barclay, who otherwise gave us an invaluable work in his *History of Methodist Missions,* couldn't resist telling a lurid tale, with all of the traditional emotional language used by white historians (e.g., "lurking" Indians, "sly," "creeping," etc.). He tells of a woman who was killed after everyone had gone to a church meeting: "[The Indians] had been lurking in the cane break, and when the people had gone to the preaching service one had slyly crept up behind the woman and killed her with his tomahawk before she knew of her danger."[21]

Historians avoid reporting on documents that present the other side of the coin. Native American tribes sought to be neutral in many cases but were drawn into conflict by colonial whites who raided Indian towns to get at the tribal granaries and other commodities needed by the armies. Atrocities committed by these white colonial raiding forces are documented in diaries and military reports dated 1778:

> That afternoon a party started off for a small Indian settlement several miles up the Mahoning at a place called the Salt Licks. Simon Girty went as pilot: They did not reach the place till in the night— found a few squaws there I took prisoner & brought her off—the others were left. A small Indian boy out with a gun shooting birds was discovered and killed—and several claimed the honor: It was left to Girty to decide—& his decision was, that one Zach. Connell killed the lad . . . an old Dutchman scalped the squaw that had been killed and put the scalp in his wallet with his provisions.[22]

Arthur St. Clair criticized the murder of Melanthy, a Shawanese headman who displayed a colonial flag and a peace treaty to indicate his friendship with the colonials. Although he was an unarmed prisoner, he was shot to death. From St. Clair's papers comes this account:

> An expedition under Colonel Logan, with nine hundred militia, went forward on the 1st ultimo. He returned to Limestone, from whence he set out in a fortnight having met with very little opposition, as all the warriors had gone to meet General Clarke. Seven of the Shawanese towns were burned, a few scalps taken [by white soldiers], and thirty women and children prisoners. Melanthy, the Shawanese King, would not fly, but displayed the thirteen stripes, and held out the articles of the Miami Treaty, but all in vain: he was shot down by one of the party, although he was their prisoner. I am sorry that this disgraceful affair should have happened, as Melanthy had always been represented as a friend to the United States.[23]

The colonial militia seemed to have an uncanny knack for overrunning Indian towns when the warriors were away hunting, or in the latter case, on a consultation with General Clarke. Their only competition in the village was women and children and old men. The immigrants on the frontier were out of control, and lawlessness prevailed in the colonial "settlement."

Such was the social condition in the colonies the day "independence" came to America. Even in the church, both lay and clergy boasted of killing Indians on the way to worship: "Jack Potter, after telling how he had dispersed a band of Indians with his Winchester, was chided by the Bishop with the scriptural quotation: 'Our weapons are not carnal.' "[25]A All these things seem to have culminated in the coming into existence of the United States of America and the nationalizing of the Methodist Church in America. Considering the brokenness of the human condition in the eighteenth century, the church had its work cut out for it.

> Following the Revolution, John Wesley had sent his circuit riders into the wilderness plodding wearily on horseback from cabin to cabin, and from church to church. They, along with the rough, self taught Baptists, and the slightly more formal Presbyterians, for years carried the torch of religion, bringing light to an individual here, and perhaps a family there, but the light was a mere flicker, often going out with their passing. As the Eighteenth Century

wore on, the riders in their discouragement regarded the frontier as abandoned to "wilderness, immorality, and infidelity."[25]

As for Wesley's view of ministry to American Indians, did he really espouse a belief that saw the Native tribes in America as the "progeny of Shem"? Probably not in the sense of their being Semitic peoples, but a point is to be made with his remark and perhaps it passed by the original recipients of the letter—that he at least recognized the Native people of the American continent as members of the family of God, just as surely as are people in other parts of the globe; and that therefore they ought to be recognized as recipients of God's grace. The first bearers of the gospel with whom the Indians broke bread should have warmly welcomed them into that family, even as the Natives on the Atlantic coasts warmly welcomed them when European feet first touched these shores.

C H A P T E R   3

TRIBULATION IN THE ANCIENT DOMAIN

The American Revolutionary War did not settle the land rights issue, in the view of Native American people. It only settled the question of which European peoples would be the principal contenders for the tribal lands. Those colonial leaders who thought that the French-American victory over England automatically gave them access and title to Indian lands soon had to think again. The Native American tribes surrendered to no one. There were hundreds of tribes possessing lands in the far West and even in the Mississippi Valley who didn't even know that white armies were fighting one another over claims to their tribal lands. As for those tribal peoples who were drawn into the war, most of them did side with the British; but when the British surrendered, the tribal people continued the pressure on the American colonists: "The fact that Indian trouble continued in many places after the Revolution indicates that their attitude was shaped by real grievances rather than by British machination, and that their role in the war was really one chapter in a long war for survival and possession of their country."[1] Neither did the colonists cease their atrocities against noncombatant tribes. Henry Knox, secretary of war in the Continental Congress, spoke out against white atrocities committed against Indians in violation of the Hopewell Treaty:

> [The Secretary of War reports] that it appears . . . that the white inhabitants on the frontiers of North Carolina in the vicinity of

Chota on the Tenessee [*sic*] river, have frequently committed the most unprovoked and direct outrages against the Cherokee Indians.

That this unworthy conduct is an open violation of the treaty of peace made by the United States with the said Indians at Hopewell on the Keowee the 30th of November 1785 . . .

That the unjustifiable conduct of said inhabitants has most probably been dictated by the avaricious desire of obtaining the fertile land possessed by the said Indians of which and particularly of their ancient town of Chota they are exceedingly tenacious.[2]

In the above report, dated July 18, 1788, Knox recommended that the Continental Congress view this as a test of the sovereign power of the Congress and take action against those "white inhabitants who have so flagitiously stained the American name."[3]

He recommended that the Congress issue a proclamation to those "inhabitants" to point out the specific sections of the Hopewell Treaty that were being violated. Further, squatters should be ordered to depart from Indian lands by a designated day. To back up this order, three hundred troops should be alerted, and if the squatters should ignore the order to leave, these troops should be dispatched to Chota to enforce the proclamation. The requested proclamation was issued on September 1, 1788.[4]

The issuance of the proclamation was pragmatic, as well as being Knox's effort to create a climate of trust between the tribes and the Continental Congress. He saw the Creeks, the Choctaws, and the Chickasaws as wielding enough power to sustain damaging campaigns over a long period of time. Knox also formulated the Continental Congress's official perception of the relationship of tribal people to their land. He was perhaps guided by declarations of the tribal people themselves. In his report of June 15, 1789, he explained:

By having recourse to the several Indian Treaties, made by the authority of Congress, since the conclusion of the war with Great Britain, excepting those made January 1789, at Fort Harmar, it would appear, that Congress were of opinion that the Treaty of Peace, of 1783 absolutely invested them with the fee of all the Indian lands within the limits of the United States; that they had the right to assign, or retain such portions as they should judge proper.

But it is manifest, from the representations of the confederated Indians at the Huron Village in December 1786, that they entertained a different opinion, and that they were the only rightful proprietors of the soil, and it appears by the resolve of the 2nd of July, 1788 that Congress so far conformed to the idea.[5]

In that report Knox enunciated the following about the Congress's understanding of Native American rights:

The Indians being the prior occupants, possess the right of the soil. It cannot be taken from them unless by their free consent, or by the right of conquest in case of a just war. To dispossess them on any other principal, would be a gross violation of the fundamental laws of nature, and of the distributive justice which is the glory of a nation.[6]

Congress, at this time, didn't have enough money to raise and equip an army to go against the two thousand or more Indian troops (warriors), and so diplomacy was the option chosen. However, Knox does express a measure of justice in his statements. He states that if the interests of the white inhabitants were the only consideration, then an expedition would be ordered regardless of the inadequacy; but in the name of impartial justice, both sides, including the interests of the Indians, should be weighed and the judgment rendered through the influence of "reason and the nature of things, and not by its resentments."[7] So at the close of the eighteenth century the issue of land was still hotly pursued by Native American tribes, as it had been pursued by Native peoples from the beginning.

The concern expressed by Knox was not without cause. Congress did seem to be unable or possibly unwilling to enforce specific ordinances based on principles enunciated by them and agreed to by tribal peoples. The Northwest Ordinance of 1787 was ineffectual in protecting the interests of Native tribes. The Northwest Ordinance declared in article three that "the utmost good faith shall always be observed towards the Indians, their lands and property shall never be taken from them without their consent."

In spite of this covenant, immigrants seeking to get something for nothing streamed into the Ohio Valley. In their arrogance they moved into areas occupied by Native tribes, where permanent tribal villages had existed for ages and where large fields of grain and vegetables were being raised.

An interview of an immigrant by Moses Austin, a miner, indicates the arrogance even of those white immigrants who had not a ghost of a chance of succeeding in achieving their goals. Austin said that if you ask the immigrants what they expect when they get to Kentucky, "the answer is 'land.'"

> Have you any?
> No, but I expect I can git it.
> Have you anything to pay for land?
> No.
> Did you ever see the country?
> No, but everybody says it's good land.[8]

Neither Austin nor the immigrants being interviewed mentioned the Native tribes and their ownership of the land as factors to be considered when moving into western lands. But western lands—as were eastern lands—were Indian lands, and tribal homes and towns had to be defended.

The newly established Methodist church in America was finding its own way under the new governmental umbrella. Just less than one year after the Christmas Conference (1785), Coke and Asbury met with George Washington at Mount Vernon. At that meeting they sought Washington's support in bringing about the emancipation of slaves in Virginia.

Washington declined to initiate personal support but said he would express himself in favor of the move were it brought before the Assembly. Coke and Asbury met with Washington again, this time in 1789, just five years after the Christmas Conference. The purpose of this meeting was to express the Methodist church's "support to the head of the new civil government."[9] Apparently the two Methodist leaders missed an opportunity to express the concern of John Wesley for the "progeny of Shem."

It is readily admitted by Methodist historians that the early Methodist leaders did not place Indian ministries very high on their list of priorities. They do point out that at least some thought was given to the subject. "Strange to relate neither Coke nor Asbury felt deeply the obligation to organize systematic missionary work among Indians."[10]

Barclay notes that Coke wrote in his journal that they had on occasion been among the Cherokees and found them to be a peaceable people. But instead of offering a mission to them, he gave a benediction: "I trust that the grace of God will in time get into some of their hearts."[11] Coke recorded that remark in 1787, the same year of the Northwest Ordinance.

In 1789, the year that John Knox was declaring the understanding of Congress that Indians, being the prior occupants, "possess the right of the soil," Asbury wrote in his journal that he wished to "send an extra preacher to the Waxsaws, to preach to the Catawba Indians [York and Lancaster Counties, South Carolina]."[12]

Coke and Asbury apparently did preach to the Catawbas themselves and apparently engaged in some preliminary discussion with the Catawba leaders about establishing a school in their midst. According to the records, nothing came of the discussion, however. An interesting comment is found in the journal of Thomas Coke. Reported by Barclay, it is as follows: "We have three Indians in the district: and who knows but they are the first fruits of a glorious harvest among that people."[13] Were these three Indians members of the white congregation in New Jersey, or were these the respondents to an attempt to start a Methodist society among Indians in New Jersey? Historians have to strain somewhat to find Methodist activity among Indian peoples during the early phases of American Methodism.

The eighteenth-century Great Awakening in the southern colonies is rendered meaningless by the continuous conflict of European nations, fighting over who would possess tribal lands, and tribal people, fighting to protect homes and families from frenzied, land-hungry colonists. Christianity could not prevent the uprooting of Native American families and the theft or destruction of their homes and crops. Missionaries occasionally made heroic efforts but sometimes paid the supreme sacrifice as white governments, in their paranoia, sought to limit the meager mission successes achieved during the middle of the eighteenth century.

Sad entries such as the following bear witness to the darkness of the times: "In 1736 Christian Priber, a Jesuit acting in the French interest, traveled among the Cherokee. He worked with them for more than five years, learned their language and their ways and was helping them organize their own government. He was arrested by the British and died while in prison."[14]

The key phrase is "acting in the French interest." Was he truly acting in the French interest, or was it just that he was *thought* to be working in the French interest? On reflection, it appears that he was simply doing what in a more enlightened time missionaries would be praised for doing.

The Presbyterians also sought unsuccessfully to establish mission work among the Cherokees. Surprisingly, even the Moravians under Spangenberg were unsuccessful among the Cherokees. Methodists were in the lands as of 1769 but did not attempt mission work among the Native peoples until much later. The incongruity of white missionaries' offering a religion of love and mercy to a people whose homes and families were being destroyed by white governments is clear enough in retrospect; but in the valley of the shadows of the eighteenth century, no one seemed able to see it.

The Revolutionary War being concluded, it did not take long for colonists to start moving west of the Appalachian Mountain range and, in the South, to start pushing toward the interior. The specter of "Indian removal" cast a shadow over the original possessors of the land. By the close of the eighteenth century, whites had moved into land areas occupied by the five major tribes: the Cherokees, Choctaws, Seminoles, Creeks, and Chickasaws. In such close proximity to these tribal groups, the immigrants—now calling themselves frontiersmen—were obliged to live under the laws of the tribes, since they were not yet numerous enough to extend their arrogance beyond encroaching on Indian land. But as their numbers increased, so did their desire to have the land occupied by the tribes. The bigotry of some of the immigrant peoples moving among these tribes unfortunately found expression in the writings of a Methodist historian: "When after the discovery of America by Columbus, it was first traversed by men from the civilized nations, it was inhabited only by beasts and birds native to the forests, and by tribes of men of savage natures, of superstitious sentiments, of rude customs, and of vulgar habits."[15]

Such inaccurate representations are common in early writings and are not sustained by more scholarly writings. The author of the foregoing quotation provided some very useful information regarding the establishment of the Methodist Church in Alabama, but this information was documented and therefore not a total invention, as were the opinions found in the preceding quoted material.

The intense coveting of Indian lands by white immigrants was never more clearly expressed than in the following remarks:

> Here at the beginning of the nineteenth century era Alabama presents a spectacle and a problem. From the beginning of creation on for fifty-seven centuries, so far as history gives information, her soil has been inhabited only by Indians, only by savages. Then for a century conquest has been attempted by foreigners, and only attempted, not achieved. During this time four different nations have engaged in strife, and have supplanted each other, but have not suppressed the powerful savages.[16]

The author of that remark was complaining that while four European nations had supplanted one another as contenders for Indian lands in America, the five major tribes in the Southeast were still solidly in possession of their lands at the beginning of the nineteenth century. These lands comprise the present states of Kentucky, Tennessee, Mississippi, Louisiana, Georgia, Alabama, Florida, and the Carolinas. Progress was measured by the degree of suppression of the Native interests in the land.

> But when the lands which were claimed by the Indians were ceded to the United States, and the Indian claims to the land were extinguished, and the Indians receded from the soil, the white settlements on the Tombigbee enlarged. . . . The administration of law commenced, and civil interest commenced. When these settlements were sufficiently developed and enlarged to be heard of in the States whence the settlers thereof came, and their surroundings guaranteed access to them, access even under difficulties, the heralds of the cross found them, and the voice of the messengers of peace was heard in the wilderness.[17]

This was not only a misrepresentation of the actual historical circumstances, it also discounted missionary initiative. As it has been documented, a few missionaries preceded white encroachment on Indian lands and worked among Native peoples. Surely they deserve to be designated "heralds of the Cross," as would those who preached only to white immigrants.

As far as the historical circumstances are concerned, there is ample documentation to show that the social and political structures of the five tribes were more than adequate to sustain the tribal people economically and militarily in a manner that would give them the internal means to remain solidly in control of their homelands "from the beginning of Creation." It can be seen that the nineteenth century would begin with Native American people's being caught between the whites who bitterly coveted the land owned by the Native tribes and a new American government that should have tried to deal humanely with both sides. The fundamental question has never been addressed, even after two hundred years of white presence on this continent: namely, the validity of the white presence on a continent already possessed and cultivated.

Certainly, private remarks had been made to justify that presence. An example is one made by Jonathan Edwards, who thought he saw theological significance in European colonization of Indian homelands; others declared that European mores were superior to Native American mores and that that was justification enough.

In 1832 an attempt was made to establish legal justification for the European presence in America. In *Caldwell vs. The State of Alabama,* an opinion was set forth that included the following statement:

> We will examine this high pretension to savage sovereignty. If a people are found in the possession of a territory, in the practice of the arts of civilization; employed in the cultivation of the soil, and with an organized government, no matter what may be its form, they form an independent community. Their rights should be respected, and their territorial limits not encroached on. From such a people, territory can only be acquired consistently with good faith, and national law, peaceably by treaty; by conquest in open war; or by forcible trespass in violation of political right. The

first mode of acquisition would be in accordance with the soundest principals of morality; the second sanctioned by uniform wages of war; the last would be morally wrong.[18]

At first glance this would seem to be an argument in favor of Indian sovereignty, since the Creeks, the tribe involved in the case, could meet all of the criteria set forth here to describe an "independent community." In addition, "forcible trespass" is declared to be morally wrong.

Instead, this is a segment of an Alabama state supreme court opinion that goes on to deny the sovereignty of the Creek tribe on the ground that the tribe was claimed to be, along with all the rest of the tribes in the country, a wandering tribe of hunters who had no territorial claims. In truth, most tribes east of the Mississippi were agricultural people, as is now generally recognized. Even schoolchildren are taught that members of the Wampanoag tribe taught the Plymouth pilgrims how to plant and cultivate crops. Yet the court opinion states, "The European powers acted on these principles: they found the country uncultivated, and inhabited by only hunter tribes."[19]

This remark is patently false. No principles were enunciated by white squatters, who simply wandered around until they found land that they wanted and who appealed for military help when they were confronted by Native residents who were using the land. No one even thought of principles until Roger Williams alienated himself from the Massachusetts Puritans when he openly declared that the Puritans were stealing land when they seized it from the coastal tribes without negotiation or compensation. One of four charges brought against Williams by Massachusetts authorities (1635) was that Williams claimed "First, that we have not our land by patent from the King, but that the Natives are the true owners of it, and that we ought to repent of such a receiving it by patent."[20] After being exiled from Massachusetts by the court, Williams wandered around without shelter or food until he was given hospitality by Indians along the Mohassuck River. After about a year, Williams purchased land from the tribe at the mouth of the river and founded the town of Providence.

As for the agricultural economy of the eastern tribes, there is ample evidence recorded in immigrant documents and even military documents to demonstrate that fact. An example of the first is an excerpt from a statement of an official of a London stock company as he exults over an excuse to attack villages of the Powhattan Confederacy in order to take their cultivated fields:

> So that we, who hitherto have had possession of no more ground than their waste, and our purchase at a valuable consideration to their own contentment gained: may now by right of Warre, and law of nations, invade the country, and destroy them who sought to destroy us; whereby we shall enjoy their cultivated places, turning the laborious Mattock into the victorious sword (wherein there is more both ease, benefit, and glory) and possessing the fruits of others labours. Now their cleared grounds in all their villages (which are situate in the fruitfullest places of the land) shall be inhabited by us.[21]

In addition, it is noted by one source that after General Anthony Wayne won a field battle against Native American defenders at Fallen Timbers (1794), he burned Indian villages and cornfields "which he described as the most extensive he had ever seen."[22]

It was the destruction of the extensive fields of grain that ultimately brought the victory to Wayne, when tribal leaders were compelled to go to Greenville in the spring of the next year to sign the Treaty of Greenville. But it was seeing their women and children suffering from hunger due to the lost crops that finally compelled the Indians to go. Tecumseh refused to go to Greenville and rejected the treaty.

The Alabama supreme court judges apparently had something else in mind that caused them to make such amateurish remarks on the subject of sociology and culture relating to the Native American tribes. They also seemed to lack adequate knowledge of the actual practice of land acquisition by the Puritans and other colonists, so they clearly misrepresented the facts when seeking to justify those acquisitions.

What they could have had in mind was the pressure being brought on the government to remove the Native tribes to the West so that the colonists could take their farms and houses. Judge Safford, after going to great lengths to show that the United States government always acted in a "liberal and humane way" in relation to the original inhabitants and that "the General and

State governments acknowledge the right of all the tribes, as well as in the States and Territories, to the occupancy of their lands," gets to the main point of his remarks:

> The facts are also identified with the history of our own Country, that the government continues its uniform practice of tendering to the Indians (such as have not yet accepted) more than just and liberal inducements to relinquish their right of occupancy within the States, and emigrate to the west; that it has evinced the utmost solicitude to avoid coercion against them; that among other means used to avoid the necessity, and tempt them to move, it has tendered an extensive grant of lands west of the Mississippi . . . where they can have, not only absolute right of soil, but different and higher assurance of less restricted empire.[23]

One could almost forget that quotation comes from a court opinion in a case that had nothing at all to do with Indian removal. The Indian Removal Act was passed in 1830, but the Choctaws and other tribes involved were not eagerly packing their bags. Alabama was and is an international state. The five "civilized" tribes all occupied recognized tribal territories in what is now the state of Alabama. Their main towns were located in the choicest areas of the state, and many tribal people owned and managed large plantations that were coveted by white immigrants.

> William Bartram, the English botanist who visited the Gulf Coast of Mississippi in 1777 said [the Choctaws] were the "most ingenious and industrious husbandmen, having large plantations, or country farms, where they employ much of their time in agricultural improvements . . . by which means their territories are more generally cultivated and better inhabited than any other Indian republic that we know of."[24]

Nevertheless, there was pressure for the Native American tribes to be removed from their ancestral homes and shifted to lands belonging to other tribes in the "Indian Territory."

During this period, from 1784 to about 1832, the Methodist Church was establishing the structural foundation through which it would do its work. It must be remembered that until 1784 there was no formal Methodist Church in America. There were no ordained Methodist clergy at the time of the Revolutionary War.

Sweet reminds us that Wesley and Asbury had always maintained that the Methodist societies in America were a part of the established church.[25] They also promoted the idea that the Church of England was the established church, even in the colonies. Later, American-based Methodists joined other religious bodies calling for the separation of church and state in America.

In 1784 John Wesley became concerned about the lack of ordained clergy in America and the fact that Methodists could not receive Holy Communion in their societies and that children were not being baptized. He explained the problem to Coke in February 1784 and asked Coke to accept ordination from him, thus authorizing Coke to ordain clergy in America. Coke accepted ordination as superintendent. Two others, Richard Whatcoat and Thomas Vasey, were ordained as elders, and in July these three were assigned to America.

On November 14, 1784, Coke and Asbury met at Barratt's Chapel in Delaware. Asbury agreed to be ordained as superintendent if the unanimous consent of the American Methodist preachers was received. At the Christmas Conference in Baltimore (December 24 to January 2), Asbury was ordained a deacon, then elder. On Monday, he was ordained superintendent.

Methodist work was not organized into Annual Conferences until 1796, when the General Conference established six Conferences with definite boundaries: New England, Philadelphia, Baltimore, Virginia, South Carolina, and Western. It would not be until 1820 that district Conferences would be created to provide an administrative connection for local preachers.

Within the framework of the formal structure that served to guide the work of the church was the actual working style of the circuit riders. The circuits were extremely large. Before they were circuits, they were "missions," which usually meant generally described territories within which there were no Methodists and no meeting places. The task of the missionary was to create a circuit or circuits through preaching, counseling, and conversion. Sweet describes the circuit ministry:

> Circuits in newly settled regions were always large, sometimes covering territory so vast that it required from five to six weeks to make the rounds. Circuits were known as two-weeks, three-weeks, four-

weeks or five-weeks circuits, according to the time required for the circuit rider to go the rounds once. . . . James B. Finley's first circuit, called the Wills Creek, was four hundred and seventy-five miles round.[26]

Circuit riders were usually single since in the beginning the work would not sustain a marriage. Those who married usually "located" and became farmers and local preachers. The circuit riders preached wherever they could get an audience—in a private home, a field, or the like—to crowds of from a few on up to several thousand. Thus American Methodism was established on this continent.

During the first thirty-five years of American Methodism, the General Conferences made no mention of Native American concerns (except Coke's remarks, previously cited); while making strong statements against black slavery, they placed primary emphasis on providing ministry to the white immigrants who now were moving westward.

Native Tribes Resist Westward Movement of European Immigrants

Sweet declares enthusiastically,

The greatest accomplishment of America has been the conquest of the continent. The pushing of population westward from the Atlantic seaboard over the Allegheny Mountains into the valley of Ohio . . . the carving of farms from the forest and the prairies; the building of roads and bridges and fences; the erection of towns and cities.[27]

There seems to be a certain blindness that prevents the white historian from seeing those parts of the historical narrative that stand in judgment on those who perpetrate the "accomplishments." When viewing the same event from the Native American viewpoint, it may be said that the greatest *tragedy* of America is the rape of the continent. The land was not at war with the colonists; and neither were the Native cultivators of the land until they were assaulted by fraudulent trade or open attack.

It is customary for historians to speak of the Ohio Valley and even the area along the Mississippi River and east of the river as vacant land, just waiting for European immigrants to come and take it. The tribes that lived in the large area called the Ohio Valley included "Sauk and Foxes, Potawatomis, Ottawas, Menominees, Kickapoos, and Ojibwas."[28] Others included the Winnebagos, Kaskas, Peorias, Illinois, Miamis, Weas, Piankshas, and Shawnees. The land was in use by settled Native peoples. There were towns, farms, and people with long-standing customs and mores. They had theologies to live by, daily sedentary routines, and hopes for the future. These were all destroyed with the coming of the white immigrants.

Efforts to defend these homelands, while successful at first, when a federation of tribes under Little Turtle soundly defeated the U.S. Army under the command of General Arthur St. Clair in 1791, failed in the long run to stop the hordes of immigrants from entering the territory:

> The wars in the Ohio country near the end of the century were the direct result of white intrusion on Indian lands. When Marietta was established at the mouth of the Muskingum in 1788, Fort Harmar was built nearby for the ostensible purpose of restraining the advance of white settlement. But this was only a temporary measure and it was soon resolved to push the Indians back.[29]

The great Shawnee leader Tecumseh was the last hope for tribes in the Ohio Valley. Tecumseh's parents lived in a Shawnee town in the vicinity of Dayton and Springfield, Ohio. Tecumseh's father, Puchishenoah, was a highly regarded headman of the Shawnees. His mother, Methoataska, was thought by some authors to have been of the Creek tribe, although her name is Shawnee.

Tecumseh apparently was born while his parents were *en route* to Chillicothe, where a conference was to be held on the question of what the Shawnee Nation should do about the intrusion of white immigrants, who were increasing in number in the Ohio Valley. It is said that he was born at the present site of Old Town in March 1786, four miles north of Xenia, Ohio. His name (in its original form, Tecumtha) translated into English is "panther-lying-in-wait." The name was corrupted in white usage to Tecumseh, a word resembling the Shawnee word for "shooting star."

As most tribal families were, Tecumseh's was a close nuclear family, structured to provide for mutual care and for education and social growth. Tecumseh and five brothers and one sister. The brothers were Cheeseekau, Sauwaseekau, Nehaseemo, Kumskaukau, and Laulewasikau. The last named became the "prophet" who figured in the efforts of Tecumseh to form an intertribal alliance to preserve the Ohio Valley from white intrusion.[30] His sister's name was Tecumapease.

Tecumseh was only six years old when the so-called Lord Dunsmore's War broke out in 1774. This war was initiated against the Indian citizens by Virginia, which claimed the Ohio Valley by virtue of its charter. The Virginia militia claimed victory on the battlefield, but the Native tribes were still in control of the valley.

Immigrant peoples continued to intrude upon Indian lands, and the tribes continued to resist. The normal family life of the Shawnee's was being infringed upon more and more. On one occasion Tecumseh's mother became alarmed when Puchishenoah did not return home when expected. She took six-year-old Tecumseh with her and went to look for him. They followed the familiar Shawnee trails, which he would most likely have traveled on. After a lengthy search, they found Puchishenoah dying of gunshot wounds on the trail.

He lived long enough to tell Methoataska what happened. He had been walking on the trail, as he had done for many years. He heard someone call out to him. He turned and saw several white men, apparently hunters, coming up behind him. He stopped and turned to see what they wanted. They approached him and opened fire on him. Thinking he was dead, they left him lying on the trail.

With his father's death, Tecumseh's older brother Cheeseekau took the responsibility for Tecumseh's education and guidance. He apparently did his teaching job well: "That the fraternal guardian faithfully executed his sacred trust the subsequent career of his pupil gave ample testimony."[31]

Being only six at his father's death, Tecumseh was first under the tutelage of his mother Methoataska, and sister Tecumapease as well. "From his mother and Tecumapease, the young Indian

learned the value of patience and the need for pity for those without power, and that cruelty for the sake of cruelty, whether to animals or man, degraded a person."[32]

Under Cheeseekau "he was taught Shawnee history, traditions
and codes of the tribe."[33] Everything he learned had to be committed to memory since it was by oral tradition that he received
his teaching. He was required to repeat each teaching until he
could do it perfectly. Like a good many young boys, his favorite
game to play with other children was the sham battlefield, where
it is said that the leadership skills that would serve him later were
very evident.

Tecumseh witnessed the savagery of the colonists for the first
time when he was only twelve years of age. The home he had lived
in for twelve years with his parents, brothers, and sister was
attacked and burned by George Rogers Clarke in 1780.

> He witnessed the destruction of his own home and devastation of
> his pretty city and the ripening crops, a havoc brought to his peo-
> ple by the invading forces of the paleface. . . . As Hannibal swore
> eternal enmity to the Romans, so Tecumseh amid the ashes of his
> home, vowed implacable vengeance upon the colonists.[34]

One might have looked with pity upon the twelve-year-old
boy standing in the smoldering ashes of his beloved family home,
gesturing to the sky, vowing to relentlessly pursue and punish
those responsible for this outrage. But Tecumseh sought no pity—
only the opportunity to offset the pain of the event. A poem by
George H. Colton, while perhaps a little overdramatic, does reflect
the spiritual preparation that may have been made by Tecumseh
as he sought to draw inspiration and guidance from the spirit of
his martyred father:

> Tecumseh stood by his father's grave
> What ere they were, deep musings gave
> To his stern face a saddened look;
> And oft his bosom heaved, as shook
> By some strong grief; till calmer wrought,
> his very life seemed bound in thought
> as he were sculptured thus, with mind
> To one eternal woe resigned

He knelt besides the moldering earth,
from which had sprung his living birth;
"O spirit of my sire! if e'er
Leaving thy blissful dwelling place
Leaving thy dance and bounding chase
Thy once loved farm thou comest near,—
Oh! now be hope and counsel one,
Thou spirit for thy father's son!
How wise, how brave how good thou wert!
Be such my tongue, my hand, my heart,
That I by speech and deeds may be
Their vengeance, fame and destiny."[35]

As eager as he was to avenge this tragedy, Tecumseh was apparently restrained by his older brother from entering into combat until Cheeseekau was sure that he was ready.

The colonial rebellion had burst into the flames of war between England and their colonies in America in 1776, when Tecumseh was only eight years old. It spanned his formative years, and he saw the Native people suffer from a brutal conflict that ultimately would be of no benefit to them regardless of who won.

In March 1782 the brutal massacre of one hundred peaceful, unarmed Delawares at Gnaddenhutten by colonial militia enraged even white residents in that vicinity along the Tuscarawa River. It is recorded in a publication of the Ohio Archives and Historical Society as follows: "In March of this memorable year occurred the horrible massacre of the hundred disarmed, peaceful and guiltless Delaware Indians at Gnaddenhutten, at the hands of the band of Virginians and Pennsylvanians under Colonel David Williamson."[36]

In May another band of colonists led by Colonel William Crawford moved into the Sandusky plains, but this time the colonial militia was met and destroyed by a combined force of British and Indian troops. The combined force was led by Captain William Caldwell, who proceeded into Kentucky, where he was met by Daniel Boone leading a force of immigrants calling themselves "Kentucky frontiersman." "It was a fierce and merciless onslaught. The Kentuckians were overpowered and routed."[37]

George Rogers Clarke rallied over a thousand militiamen and led an expedition into Miami country. But instead of seeking out

Indian fighting forces, he made his moves against defenseless Indian towns, which he burned, leaving surviving families homeless and without crops.

The ceaseless warfare caused some tribal families to start moving westward in an attempt to move out of the line of fire. It was a futile attempt. Tecumseh and his family stayed in the traditional homeland with Cheeseekau at the head of the family.

In 1783 Tecumseh's military career was launched. In his first battle he outshone even the seasoned fighting men of the Shawnees and won a place of respect among his peers. He was only fifteen years of age. Observing the brutal killings of colonists who had been taken prisoner by the Shawnees, Tecumseh rose in protest and in an angry speech to his fellow tribesmen declared that "such cruelty was unworthy of real men, of Shawnees."[38] He vowed that he would never be a party to such degrading acts. It is reported that he kept that vow. "Tecumseh never altered his resolution. Time and again he protected women and children from his infuriated followers."[39] A major test of character for a fifteen-year-old; but his resolve remained intact throughout his life.

Tecumseh was only nineteen when he made his first journey south with his brother Cheeseekau in command of the Kispokotha party in 1787. They joined the Cherokees in a campaign against the colonists, and once again Tecumseh proved himself an able and skilled fighter. Cheeseekau was killed in this campaign (April 1788), and Tecumseh assumed command of the Kispokotha Shawnee. Concluding this campaign, the Kispokotha traveled throughout the South. They then returned to Ohio. Tecumseh wanted to stop for a nostalgic visit to his boyhood home on the Mad River. By now it was 1790, and things had changed; there were signs of difficult times ahead.

As he looked over his homeland, saw the changes that had come about, and empathized with the anguished people of his tribe and the other tribes, whose lives were being disrupted by the destruction of their homes and crops by groups of whites suddenly appearing on their homelands, he knew that something had to be done. The colonial militias would be coming in strength, and if no steps were taken, all of the tribal homelands would be lost.

A number of "treaties" had been made with various tribes as the U.S. government began to try to gain a hold on Indian lands after signing the Treaty of Paris in 1783. Congress assumed (incorrectly) that by wresting the paperwork from England, the Indian-owned lands would automatically come under U.S. control. The tribes occupying the land quickly cleared up that misconception. The "treaties" that had been made with a few tribes were repudiated by the major tribes of the Ohio Valley. The Shawnees for the most part refused to be a party to treaty conferences and refused to confine themselves to a United States defined territory. The dissenting tribes rejected the "treaties" because they were negotiated with individual tribes, and no tribe was authorized to speak for any other tribe. If the colonials wanted to make a deal on land occupied by Indian tribes, they should deal with all tribes together and not individual tribes. When one by one the tribes began to refuse to participate in treaty sessions unless the other tribes were involved, the situation became tense.

The tribal leaders were courteous and polite in their rejections of the treaty offers, as is evidenced in Blue Jacket's response to Governor St. Clair

> My friend, by the name and consent of the Shawnees and Delawares I will speak to you. We are all sensible of your speech, and pleased with it; but, after consultation, we cannot give an answer without hearing from our father at Detroit.

and also the response of the Weas on the Wabash

> We approve very much our brethren for not giving a definite answer without informing of it all the Lake nations; that Detroit was the place where the fire was lighted; then it ought first to be put out there.[40]

Rather than yield to the pressure to treat with the tribes as a single body, the Continental government made the next move by military force. General Josiah Harmar, a Revolutionary War veteran, now commander in chief of the U.S. Army, was ordered into action against the Ohio Valley tribes. With an army of fifteen hundred men, he moved into Native territory at the headwaters of the Maumee and the Miami. The tribal leaders in the area had anticipated the U.S. action and under the able leadership of Miami headman Me-Che-Cannah-Quah (Little Turtle) had made military preparations. Arming themselves with weapons secured from the English and organizing according to strategy designed by Me-Che-Cannah-Quah, they moved to intercept Harmar's forces near the upper Miami towns where Miami runners had calculated the course of the U. S. Army's movement. An article by E. O. Randall in *Ohio Archaeological and Historical Society Publications* describes the result of the battle:

> The Indians, in far less numbers than the American army, were led by the renowned Miami chief Me-che-cannah-quah, better known as Little Turtle, who by wily strategy divided Harmar's army and defeated and routed the expedition. Harmar, chagrined and humiliated, retreated to Fort Washington after suffering great loss of men.[41]

Shortly after the defeat of the U.S. Army by Little Turtle, Tecumseh returned to the Ohio Valley. He noted the change in circumstances and saw the beginnings of a new style of Native offensive (for the Ohio Valley). Word had reached the various tribes in 1791 that the U.S. government was preparing another military expedition against the Ohio Valley tribes. Tecumseh was the leader of a small party of scouts sent to track the progress of the U.S. forces.

The army force, this time under the command of Governor St. Clair, numbered fourteen hundred men. Tecumseh followed their progress and projected the probable location of their encampment. With this information the tribal headmen, Little Turtle, Blue Jacket (Shawnee), and Buck-Ong-A-Helas (Delaware), prepared their strategy; tribal forces were in place, waiting for the appointed time. At a little before sunrise, they attacked the U.S. encampment.

> The story of the dire result is a tale that has often been rehearsed. It was a desperate, irregular combat, the troops were completely demoralized and stampeded. They sought refuge in hasty flight, but less than half escaped. The camp and artillery were all abandoned; not a horse was left; the soldiers threw away their arms and accoutrements as they fled, strewing the road for miles. . . . This disaster, in the extent of its loss, was equal to, while its frightful details far exceeded, the defeat of . . . Washington at

Germantown, which was one of the worst repulses the colonists received.[42]

Governor St. Clair never recovered from this humiliating defeat at the hands of the Miami tribe. He resigned his army command, and several years later, in a dispute over the law making Ohio a state, he "had to resign as governor."[43]

Three years later General Anthony Wayne took great care in training his troops for the encounter with the Ohio Valley tribes; making sure he had at least twice the number of fighting men that the Ohio tribes could muster, he entered tribal lands in the Ohio Valley.

Tribal forces were waiting, numbering about fifteen hundred under Little Turtle. Wayne's forces numbered three thousand. The encounter took place in an area along the north bank of the Maumee River. A severe storm had left numerous trees strewn on the ground. The battlefield would be known as Fallen Timbers (August 20, 1794). This resulted in the first major defeat of the tribes in the "Northwest Territory," and a year later the Treaty of Greenville was signed by some of the participants.

Tecumseh adamantly refused to attend the meeting and never recognized the treaty. By the terms of the treaty, some two-thirds of the Ohio Territory was to have been lost to the colonists, and there would have been territories reserved for the participating tribes. Tecumseh, declaring that the Treaty of Greenville was the "effect of force and not of justice," planted his foot firmly on the ground and vowed not to give another inch to the intruding colonists. Immigrants began to pour into the Ohio Valley in large numbers.

Tecumseh was not idle in the intervening years. Even while the various tribal representatives were meeting in Greenville, he was initiating a new resistance that would invoke a massive inter-tribal federation. If the traditional leaders of the tribes chose to honor the Treaty of Greenville, then others who chose to continue the resistance to colonial intrusion on Native lands would be invited to join his movement.

Tecumseh made numerous journeys throughout the Ohio Valley. He accepted an invitation from the Delawares to live on land they controlled on the White River. He gladly moved his contingency among the Delawares, and this became his base of operation for seven years. While in this vicinity he would make occasional visits to the site of his boyhood home north of Xenia, Ohio. The Galloway family (a white family) was living in the vicinity, and they and Tecumseh became friends.

It is said that James Galloway had a personal library that he shared with Tecumseh, and they would spend hours in conversation on various subjects of mutual interest. It is also said that Tecumseh learned to read during their friendship, but it was James Galloway's daughter, Rebecca, who could speak the language of the neighboring tribes, who spent a good deal of time reading with Tecumseh. It was probably through her that he became knowledgeable about the New Testament. His references to the heart of the New Testament in later speeches were due to this friendship perhaps more than to missionaries whom he must have encountered during his career.

In the meantime, the immigrants were also active. William Henry Harrison had somehow managed to get himself appointed as the territorial governor of Indiana. He took office in 1801 and immediately began carving more land away from the tribal people. "Harrison had little sympathy for the Indians and was convinced that the only possible way to deal satisfactorily with them was to destroy them."[44] His goal was total dispossession of the tribal people of their land. When Tecumseh's travels began to yield results, Harrison began a campaign to discredit the movement.

Tecumseh's brother Laulewasikau, through a religious experience, assumed the role of "the prophet," perhaps filling the spiritual vacuum left by the death of the Shawnee prophet Penagashega, a respected spiritual advisor. Laulewasikau changed his name to Teuskwatawa, which is said to mean "the open door," reflecting a popular Christian metaphor.

Through Tecumseh's promotion and the prophet's devotion to his role, the prophet had gained considerable influence among the Shawnees. This influence, coupled with the compelling charisma of Tecumseh, established a trend of growth among the followers of Tecumseh. This made Harrison uncomfortable. He stepped up his campaign to discredit the prophet by seeking to sow doubt among his followers. To a group of Delawares Harrison said,

"Why don't you ask him to prove his powers as a prophet. Ask him to make the sun stand still."

This matter was laid before the prophet, who asked Tecumseh for advice. Tecumseh told his brother, the prophet, to announce that "fifty days from that day the sky would turn black at noon, the night creatures would stir and the stars would shine."[45] The prophet did as he was told, and all the tribal people assembled to watch this spectacle. At noon on the appointed day (June 16, 1806), a shadow passed over the sun, the sky became black, and for a period of time, the sound of the night creatures was heard and the stars shone in the sky. Harrison had lost this round. It was Tecumseh who knew that a solar eclipse was to take place that day.

Tecumseh sought to reason with Harrison and persuade him not to make any more treaties with any tribe that involved land cessions. Harrison arrogantly refused to consider such a suggestion. He launched into the standard rhetoric that "the United States was their friend, while all other countries had been their enemies." Harrison apparently made a remark that brought the Shawnees to their feet, weapons raised. Tecumseh calmed them, turned his back on Harrison and said to the interpreter, "Tell him—he lies," and walked out of the meeting.

Tecumseh returned and sought once again to persuade Harrison to abandon the immoral theft of Indian lands through sham treaty cessions. During this meeting at Vincennes, Tecumseh stated his credo as follows:

> I have made myself what I am, and I [wish] that I could make the red people as great as the conceptions of my mind, when I think of the Great Spirit that rules over all. I would not then come to see Governor Harrison to ask him to tear the treaty, but I would say to him, Brother, you have liberty to return to your own country. Once there were no white men in all this country; then it belonged to the red men, children of the same parents, placed on it by the Great Spirit, to keep it, to travel over it, to eat its fruits, and fill it with the same race—once a happy race, but now made miserable by the white people, who are never contented, but always encroaching. They have driven us from the great salt water, forced us over the mountains, and would shortly push us into the lakes— but we are determined to go no farther. The only way to stop this evil is for all the red men to unite in claiming a common and equal

right in the land, as it was at first, and should be now—for it never
was divided, but belongs to all. No tribe has a right to sell, even to
each other, much less to strangers, who demand all and will take
no less. The white people have no right to take the land from the
Indians, who had it first; it is theirs. They may sell it, but all must
join. Any sale not made by all is not good. The late sale is bad—it
was made by a part only.[46]

In that statement Tecumseh identifies with all tribal peoples
who have ever experienced injustice at the hands of the colonists,
from the Atlantic coast to the Mississippi River. He expresses his
vision of a massive united front involving all tribes to reinstate—
by force if necessary—"a common and equal right in the land—
as it was at first—and should be now." The remark did not fall on
deaf ears. Harrison heard it all too clearly and was troubled. The
tribal people heard, and thereafter, Prophet Town (established
by Tecumseh as an intertribal village and first located near
Greenville, then moved to a site on the Tippecanoe, a tributary of
the Wabush River) increased in population day by day.

Tecumseh was again on the road, accompanied by his best lieu-
tenants and fighting men. He decided to make the southern
rounds to seek the support of the Choctaws, Chickasaws, Creeks,
Cherokees, Seminoles, and other great tribes of the South.
Because his military leaders would be accompanying him and
because no conflict of whatever size must take place that might
compromise the positive trend of preparation that had been established, Tecumseh ordered the prophet to avoid all conflict at any
cost. He then headed south. Harrison noted his departure.

Tecumseh was more successful in the lake country than in the
South. The Choctaws—at least Pushmataha—refused to cooper-
ate. Some of the Creeks and other tribes responded, but the massive manpower that could have come from the South was not
offered. It is related that Tecumseh perceived that one of the
Creek towns under Big Warrior was not going to join his resistance movement, because they didn't believe that he was sent by
the Creator. He told the council and assembly that he was returning to Detroit, and on the appointed day, he would stamp his foot
on the ground and "shake down every house in Tuckhabatchee"
(the Creek town). Tecumseh had made this remark to other tribes

in the lake area and in the east. He also said that great trees would fall, and the water in the river would reverse its flow. "Lakes would be swallowed up and new lakes would appear."[47]

Governor Harrison, seeing that Tecumseh was absent for a considerable length of time, saw an opportunity to move against the defenseless Prophet Town and perhaps put an end to the prophet and his movement. With a force of one thousand men, on September 26, 1811, he started off in the direction of Prophet Town. Reaching the vicinity on November 6, he camped on the banks of Tippecanoe Creek. The prophet sent a delegation to arrange a peace party with Harrison. Harrison agreed to it, but the prophet committed a major blunder. He persuaded the inexperienced warriors to attack Harrison's encampment since they would be under his magical protection. The handful of Indian troops fought valiantly, killing and wounding 20 percent of Harrison's troops, but the battle ended inconclusively when the Indian forces withdrew. Harrison and his troops also retreated quickly.[48]

Tecumseh returned to find Prophet Town abandoned, and his brother in disgrace. Tecumseh's anger was so severe that he came very close to killing the prophet, whose blunder had destroyed the resistance by undermining the spiritual fabric that held it in place while the build-up was in progress.

> On December 16, 1811, a deep, terrifying rumble was felt in the south of Canada. Trees fell and huge trees toppled. Lake Michigan and Lake Erie trembled and great waves broke on the shores, though the day was windless. In the west the earth shuddered so fiercely that great herds of bison staggered to their feet and stampeded, and in the south whole forests fell. In Missouri the town of New Madrid was destroyed, the Mississippi River turned and flowed backwards. The earthquake lasted for two days and filled the atmosphere with choking dust.[49]

It is reported that the Creeks remembered the words of Tecumseh as the houses in Tuckhabatchee came crashing to the ground. While Tecumseh was experiencing the undermining of his resistance movement by the events at Tippecanoe, this seemed to many who heard the great orator to confirm and authenticate his leadership.

In addition to the rumble of the earthquake, other rumblings were heard. A new war was brewing between the Americans and the British. When in 1812 it was certain that war was imminent, William Hall, governor of Michigan Territory, appealed to the Native tribes to maintain a neutral stand. Wyandotte headman Isadore spoke in favor of tribal neutrality and offered a peace pipe in a peace council with Tecumseh. Tecumseh broke the peace pipe, saying:

> And what are we to gain by remaining neutral or if we are all to take sides with the Big Knives? Would our rights to the soil of our fathers be respected, or will our hunting grounds that have wrongfully been taken from us be restored to us after the war? No! As well might you think of recalling some of the years that have tolled over your heads as to think of getting back any of your lands that have passed into the hands of the white man.[50]

He left the council and headed for Detroit and then to Canada, where he aligned himself with the British under Major General Sir Isaac Brock.

So began the final scene in the fateful struggles of Tecumseh. His dreams of a massive assault on those who were taking Native American lands were dashed by the inexcusable blunder of his brother, the prophet. But he saw in the new war between the British and the United States an opportunity to retrieve that lost impetus. At Fort Malden, when "American" agents sought to keep Tecumseh neutral, Tecumseh broke the peace pipes that were handed to him, saying it was

> a chance such as will never occur again—for us Indians of North America to form ourselves into one great combination and cast our lot with the British in this war. And should they conquer and again get the mastery of all North America, our rights to at least a portion of the land of our fathers would be respected by the King. If they should not win and the whole country should pass into the hands of the Long Knives—we see this plainly—it will not be many years before our last place of abode and our last hunting ground will be taken from us, and the remnants of the different tribes between the Mississippi, the Lakes, and the Ohio River will all be driven toward the setting sun.[51]

The tribal groups that worked closely with Tecumseh knew the truth of his remarks. The inhabitants of Prophet Town had included Shawnees, Ojibwas, Kickapoos, Delawares, Wyandottes, and Ottawas. Others who added considerable strength were the Potawatomis, Illinois, Weas, and Piankasaws. While there was no guarantee that England would honor Native claims to a land base, the rest of the statement reflected distrust in the U.S. government's ability to deal fairly with the Native tribes.

Tecumseh also expressed disappointment in the failure of several significant tribes to pledge support for a large confederation of tribes. On one occasion he described his feelings when he returned from a trip among the southern tribes: "My mission to my mother's land had failed. I could not induce them to come where the water turns to stone and the rain comes from the clouds in showers of white wool to bury everything in sight. I had to shut my eyes all the way so as not to see the beautiful country that would soon be trampled under the feet of the hated white men."[52]

It had all come down to one last effort. Tecumseh would have preferred to be leading a combined force of tribal armies against the colonists, but instead the Ohio Valley tribesmen would enter the war of 1812 allied with the British against the Americans. At first the staunch supporters of Tecumseh's resistance alongside the Shawnees were the Wyandottes, Kickapoos, Potawatomis, Ottawas, and Winnebagos. These were the tribes present at Vincennes when Tecumseh told Harrison that the Native tribes had just as much right to form confederations of tribes as the thirteen colonies did. Other tribes would rally as the issue was joined on the battlefield.

General Brock was, from some accounts, a competent officer who led his troops well and depended on Tecumseh's skill as a field general many times. British and Native American forces captured Detroit when General Hull raised the white flag and surrendered on August 16, 1812.

Two thousand American soldiers were taken prisoner that day. Not having any adequate means to take care of that many prisoners of war, the Americans were released in several different locations. In recognition of Tecumseh's leadership, General Brock took his personal sash and gave it to Tecumseh. Tecumseh in turn expressed his appreciation for one of the tribal leaders who had rendered good and inspiring field direction—he gave the sash to Roundhead, leader of the Wyandottes.

While Brock was in command of the British forces, the combined efforts of Brock and Tecumseh yielded hopeful results. On October 12, 1812, Brock was killed at the battle of Queenstown. He was succeeded by General Henry A. Proctor. Tecumseh and Proctor began their campaign together in April 1813. Fort Meigs was to be their objective and target. Harrison and his troops were maintaining control of Fort Meigs.

The British–Native American forces laid siege to the fort. Colonel Dudley brought his troops and captured the British batteries but found himself victim of an ambush that had been prepared for him and his troops. Tecumseh's forces attacked and retook the batteries; they destroyed Dudley and six hundred of his troops. Colonel Miller brought a force against the British–Native American troops but were driven back.

The siege on Fort Meigs lasted two weeks, and then General Proctor began to withdraw. Harrison at this time refused to emerge on the battlefield, even though Tecumseh sent him a personal message challenging him to come out and do battle. His message to Harrison pointed out that they had equal numbers of troops and that though Harrison had talked big at Vincennes, "now you hide behind logs and in the earth like a groundhog."

It was the Fort Meigs siege that was the scene of the eyewitness report of the incident in which Tecumseh came upon a group of "American" prisoners being brutalized and killed by Tecumseh's own men. Tecumseh broke up the carnage and placed the remaining prisoners under protective guard. He angrily demanded to know why Proctor, who had been standing nearby all along watching the brutality, didn't stop the brutal killing of the prisoners. "Sir," Proctor said, "your Indians cannot be commanded." Tecumseh ordered him out of his sight, telling Proctor, "You are unfit to command; go and put on petticoats."[53]

Tecumseh and Proctor returned to Malden, reinforced their troops and at the end of July returned to Fort Meigs for another attempt to capture the fort. Efforts to draw the American troops out to do battle were in vain.

Apparently perceiving Proctor's weakness as the fatal flaw in their military strategy, Tecumseh began to indicate that he foresaw serious problems ahead. He is said to have shared his feelings with the Native American troops, perhaps giving them a chance - to withdraw if they should choose to do so. They declared their commitment to see it through, and Tecumseh went to Proctor to work out the next offensive. Proctor informed Tecumseh that the British under Proctor were going to return to the Thames, regroup, and start again.

Tecumseh knew that Proctor was going into a retreat. He assembled the Native American fighting forces and insisted that Proctor be present. Tecumseh challenged Proctor not to desert the campaign. The war was proceeding elsewhere, and it would be unseemly to retreat from the battlefield without ever seeing the enemy. Nevertheless, Tecumseh continued, "We must compare our parties condition to a fat dog, that carries its tail on its back, but when affrighted, drops it between its legs and runs off."[54]

Proctor declared his support for the Native American allies and promised that if they would accompany him to the Thames, he would supply their needs, including a fort for their use. Tecumseh reluctantly agreed to go to the Thames.

Retreat was not a part of Tecumseh's battle plan, however, and finally he stopped with his troops and refused to retreat any further. On October 5, 1813, he took command of both the British and Native American troops and dictated the strategy to be used against Harrison's troops, which were in "slow pursuit" of Tecumseh and Proctor's forces. When he had placed the troops in position, he addressed the Native American allies:

> Brother warriors, we are now about to enter an engagement from which I shall never come out. My body will remain on the battle field. To Proctor he said, "Tell your young men to be brave and all will be well." Unbuckling his sword, he handed it to a chief saying, "When my son becomes a noted warrior, give him this." He then removed his British military uniform and took his place in line, attired only in the ordinary buckskin hunting suit of his people.[55]

In the fierce battle that followed, not one Native American wavered. Tecumseh fell on the battlefield, and the vision of liberty in the Ohio Valley perished for the citizens of the Ancient Domain.

EXILE FROM THE ANCIENT DOMAIN

American Methodism, while planted firmly on the continent, was not without its organizational problems. Just four years after the Christmas Conference, the "first" General Conference met in Baltimore (1792) (John Wesley had died in 1791). In this General Conference James O'Kelley, a Methodist clergyman from Virginia, presented the church with its first major schism.

O'Kelley, a popular and forceful clergyman with a strong following among the Virginia clergy, opposed the absolute powers of the bishop. He sought to modify those powers through a resolution that, if approved, would grant the right of appeal for clergy in the appointive process. The resolution did not pass. This resulted in a schism in the church, centered mainly in Virginia. The schism was eventually resolved, but not before it contributed to a serious decline in church membership. The O'Kelley incident and a general disinterest in religion on the part of the immigrants were responsible for a drop in Methodist membership during the years 1794 to 1797.

The General Conference also busied itself with the issues of slavery and temperance. The church always seemed clear in its stance against slavery, with Wesley himself having been militantly opposed to slavery in the colonies. On the issue of temperance, the General Conference in 1796 passed a rule forbidding Methodist preachers to sell liquor. The most important contribution of the 1796 General Conference was the establishing of Annual Conferences with definite geographical boundaries. There were six formed at this session. The Western Annual Conference had as its western boundary the Mississippi River.

The turn-of-the-century General Conference in 1800 dealt with the foregoing matters in addition to other contemporary events. Apart from the consideration of the slavery issue in the Methodist Church, there were movements against slavery being activated by blacks in other ways. Philadelphia's free blacks submitted to Congress a petition opposing slavery and the slave trade. The Fugitive Slave Act of 1793 died in committee on January 2, 1800. Later in the year (August) a movement for freedom led by a slave named Gabriel was betrayed. Gabriel and twenty-five of his followers were hanged. The American population in 1800 was 5,300,000, and about 900,000 of these (one-fifth of the total) were slaves.[1] The 1800 General Conference took definitive action on the matter of missions to slaves and authorized the ordination of black clergy as local deacons to help facilitate that mission. This was not to say that the Methodist church was not active before then. It is reported that during the first three years of American Methodism, "more than six thousand Negroes" were enrolled in the total membership of the Methodist Church.[2]

The General Conference of 1808 provided for representative government. The provision was for one delegate for every five members of each Annual Conference. These were clergy delegates, as lay representatives were not in the picture at this time. At this General Conference, William McKendree was elected to the episcopacy, signaling some high-level support for moderation in the aristocratic governmental system of the church.

At the beginning of the nineteenth century, students at Williams College formed the Society of Brethren to initiate missions to the "heathen." In 1810 it became known as the American Board of Commissioners for Foreign Missions, "originally organized as a secret society because of the indifferent and hostile attitude of a church which could see in foreign missions only overheated religious zeal and fanaticism."[3]

The General Conference of 1812 met in New York City, the only time between 1784 and 1824 that it did not meet in Baltimore. This was the first delegated session of the General Conference, and there were ninety delegates from eight Annual Conferences present. This Conference met on May 1 in the John Street

Methodist Church. At this Conference, two new Annual Conferences were formed. This involved a division of the Western Conference to form the Ohio Conference and the Tennessee Conference. The first session of the Ohio Conference took place on October 1 at Chillicothe; the Tennessee Conference had its initial meeting on November 12.

On June 18, 1812, the American Congress declared an irrational and useless war. Claiming maritime offenses by Britain, in which American merchant ships were boarded and American sailors pressed into service for the English Navy in its war against France, plus various alleged offenses in the old Northwest, Congress voted halfheartedly to go to war against England.

Most commentators agree that the unofficial yet overriding reason for the War of 1812 was the American desire for expansion, even to the extent of wanting to seize Canada and drive the English from North America. John Randolph, a strong opponent of the war, pointed out weaknesses in attempts to rationalize this particular war against England. He struck hard at the general practice of the U.S. government in claiming Indian attacks on the frontier as justification for just about anything they needed an excuse for.

> This insinuation was of the grossest kind. A presumption the most rash, the most unjustifiable. Show but good ground for it, he [Grundy, a proponent of the war] would give up the question at the threshold—he was ready to march to Canada. It was indeed well calculated to excite the feelings of the Western people particularly, who were not so tenderly attached to our red brethren as some modern philosophers; but it was destitute of any foundation, beyond mere surmise and suspicion.[4]

It was true that the tribal peoples in the Ohio Valley were seeking ways to defend their homelands against white intrusion, but their actions were, in the beginning and in the long run, independent of British instigation. Tecumseh's move to form a confederacy among the tribes was taking place at this time, but it was not related to the British-American conflict. It was clearly and firmly aimed at preserving the Ohio Valley for its original owners and cultivators. Randolph's remarks recognized the legit-

imacy of Native American grievances and sought to put things in
perspective.

> Advantage had been taken of the spirit of the Indians, broken by
> the war which ended in the Treaty of Greenville. Under the ascen-
> dancy then acquired over them, they had been pent up by subse-
> quent treaties into nooks, straightened in their quarters by a blind
> cupidity, seeking to extinguish their title to immense wilderness-
> es, for which (possessing) as we do already, more land than we can
> sell or use) we shall not have occasion for half a century to come.
> It was our own thirst for territory, our own want of moderation
> that had driven these sons of nature to desperation, of which we felt
> the effects.[5]

If the colonies had fallen onto bad times economically, it was
through mismanagement on their part and not the interference of
external powers, said Randolph. He said that the only people
who would profit from the war would be speculators, merchants,
commissaries, and contractors.[6]

Opposition to the declaration of war in 1812 was not limited
to members of Congress. It was very unpopular in the East. Says
Barclay, "No war in American history has been more unpopular.
Opposition was strongest in the New England states and New
York. Nathan Bangs records that 'ministers of the gospel . . .
refused even to pray for their rulers and country.' "[7]

Most opponents of the war believed that the United States
had legitimate course to take action for grievances against the
British, but there was nothing that could not have been settled
through statesmanship.[8] The effect of the war was felt by the
Eastern Annual Conference, but it had little or no effect on Annual Conferences in the Ohio Valley, where agitation for war was
highest. The Genessee Conference (July 23) met without the
Canadian clergy. The Ohio Conference met on October 1, and the
Tennessee Conference met on November 12.

In spite of contemporary educational impressions, the United
States did not win the War of 1812. Neither did England. The
Treaty of Ghent signed in Belgium on December 24, 1814, had
both sides agreeing to resume pre-war conditions as far as land
acquisitions with Native tribes were concerned. The issue of
"impressment" that dominated James Madison's war message as

the principal reason for declaring war on Britain was not mentioned.

The war did considerable damage to Methodist work already under way in Canada, and it was with some difficulty that the work falling in the jurisdiction of the Genessee Conference was reestablished. British Methodism in North America became stronger, reflecting the inconclusiveness of the War of 1812.

The General Conference of 1816 saw a new reform movement emerge. The agitation for lay representation was very pronounced; also, the movement to modify the powers of the episcopacy emerged stronger than ever.

William McKendree, in response to Asbury's declaration that bishops should reserve all appointive powers to themselves, said, "I refuse to take the whole responsibility upon myself, not that I am afraid of proper accountability, but because I conceive the proposition . . . highly improper."[9] McKendree is credited with introducing the cabinet process into the Methodist appointive systems.

The Missouri Conference was formed in this General Conference (1816).

In 1819 Alexander Talley was appointed by the South Carolina Conference as missionary to the Alabama territory. His appointment signaled the introduction of Methodism among the Choctaws, although his first assignment was not for that purpose. Alabama became a state in 1819, but an Annual Conference was not organized there until 1832.

The 1820 General Conference exhibited more than usual interest in missions, as it achieved two landmark decisions. First, it approved a mission to Liberia that eventually would develop very significantly. Second, it established the Methodist Missionary Society. Two things seemed to prompt the action, both in the field of Native American work. First, the federal government, at the request of John C. Calhoun, established a "civilization" fund amounting to ten thousand dollars in 1819, and it appeared that churches that were willing to establish schools among Native American tribes would be the recipients. Second, the Wyandotte Mission was underway, and the means to firm up that work had yet to be put in place. Among the church's peripheral actions in

1820, the Kentucky Conference was authorized. There was no bishop elected at the 1820 General Conference.

In the 1824 General Conference three Conferences were formed: the Canada Conference, the Maine Conference, and the Illinois Conference. The final appearance of the effort to make presiding elders subject to election occurred and was firmly defeated. In the General Conference of 1828, the Oneida Conference was formed, and the South Carolina Conference was divided. At this General Conference, the church faced a major schism resulting from the defeat of reform measures allowing for lay representation. The reaction by the proponents was very severe. Out of this turn of events came the formation of the Methodist Protestant Church (1830), and the Methodist Church lost between twenty-five and thirty thousand members.

In the 1832 General Conference, the Alabama Conference, and the Indian Conference were formed. There appeared to be a high interest in missions as the General Conference approved the hiring, by Annual Conference, of missionary agents. It also called for a missionary survey of South America.

The 1836 General Conference formed the Black River Conference (which absorbed the Oneida Conference); it also formed the Erie Conference, the New Jersey Conference, the Michigan Conference, and the Arkansas Conference. The question of qualifications for designation of "mission circuit" arose, resulting in the following action of the General Conference: "Each Annual Conference [is] to examine strictly into the state of the domestic missions within its bounds and to allow none to remain on the list of its missions which in the judgement of the Conference is able to support itself."[10]

This General Conference also created the Liberia Mission Annual Conference. This was an institutional innovation for the church. The Liberia Mission Annual Conference had all the rights and powers of other Annual Conferences except that (1) it had no representation at General Conference, (2) it had no participation in the profits of the book concerns, and (3) it could draw no support from the chartered funds.

The 1840 General Conference continued the trend of institutional expansion by adjusting the boundaries of Annual Conferences and creating new Annual Conferences, including the Texas

Annual Conference. It also emphasized administrative responsibility over mission activity in the church by establishing three corresponding secretaries for the Missionary Society.

The 1844 General Conference was significant in several ways. Several Annual Conferences were formed, including the Indian Mission Annual Conference, to be based in "Indian Territory" west of the Mississippi River. The issue of slavery came to a head at this General Conference, and a plan of separation was adopted that formed the Methodist Episcopal Church and the Methodist Episcopal Church, South. •

The era beginning at the turn of the century and extending well into the nineteenth century was a period of powerful contradictions. On the one hand, church denominations geared themselves up to take the souls of Native American peoples into a brotherhood of love and peace; on the other hand, they were a part of a white nationalist movement that geared itself up to take away the land and livelihood of Native American people by treachery and force. Again, on the one hand, the American national leaders were proclaiming America to be a land of freedom and justice, while on the other hand, citizens were mired down in the moral degradation of the practice of slavery.

In the first case the church was powerless to stop the wholesale theft of land by the federal government and the colonial states. Instead it contented itself with following the "settlers" and establishing churches among them. In the second case the matter would be complicated by the possibility of division of the nation into two nations as the dispute over slavery heated up and became a regional conflict. The federal government might then use its military power to try to resolve the issue.

But there would be no civil war fought over the rights of the Native American tribes as hordes of European immigrants began to crowd into the territories of the five major tribes of the Southeast. In the spring of 1803 the Louisiana Purchase was negotiated, whereby France sold land it didn't own in the first place to the United States, who didn't own it in the second place. Nevertheless, the floodgates were opened. The clamor for lands owned by the five major tribes of the Southeast was heard in the old West. A flurry of proposed treaties followed—some of them completed—that were all designed to wrest land from the various tribes.

> Since the Louisiana Purchase, no less than nine "treaties" had been made with the Cherokee Indians, by which they had been induced to release parts of their territory or agree to new boundary lines demanded by the whites; six with the Creeks, four with the Choctaw, three with the Chickasaw, and one with the Seminole.[11]

Removal concepts were first enunciated by Thomas Jefferson but not seriously developed until the administration of Andrew Jackson. These were not treaties in the accepted sense of the word but agreements gained through bribery, threats, and extortion. The Treaty of Hoe Buckintoopa (August 1803) was one in which Thomas Jefferson had recommended using the government trading houses to push the tribes into debt, which would then be canceled if the tribes would cede their land. The Choctaws ceded 853,760 acres of land in southwestern Alabama when the firm of Panton, Leslie, and Company presented a bill to be paid on demand. They lost 4,142,720 acres to the U.S. government in the Treaty of Mount Dexter (1805) involving the same trading company. Thomas Jefferson conceived the idea of using methods that he described as bribery: "Jefferson himself described the policy as bribery, and he had expounded it long before he won the presidency in 1800. . . . He had advocated in a letter to James Monroe that, after the government successfully subdued the recalcitrant Indians, it should change its policy from 'war to bribery.' "[12]

It would be up to John C. Calhoun to establish a policy in tune with the times and circumstances. While he advocated a humane policy toward the Native tribes, his racism would not allow him to see any solution short of stripping the Native tribes of their cultural identities: "Indians should be subject to the same controls exercised by the government over all other people living within its national borders. 'By a proper combination of force and persuasion, of punishments and rewards, they ought to be brought within the pales of law and civilization.' "[13]

President Monroe enunciated the Calhoun policy in his first annual message to Congress: "It is our duty to make new efforts for the preservation, improvement, and civilization of the Native inhabitants."[14]

At the beginning of the nineteenth century, the Methodist Church finally began to face up to the question of how it should relate to the Native American people in whose land it existed. In 1819 the South Carolina Conference appointed Alexander Talley to the Catawbah District of the Mississippi Conference. His appointment was to serve as a missionary to white inhabitants of Alabama territory. This appointment placed him in the immediate vicinity of the Choctaw Nation. It may be that he initiated a relationship in ministry to the Choctaws that would later serve him well when he was appointed as missionary to them.

Another name that appears in the annals of Native American missions of this period is that of Jesse Walker. On the appointment list of the Illinois Annual Conference of the year 1819, he is designated "Jesse Walker, Missionary to the Missouri Conference, to extend his labors to the farthest bounds of civilization."[15]

The person generally credited by the Methodist Church with igniting the fires of institutional missions among Native Americans is John Stewart. In September 1814 Stewart, seeking relief from a life of poverty and drunkenness, made his way to a camp meeting during which Methodist evangelist Marcus Lindsay provided the words and message that brought him to repentance.

With the help of Marcus Lindsay, pastor of the Marietta circuit in the Ohio Conference, John Stewart gained in spiritual and physical health. He established himself in a small business as a dyer and became a member of the Methodist Church in Marietta. He received his license as an exhorter and became excited about the prospect of preaching the gospel.

Hearing a call to "declare my counsel faithfully," Stewart packed is knapsack and walked in a northwesterly direction because a voice seemed to point him in that direction. He arrived at a Delaware settlement of Moravians on the Tuscarawas River and was directed further north. Arriving in upper Sandusky, he came to the home of William Walker, a U.S. subagent and interpreter. Mrs. Walker, herself of the Wyandotte tribe, encouraged Stewart in his mission, and he began his ministry among the Wyandottes.

The Wyandottes were one of the loyal tribes in the Lake Confederacy. This tribe struggled valiantly to maintain control of its tribal lands. Their last great effort to protect their homeland from theft by European immigrants was in the War of 1812. They were part of the confederation of tribes led by Tecumseh. Losing in their effort, they were destined to eventually move west of the Mississippi River.

Between the years of John Stewart's ministry and the time of the forced removal of the Wyandottes, the Methodist Church conducted a successful ministry among this people. First, of course, was the faithful work of John Stewart and his interpreter Jonathan Pointer. Through their work the principal leaders of the tribe were converted. Stewart was black, as was Pointer. The latter was a resident among the Wyandottes and knew the language as well as any tribesman.

Stung by criticism that he was administering ministerial functions without having been ordained or licensed, Stewart applied to his Quarterly Conference for a license to preach in 1818. He was granted the license at the Quarterly Conference held near Urbana in that same year. The vote in Stewart's favor was unanimous and inspired several local preachers to volunteer to assist him in his work. From the time of the ensuing Annual Conference onward, Stewart was not the official missionary-in-charge. While he continued to minister to the Wyandottes, he did so "in association with missionaries placed in charge."[16] In August 1818 the Ohio Conference, meeting in Cincinnati, officially established the Wyandotte Mission.

In the meantime, representatives of the church in the East were striving to create some organizational commitment to the missionary character of the Methodist Church. While hearing such stories as those that appear in the journal of Thomas Ware, a white Methodist clergyman, might have brought a momentary feeling of inspiration, this was not reflected in any kind of innovative outreach ministry of the church: "In his autobiography he relates a conversation with a clerical opponent who overtook him as he was riding and inquired if he was a missionary. 'I replied,' says Ware, 'that I was a Methodist, and we were all missionaries.' "[17]

It is true that all appointments at the time were listed as "missionary," but it was believed by many that the church needed to be more deliberate and creative in its outreach and expansion work. As Nathan Bangs explained it, "as the church had grown—many new Districts and Conferences having been formed—it had lost somewhat of its original missionary character and needed new missionary stimulus."[18]

On April 5, 1819, the committee of New York clergy reported in an open meeting of New York Methodists that a constitution had been prepared for approval in chartering the "Bible and Missionary Society of the Methodist Episcopal Church." It was adopted by those in attendance, with some amendments. The structure of the society would include thirty-two "managers" and seven officers. Bishop McKendree was elected president, although he was not present at this meeting. Three of the seven officers elected were bishops. None of them were present.

Interest in the society waned almost immediately. The New York churches failed to respond with adequate numbers of membership subscriptions, which would have been used to send out missionaries. Even the organizing group, says Barclay, could not sustain its interest.[19] Eleven of the original thirty-two managers resigned before the close of the first year. The quorum initially set for society meetings, fifteen, had to be lowered to thirteen. Then there were the dissenters:

> Some of its opponents contended that the Church itself was so definitely missionary in character that a special organization was quite unnecessary. Others insisted that the members of the Church were too poor to support any other organization than the local church. Still others voiced opposition to "foreign" missions, insisting that the churches had more opportunities for urgently needed service in their local communities than were being met.[20]

Nevertheless, this became the model that was submitted to the General Conference in 1820. The plan of the New York Conference was approved by the General Conference and commended to all Annual Conferences for implementation. The name was changed to the Missionary Society of the Methodist Episcopal Church, in the City of New York—the words "Bible" and "in America" being removed to accommodate the concerns of the American Bible Society.

The effect of the General Conference action in 1820 was to approve a way to approach new mission fields through a generally authorized structure. Other Conferences could follow the lead of New York but were offered principally a model and official authorization.

It has been suggested many times that one of the reasons for the General Conference action was that John C. Calhoun, secretary of war under President Monroe, had established a "civilization" fund in 1819 amounting to ten thousand dollars per year for the purpose of "civilizing" Native American people, thereby preventing their extinction from the face of the earth. The church possibly anticipated sharing that fund. There is no question that it was in the mind of some of the promoters of the Missionary Society, and the Methodist Church did eventually share in that federal appropriation, plus other federal funds.

> The 1820 Methodist General Conference authorized "the establishment of Indian schools in conformity with the circular issued by the Secretary of War," and the committee appointed by the conference was authorized to apply for a share of the government appropriation. In March 1824, the Secretary of War was able to report that there were in operation twenty-one Indian schools, all but four of which had been opened since the first appropriation was made from the Civilization Fund. A year later it was reported that six additional had been opened.[21]

Bishop McKendree raised another issue that led to a more general concern for a greater outreach ministry. In the episcopal address McKendree said,

> Perhaps we have not paid sufficient attention to the voice of Providence, calling to a more general as well as a more detached spread of the Gospel among the Indians, and among the destitute of our cities, and of many remote and scattered settlements. . . . at this moment your attention is emphatically called to their subject by an address from the Wyandotte Indians, requesting us to send missionaries among them.[22]

There seemed to be considerable interest in missions among Native American people and the Wyandotte Mission of the Ohio

Annual Conference was to be the launching ground for Methodist missions among Native Americans. "With the increased sense of responsibility for Indian evangelization expressed by the 1820 General Conference, Methodism was ready for a wide expansion of its Indian Missions."[23]

That is not so difficult when you only have one mission, but nevertheless, from this point on, mission work among Native American tribes did increase. The Wyandotte Mission was in fact a model for the times in which it flourished, and it may still provide important instructions and inspiration for us today.

The spiritual foundation for the Wyandotte Mission resided in the labors of John Stewart, Mononcue, Between-the-Logs, Hicks, and Peacock, the latter four being Wyandotte headmen. From the time he was licensed to preach until his death in 1823, Stewart's health was a problem for him. He suffered from tuberculosis but continued his ministry as much as his health would permit. He married in 1820, and the bishop of the Ohio Conference raised enough money to purchase property adjacent to the Wyandotte land. A log house was built on the property. When Stewart died, he was buried on this property, but the Wyandotte people, sensing their impending forced departure, took Stewart's remains and reburied them on the south side of the Wyandotte Mission Church.[24] It was deemed fitting that he become a part of one of the Methodist national shrines. Two years after he died, he was remembered in a sermon by one of the Wyandotte preachers:

> My friends! A colored man first brought us the word. We were assembled feasting and singing and dancing. He tried to reason with us, but we continued our merrymaking until he knelt down to pray. Then we paused to look on and see what would come of this strange ceremony.
>
> Papacy was taught among us fifty years ago. Few only received it. It benefited those who obeyed its precepts. We care not how or from whom the word comes. We only rejoice in its blessings.
>
> My friends! the colored man was soon called to the reward of his labors; and immediately a white man, Finley, occupied his place.[25]

It was the Reverend James B. Finley who, with the energetic ministry of the Wyandotte ministers Mononcue and Between-the-Logs and many other Wyandottes, made the Wyandotte Mission effective, not only in upper Sandusky but also in southern Canada of the Lakes region and the Michigan Territory as well.

In 1819 Finley, as presiding elder of the Lebanon District in Ohio, became personally involved in the Wyandotte Mission and initiated himself into a relationship with the people of the tribe that bore fruit for a number of years. He assigned Moses Hinkle, Sr., to take the place of a clergyman who left to take another assignment. Finley personally appeared at the Wyandotte Mission and preached through an interpreter. He introduced Hinkle, who preached in the evening service.

There was apparently some discontent within the tribe about whether the mission should continue. The Wyandottes met several months later in their traditional council with tribal headmen and women leaders. They debated the matter at length and presented their decision to Finley. Their decision was to request the continuance of the mission and affirm the appointment of Hinkle. They requested the continuance of the interpreter Armstrong, John Stewart, and Jonathan Pointer.[26]

Finley proposed in 1821 that a "competent full-time resident missionary" be stationed among the Wyandottes and that a school be established among them.[27] The Wyandottes, in council and in consultation with tribal members, approved the proposal, and it was transmitted to the Ohio Annual Conference. The Ohio Conference approved the proposal and appointed Finley as the "competent full-time resident missionary."

The missionary wasted no time launching his ministry among the Wyandottes. The Wyandotte leaders themselves had approved the school and missionary proposal only after they had assured themselves that they could make the most basic contributions. Their statement reads as follows:

> [We, your Wyandotte Brethren] inform you that lately our council resolved to admit a missionary school, to be established amongst us, at upper Sandusky; and have selected a section of land for that purpose, at a place called Camp Meigs, where there is spring water and other conveniences; and all other necessary privileges that may be required for the furtherance of said school, shall be freely contributed. . . . Moreover we will endeavor to supply the school with scholars of our own nation sufficient to keep it in action; and we will admit children of our white friends who live amongst us. . . .

We would further let the conference know that we wish our teacher to be a preacher, that can teach and baptize our children and marry our people; a man that loves us and our children.[28]

The statement was signed by seven headmen and witnessed by William Walker and Moses Hinkle.

Treaties with the U.S. government by which the Wyandottes secured the land they were presently occupying also provided for the establishment of a blacksmith shop, a gristmill, a sawmill, and other implements. These were in place and operating. The Wyandottes donated land for the farm and in general committed themselves to participation in the further development of the Wyandotte Mission. The total contribution of the Ohio Conference (1821) for the initiation of this project was two hundred dollars "for mission support, including missionary salary."[29]

It was Finley who formed the Wyandotte Mission into a chartered Methodist Society, although ministry among the Wyandottes had been going on for five years. Beginning with thirty persons who responded to the invitation to form a Wyandotte Methodist Society, the little church grew quickly to sixty. By 1829 there had been considerable progress due to Wyandotte tribal participation and Finley's organizational skills. The school was administered with the oversight of Between-the-Logs, Mononcue, John Hicks, Peacock, and Squire Grey Eyes. The condition of the Wyandotte community in the vicinity of upper Sandusky may be glimpsed in a letter from John Johnston, agent for Indian Affairs to Bishop McKendree.

The buildings and improvements of the establishment, are substantial and extensive. . . . The farm is under excellent fence, and in fine order. . . . There are about fifty acres of corn, which from present appearances, will yield three thousand bushels. It is by much the finest crop that I have seen this year—has been well worked and is clear of grass and weeds. There are twelve acres in potatoes, cabbages, turnips and garden. Sixty children belong to the school, of which number fifty-one are Indians. These children are boarded and lodged at the mission house. . . . They are orderly and attentive. . . . They attend with the family regularly to the duties of religion. A better congregation in behavior, I have not beheld. . . . I believe there are very many persons. . . . in the Wyandotte nation who have experienced the saving effects of the Gospel upon their minds.[30]

It appeared that this mission of the Wyandottes in the Methodist Church had only prosperity, both spiritual and temporal, to look forward to. Some of the most compelling examples of Christian witness were expressed through the work and sayings of the Wyandotte people themselves. Since they promoted the mission at the Annual Conference themselves, their activities are a matter of record.

A letter from G. R. Jones reports on one such happening at the Ohio Annual Conference held in Urbana, Ohio, in 1823. After several interviews between the Wyandotte delegation and "General Superintendents," one of the interviews was held in the room of Bishop McKendree. The visiting delegation from the Wyandotte Mission included Mononcue, Between-the-Logs, Jonathan Pointer, and possibly John Stewart. If Stewart was present, it would have been his last appearance at an Annual Conference. He died in December 1823. The meeting with Bishop McKendree is recorded as follows:

A few friends were invited to be present at the interview. As breaking bread together has been a token of hospitality among most nations, a cup of tea was prepared by the family and at a suitable time they were waited on with it. Bishop McKendree, without any previous arrangement or design, appears to have been made a kind of Master of Ceremonies—he was waited on first. The sagacity of our red brethren was quite observable, they kept their eye on him and conformed in every particular. Jonathan, a man of colour (who has served the mission from the beginning as an interpreter, and has, while engaged in this work, become convinced of sin, and happily converted to God) was one of the company; he modestly declined partaking with them but being pressingly solicited by Bishop McKendree, yielded. After the repast was over, the red brethren joined in singing several hymns in their own tongue, during which a number in the house within hearing crowded into the room until there might have been as many as forty present. Mononque (a chief) rose, and approaching Bishop McKendree respectfully, held out the hand of friendship, which was cordially received, and a warm embrace took place; this appears to have taken off all restraint. Between-the-Logs (another chief) followed his example, and they proceeded around to all in the room, while sighs and tears witnessed the feelings of most who were present; but they were sighs of gratitude and astonishment, and tears of joy. The spirit of hostile foes in the field of battle was lost in the spirit of harmony and Christian love, which appeared to fill the room. I have witnessed few scenes which carried stronger conviction to my heart of the truth and excellency of the religion of the meek and humble Jesus.[31]

There can be no question about the depth of commitment of the Wyandotte people, as time after time they initiated the expressions of Christian faith that eased tensions and turned a room full of people into an appreciative fellowship. In the latter years of the Wyandotte Mission, the Native leaders seemed to sense that things, as they were, would not last. Christianity had become important to a significant portion of the Wyandotte tribe, if the reports are accurate. Agent John Johnston wrote concerning the effect of Christian leadership among the Wyandottes: "A spirit of order, industry and improvement, appears to prevail, with that part of the nation which has embraced Christianity; and this constitutes a full half of the whole population."[32]

At the time there were 260 on the class register, and it was said that "the houses were too small to contain the congregation." In August 1824 Bishop Soule and Bishop McKendree visited the Wyandotte Mission. They spent a week looking over the plant, visiting in Wyandotte houses, attending worship services, and interviewing the Native leaders. On a Tuesday, according to the account, the bishops met with the Native leaders.

> After opening the meeting with prayer, Bishop McKendree informed them that we should be glad to hear from them how the church was prospering, the state of the school and whether anything more could be done for its prosperity, with any other matters which they might wish to communicate, assuring them that we were their friends, and would be glad to do them all the good in our power.[33]

Mononcue was the first to respond. After his personal testimony of faith, he assured the bishops that "Brother Finley" was loved and appreciated and said that he hoped that Finley could remain as missionary to the Wyandottes. Mononcue's insight is instructive: "They might send a better man, but they cannot send one so well acquainted with the affairs of the Indians."[34] One after another, each Native leader echoed the testimony of Mononcue, expressed his own faith, and affirmed Finley. One of the spokesmen, Driver, spoke of the school:

> Sometimes through the eye of faith I can view the beauties of heaven, and I rejoice in the prospect of it. I believe God who has begun this work will carry it on; and that the school is the place from which the word of God will start out. And I pray God to bless the children, and make them teachers and leaders of the nation.[35]

In Zanesville, Ohio, on September 5, 1824, an unidentified Wyandotte tribesman gave his personal testimony and spoke of the spiritual benefits of Christianity, as Christ had brought the power of salvation not only to one man but also to a whole community of people: "Our eyes never melted into tears while worshipping, until we heard the name of Jesus."[36]

He expressed a hope, the fulfillment of which seemed evidenced by the Wyandotte Christian community: "The young walk in straight paths, and the aged rejoice in the prospect that our race shall not be altogether lost from the face of the earth. The white and red man will become one people."[37]

But was there a concern—a muted fear—that found expression for those who could perceive it? This same spokesman, in the same speech, raised the Bible in his hand, pointed to it, and said, "This book brought the truth into the wilderness. Oh, that we might all walk in its precepts. There are two classes in the wilderness, one opposes, and reviles, and would destroy the word. I fear there are two classes among you."[38]

Bishop McKendree expressed a desire to open new work in Michigan Territory. The Wyandottes of upper Sandusky, along with Finley, made a trip to a Wyandotte settlement on the Huron River, just north of Flat Rock, Michigan, and established what Finley reported to be the first Indian Methodist class in Michigan Territory. Their group also established work in Canada on the Aux Canards River. Finley describes this as the first Methodist Indian

Society in Canada, but Barclay shows that Alvin Torrey organized one in the East at about the same time.

The year 1824 was when trouble began for the Wyandotte Mission. The prophetic fear that there were "two classes" among white Americans was justified when the War Department began its efforts to gain cessions of land from the Native American tribes— so vigorously that "government agents are said to have threatened his [Finley's] life."[39]

Faced with wholesale discouragement among the Wyandottes, Mononcue and Between-the-Logs, now both licensed clergymen, worked even harder to maintain the progressive trend of the mission. Their trips to the East in 1826 to promote the mission with Brother Finley "created considerable interest." Their efforts were successful for a while. When Finley's relation with the Wyandotte Mission first terminated in 1826, the mission reported "300 church members, seventy pupils in the school, fifteen class leaders, and four Native preachers."[40]

In 1831 the Ohio Conference placed the Wyandotte Mission on a two-point circuit, the other church being white. Predictably, the Wyandotte Mission was neglected. Bishop John Emory visited the Wyandotte Mission in 1832. He requested a meeting with the church leaders and its members. The Wyandottes had chosen James Harryhoot as their spokesman. He criticized the new appointment policy of the Ohio Conference:

> For the last two years, the Mission . . . has been thrown into a circuit, embracing a large extent of country; and the missionaries have been obliged to attend to this large circuit and at the same time to the affairs of the Mission, and the mission school, - the whole together being a task too heavy to be well managed by any two missionaries. We have thought . . . that [since] we have discovered a serious decline in the school . . . and a great diminution in the number of scholars has taken place . . . the task imposed on . . . the [missionaries] was too heavy; more than they could attend to. . . . Another discouraging circumstance to our people [is] the efforts of the government . . . to induce us to remove to the west of the Mississippi. This keeps the minds of our people in a constantly unsettled state, and many have been induced to believe that their friends and the former patrons of the Mission had

become discouraged, and were about to abandon them to their fate.[41]

From 1828 to 1844 the Wyandotte Mission lost the tendency toward growth and development that characterized its precircuit days. In 1842 a "treaty" was concluded with the Wyandottes that wrested all of the Ohio lands from the tribe. They began their exile in July 1843. Following a farewell service on the eve of their departure, the historic Wyandotte Mission Church was closed. The last missionary to be appointed by the Ohio Conference, James Wheeler, preached the farewell sermon, which, it is said, was the same sermon preached at the funeral of John Stewart. Jonathan Pointer was the interpreter in this service. Testimonials were made by the Wyandotte leaders whose struggles had brought the mission to its peak, and then the door of the old Wyandotte Mission was closed to the community for which it was opened to serve. "The journey took about three weeks in July, 1843. Of the total 700 emigrants about 200 were members of the Methodist Episcopal Church, including nine class leaders, three local preachers and several exhorters."[42]

Potawatomi Missions

Jesse Walker, under appointment in the Illinois and Missouri Conferences from 1819 to 1832, was listed as "missionary" in almost all of his appointments. His appointments were generally not to established stations but to unchurched territories. His involvement in "Indian" missions began in 1823, when he was appointed by Bishop McKendree to open work among the tribes living within the bound of the Conference.

In a letter dated October 25, 1825, he reported to the Missionary Society secretary that because of the need to be at General Conference, he was unable to follow through on a conversation he had had with the Potawatomi tribe. A record of that meeting with the Potawatomi leaders provides some insight into the methods by which missionaries established new work among the eastern tribes. In 1823, after receiving his instructions, Walker set out to look over his territory, which covered Missouri and Illinois. He knew of the location of the Potawatomi people, so he made his way to an area between the Illinois and Mississippi rivers. Most of the tribe were away on a hunting expedition in Iowa. Walker set out with his interpreter and sought to overtake them. He arrived at their encampment and requested a council with the Potawatomi leaders.

The headman of the Potawatomi sent runners to the neighboring encampments, and the council assembled. The headman's wife brought food—a bowl of meat and broth—and passed it first to the headman and to Jesse Walker and then to the rest of those assembled. The pipe of peace was passed; Walker held the Bible up and then passed it to the headman and said he wished to teach it to the Potawatomi children. The tribal leader took it respectfully and said, "The white children's father has given them a book and they will do well to follow it."[43]

Besides going to General Conference, Walker also laid out his plan to Secretary of War John C. Calhoun at the national capital in an effort to clear the way for entry into Indian territories, and also to apply for financial aid from the "civilization" fund.

The account shows without explanation that Walker returned in the spring of 1825 accompanied by five white families. After securing permission from tribal leaders, he and the white families built log cabins (the location of these cabins was on the site of present-day Ottawa, Illinois). Unfortunately, the cabins were not on Indian land; Walker had miscalculated the location. The Native American settlements were much farther north.

Crushed, Walker went to a private place and knelt to pray and seek help for his next decision. He glanced up from his prayer and saw Shabbovee, a tribal leader, smiling at him but with an expression of concern. Overcoming the language difficulties, they began to communicate well enough to understand each other. Shabbovee went away for a while; when he returned, he brought food—deer and wild turkey. He also brought another tribesman with him to be a guide and interpreter for Walker. With the help of Furkee, Walker was able to locate a suitable place to build the mission, at Mission Creek in Lasalle County.[44]

The Salem Mission among the Potawatomi was established. The plant, which included buildings on another site, is described as having a house to shelter eighteen persons, a blacksmith shop, a poultry house, a springhouse, four hundred acres of land in cultivation, seven acres fenced for pasture, and one acre in a garden. At the time of the report, the school had fifteen children enrolled, the goal being one hundred.

Critics of the Conference began to question whether the successes of the Salem Mission were sufficient to balance off the expenditures in human services provided by the missionary family, and especially the money expended. Unfortunately, the Conference forgot that the Potawatomis had major investments in the Salem Mission too. Their children were the immediate object of the mission, and it was the children plus Potawatomi adults who provided the labor that resulted in excellent farm production. It was the tribal leaders who had to counsel privately with tribal members to assure them that it was all right for the missionaries to be there and that the Potawatomi children would be well taken care of if they went to the mission school. In a letter, Peter Cartwright wrote about the financial difficulties of the mission but concluded, "We have endured great hardships this year, but the God of missions has supported us, and with the appropriations made by our bishops, we have met the current expenses of the year."[45]

But trouble was coming for the Salem Mission from sources not unknown to the Native American tribes—nor to the church. The U.S. government, yielding to the greed of the land-grabbing European immigrants, began to move the Potawatomis and other tribes to the west of the Mississippi River (1828). The entry in the 1829 Annual Conference minutes (Illinois) reads: "On motion resolved that whereas the Potawatomi Indians have disposed of their lands where the Mission was located, it is inexpedient no longer to continue a Mission among them, and the same is hereby discontinued."[46]

In a short time Walker had made some inroads and, most of all, had made friends among the Potawatomis by treating them with respect. The lack of conversions seemed to bother some in the Annual Conference, but no one found fault with Walker's work. He provided another insight that is sad but shows what suffering the Potawatomis and other tribes endured as a result of being forced out of their homelands.

When he arrived in Chicago to meet with tribal leaders, apparently on a pastoral mission as much as anything, he found a demoralized and grieving people. The government had delayed paying them because the local agent had just taken ill and died. When the tribes finally received part of their compensation, "all broke up into confusion."[47]

For several days he worked among them, seeking them out and visiting with them. He found that those who associated with the church as Christians had come together for mutual support. He expressed hope that these tribal people would someday have their place to read the Word of God and till the soil. Peter Cartwright expressed his feeling as follows: "We expended several thousand dollars of missionary money in improving these Mission premises, and succeeded in civilizing and Christianizing a few of these Indians, but the whites kept constantly encroaching on them till they became restless, and finally the government bought them out."[48]

Missions in the Great Lakes Region

The Chippewa Nation in the Great Lakes region had for years been the subject of mission activity by French Catholics and also the Church of England. There seems to be some confusion about when the Methodist Church actually began work among them. Chippewa clergyman Peter Jones (Kah-Ke-Wa-Quo-Na-By) places the beginning of Chippewa Methodist missions in 1822 and credits Seth Crawford, a Methodist from the Genessee Conference, with making the initial contact and laying the groundwork. In his autobiography Peter Jones writes:

> About this time [1822] Seth Crawford from the states, came amongst us for the express purpose of learning the Mohawk language, that he might be enabled to preach the Gospel to the Indians in their own tongue. He stated that he received an impression on his mind it was his duty to preach to the Indians. He hired his board at one of the Indian houses, and commenced his studies.[49]

Seth Crawford was apparently part of the missionary team under Alvin Torrey, who in 1822 was sent from the Genessee Conference to minister to "the scattered and destitute inhabitants on the Grand River."[50] William Case, the presiding elder, wrote in October 1823, "It was not at first commenced with the professed design of converting the Natives (though they were had in view) but for the benefit of the white inhabitants scattered over the Indian land."[51]

But nevertheless he was pleased to report that thirty Natives (Mohawks) were converted, along with an equal number of whites. Most of the team's work took place in southern Ontario, Canada, in the vicinity of present day Brantford. While a number of tribes inhabited the area, the predominant tribe was the Mohawks. Torrey, in a letter dated January 26, 1825, reported that the work was going along very well. He reported that the mission house was usually filled for worship services. The membership of the Mission Society, however, was forty-four, of whom seven were white.

> There is one thing we should keep continually in view, in order to extensive usefulness to the Indian tribes, i.e. the raising up of Native teachers, whose piety and zeal shall be commendable, to preach the Kingdom of God to their brethren in their native tongue. . . . The conversion of Peter, a youth of about twenty-one, has already been mentioned. He speaks the Chippewa, (Missisongah dialect) and has already been useful in bringing in from the woods several of his relatives, both to the school and the society.[52]

So the beginnings of Methodism among the Chippewa occurred early in the nineteenth century as a part of the Genessee Conference mission to the Mohawks.

The autobiography of Peter Jones deserves a closer examination because it provides a view of the Native American people and their response to Christian missions in the context of white encroachment and removal of Native American people from their traditional homelands.

Peter Jones identifies himself as a member of the Missisongah tribe of the Ojibwa Nation. His mother taught him the traditional ways and beliefs of the tribe. At the appropriate age he was given the name Kah-Ke-Wa-Quo-Na-By and was dedicated to the Thunder God, whose symbol was the eagle. He went through the usual tutelage a young man goes through to guide him into manhood. He remembered that as a youth he was frightened while walking in the woods with "old Peter," who explained that the shrieking sounds they were hearing were the shouts of Pahguk, a flying skeleton. Another uneasy experience was during a period of unrest among tribes, when "a strict watch used to be kept up during the night at each wigwam, in order to prevent our being fallen upon by surprise."

Jones wrote that when the War of 1812 broke out, the belief in the villages of the Ojibwa was that "the Yankees were coming into Canada to kill all the Indians." His grandmother, Puhgashkish, was believed to have been killed by American colonists because she was crippled and unable to move to safety during the battle at York.

Jones spent nine months in an English school in 1816 and learned to "read, write, and cipher." His family then settled among the Mohawks. The Church of England had a mission among the Mohawks, and Peter Jones was baptized, at the urging of his father, by the Reverend Ralph Leeming of Ancaster, a clergyman of the Church of England.

> The principal motives which induced me to acquiesce with this wish, were, that I might be entitled to all the privileges of the white inhabitants and a conviction that it was a duty I owed to the Great Spirit to take upon me the name of a Christian, as from reading a sermon, I began to believe that the Christian religion was true.[53]

Peter Jones was very sensitive to the commitments he was "induced" to fall into. He was dissatisfied with his baptism experience and began to doubt that it would help him, since it didn't seem to help or change the whites for the better.

> Sometimes whilst reading the Word of God, or hearing it preached, I would be almost persuaded to become a Christian; but when I looked at the conduct of the whites who were called Christians, and saw them drunk, quarreling, and fighting, cheating the poor Indians and acting as if there were no God, I was led to think there was no truth in the white man's religion, and felt inclined to fall back again to my old superstitions. My being baptized had no effect upon my life. I continued the same wild Indian youth as before. I

was only a Christian outwardly, and not in heart, not yet having received the baptism of the Holy Ghost.[54]

While continuing his spiritual quest, he also sought to get more education for himself, with the view of working at an "Indian trading establishment." At the age of twenty, he hired himself out as a brickmaker to support himself in the meantime. He paid for his room and board in the home of a Mr. E. Burnell and attended school at Fairchild Creek. He returned home to his family.

It was about this time (1822) that he met Seth Crawford, who was living with an Indian family to learn the language of the Mohawks. He says about Crawford, "The piety of this young man, together with his compassion for the poor Indians, made a deep impression on my mind."[55]

Jones writes that in the spring of 1823 the word was circulated that Methodist preaching was to take place at the house of Mohawk leader Thomas Davis. From that experience he notes, "It is quite evident that the Spirit of the Lord had already begun to move upon the hearts of their people." In June 1823 he and his sister Mary were invited to attend a Methodist campmeeting in the township of Ancaster. "I was prompted by curiosity to go and see how the Methodist worshipped the Great Spirit in the wilderness."[56]

After all his searching, Peter Jones's soul was fertile ground for a spiritual experience. He and Mary arrived at the encampment and heard the sounds of people singing and saw groups gathered in prayer.

> Some strange feeling came over my mind, and I was led to believe that the Supreme Being was in the midst of his people who were now engaged in worshipping him. We pitched our tent upon the ground allotted to us; it was made of course linen cloth. The encampment contained about two acres enclosed by a brush fence. The tents were pitched within this circle; all the underbrush was taken away; whilst the larger trees were left standing, forming a most beautiful shade. There were three gates leading into the encampment. During each night the whole place was illuminated with fire-stands, which had a very imposing appearance amongst the trees and leaves. The people came from different parts of the

country, some ten, some twenty and some even fifty miles in their waggons, with their sons and daughters, for the purpose of presenting them to the Lord for conversion. I should judge there were about a thousand persons on the ground.[57]

This campmeeting was generally supervised by the Reverend William Case, who, as James Finley did, became deeply involved in the work of the administrative territory he served as presiding elder. As is usual in campmeeting evangelism, there were several preachers present, and they took turns preaching from the "preacher's stand." Several sermons were usually preached during the day. Following each sermon were the exhortation and prayer meeting, during which penitents were helped through prayer and counseling to come to terms with their spiritual selves. Peter Jones was deeply affected by the preaching and exhortation at this particular campmeeting and wrote in his journal:

> The meeting continued all Monday; and several discourses were delivered from the stand. My convictions at this time were deep and powerful. During the preaching I wept much. This, however, I endeavored to conceal by holding down my head behind the shoulders of the people. I felt anxious that no one might see me weeping like an old woman, as all my countrymen consider this to be beneath the dignity of an Indian brave.[58]

He struggled all day with his desire to seek prayer from those assembled, and in the evening he sought a solitary place in the woods where he might pray privately. When he knelt by a fallen tree, something unusual about the way the leaves rattled in the trees made him feel uneasy. He went deeper into the woods. He knelt to pray. A voice said to him, "Do you wish to obtain religion and serve the Lord?" Peter Jones looked up. It was old man Reynolds, who was known by Jones. "Yes," he replied.

They walked back to the campmeeting, where prayer and exhortation were offered for Peter Jones. He said that strangely his heart, which was melting with religious fervor, suddenly became hard as stone. He tried to look up, but "the heavens seemed like brass." He finally arose and went back to his tent and went to sleep.

He was later awakened by the Reverend E. Stoney, who encouraged him to complete his quest because Peter's sister Mary had herself just "obtained the Spirit of adoption." On hearing about Mary, Peter sprang to his feet and went to look for her.

> On arriving at the prayer meeting, I found my sister apparently as happy as she could be; she came to me and began to weep over me and exhort me to give my heart to God, telling me how she had found the Lord. These words came with power to my poor sinking heart, and I fell upon my knees and cried to God for mercy. . . . At the dawn of day I was enabled to cast myself wholly upon the Lord and claim the atoning blood of Jesus.[59]

He dates his conversion experience as "morning of 5th of June 1823!" This camp meeting apparently marked the beginning of Methodism among the Mohawks and apparently the Ojibwas (Chippewas) as well. Peter Jones notes in his autobiography, "Shortly after this the Rev. A. Torrey, a Methodist missionary came and preached at Thos. Davis' and gave notice that he would hereafter visit us once a month."[60]

Peter Jones went on to become an effective worker in both Canada and the Lakes region of the United States. He is mentioned by Barclay as one of the initiators of the Methodist Church among the Chippewa at Sault Ste. Marie. Working with John Clark, Jones met up with another Chippewa Methodist who had been conducting services in Sault Ste. Marie for two years previous to the arrival of Clark and Jones (June 1833). After receiving permission from the Chippewa headman, they established a day school and a Sunday school. A Methodist class was also initiated. Before long the Methodist class had grown to fifty-nine members, nineteen of whom were whites. "The employed staff included three Indian exhorters and an interpreter."[61]

In the meantime John Sunday (Shahwundais) was asked by a post trader (John Holliday) at Keweenaw to establish work at Kewawenon using his house. Sunday traveled the distance of 250 miles and started his work. Meeting resistance at first, he succeeded in 1832. Native workers Thomas McGee and Thomas Frazier succeeded him. The Kewawenon Mission was added to Clark's assignment. An attempt to start a Methodist mission at

Grand Traverse Bay was not successful due to the antagonism of the mission of another denomination.

By 1834 Clark was able to report two successful missions at the Sault, one at the fort and one at Missionville. In August 1834 the Reverend Daniel M. Chandler of the Troy Conference came to Sault Ste. Marie as a volunteer. Clark assigned him to Kewawenon, with Chippewa ministers George Copway and John Taunchy as his assistants.

Efforts to evangelize the Chippewa people in Michigan are credited to John Clark, whose assignment by the New York Methodist Episcopal Missionary Society seems to signal that the Missionary Societies were developing into sending agencies rather than support agencies. While Clark was apparently the official missionary, the actual evangelization seems to have been accomplished by several Native American evangelists. These were John Sunday (Chippewa clergyman), Henry Snake (interpreter), Thomas Frazier (clergy), and Thomas McGee (clergy) at Kewawenon.

In August 1834 Native American clergy attempted to open Methodist work among the Chippewa in the Grand Traverse Bay area. These were John Taunchy, John Cahbeach, "and one other." They established preaching services and a small school. The work looked promising until they came under attack by the Catholic Church. Clark withdrew the Native missionaries and for the time dropped efforts in the Grand Traverse Bay area. Other Native American clergy working with Clark were William Herkimer (whose wife also gave full-time to Christian work), John Johnson (trained under William Case and at Ebenezer Manual Labor School), and George Copway and Peter Marksman, both of whom were also trained under the ministry of William Case.

The Herkimers and John Johnson developed new work at Ontonagon River. In 1835 Clark sent John Taunchy, George Copway, and Peter Marksman to establish new ministries among the Chippewas at Ottawa Lake (Lac Court Orielle). They spent the winter with Sherman Hall, an American Board of Commissioners for Foreign Missions missionary in La Pointe. It is said that Copway assisted Hall in translating the Gospel of Luke into the Chippewa language.[62]

In 1836 they were granted permission to establish mission work by the tribal leaders and proceeded to do so. Clark saw this as an important achievement, since this was the largest settlement of Chippewas "in the entire Northwest." Later the same year the mission was established, it was "transferred to the Illinois Conference, Galena District, under the supervision of Alfred Brunson." In 1837 it failed without leadership and is no longer listed as an appointment.[63]

In 1839 the Michigan Conference sought to strengthen its efforts among Native Americans by establishing the Indian Mission District under the supervision of William H. Brockway. The primary foci of Chippewa missions up to 1844 were Kewawenon and Sault Ste. Marie, with outreach ministries carried out by the Native clergy.

As Annual Conferences began to realign themselves, Indian missions were effected. Some ultimately failed under new administration, while others lingered on for a while. Alfred Brunson was appointed as "Presiding Elder of the Galena District [Illinois Conference] and missionary to the Indians on the upper Mississippi."[64]

At Brunson's request in 1837, he was relieved of all responsibility for white settlements and was appointed solely as a missionary to Native American people. The Indian Mission District was created. As a result of his work (he had a staff of twelve persons) and that of his successor, B. T. Kavanaugh (1839–42), a program of missions was established at Kaposia, near Fort Snelling, Minnesota.[65]

Methodist missions among the Oneida began in 1829 in the vicinity of Vernon, New York. Daniel Barnes was appointed as presiding elder and "superintendent of the Welsh and Oneida Missions."[66]

It was Daniel Adams, a Mohawk clergyman, who at the request of Barnes performed the evangelistic work that resulted in the establishment of the Oneida Methodist Society. In the first year his preaching resulted in the conversion of over one hundred of the Oneida people. Adams formed a Methodist society of 111 persons and opened a school.[67]

Two years later, forced removal of the Oneidas began when a reservation was created by a "treaty" in Green Bay, Wisconsin. Of the one hundred Oneidas who made the long journey to Green Bay, it is said that about thirty of them were Methodists. From this core group of thirty, the historic Oneida work grew during the nineteenth century.

In New York the ministry of Daniel Adams also reached the Onondaga, and a society was formed among them. It was interrupted shortly after its beginning due to the alleged interference of "unscrupulous white men."[68]

John Clark, attending the General Conference in 1932, became aware of the Oneidas in Green Bay. He was sent by the Methodist Missionary Society to reestablish work among the Oneida people. He had the presence of mind to secure the help of the successful Mohawk evangelist, Daniel Adams, in this work. The date for the official beginning of the first Oneida Methodist class in Wisconsin was September 15, 1832, on the Fox River near Green Bay. There were twenty-five in the class.[69]

The mission house was a long structure, twenty-four by thirty feet. A school was also organized, with thirty children enrolled. The settlement on the Fox River also included some of the Tuscarora and the Stockbridge (Housatannuck) tribes. Electa Quinney, a young Housatannuck woman, was the first teacher employed. Interrupted again by a treaty of cession, the Oneidas moved to Duck Creek (1833). The school, very successful under the guidance of Miss Quinney, was reestablished, and the work continued. Daniel Adams and Electa Quinney were married and in 1837 went to the Seneca Mission in Indian Territory.

The tribes in the upper Mississippi were experiencing tremendous anguish in this period of history as whites continued to intrude upon their homelands. Even those recently arrived due to forced land cessions in the so-called New England area and New York were now being hounded by the federal government to move again to make room for whites who wanted their lands. Resistance to oppression is inevitable among any self-respecting people, and for the small, virtually defenseless tribes, it was often costly in loss of lives.

The story of the Sauk leader Black Hawk and the final struggles of his people illustrates a point that is often difficult to explain. The Sauk and Fox people controlled an extremely large area of land. Their traditional means of livelihood was agriculture. They planted extensive fields of corn and a wide variety of vegetables. They also depended on an annual hunting expedition to provide them with meat and other products such as furs, used to trade for other essentials with other tribes and at European trading posts.

It was during a time that they were on an annual hunting expedition in 1832 that Black Hawk received word that white families had entered the Sauk village. He left the hunting camp and returned to the village and discovered that there were several white families living in the Sauk lodges. One family was actually living in Black Hawk's family lodge.

Instead of ordering them out immediately, he sought to communicate to the white families that they should vacate the village since the people who owned the lodges would be returning soon. Thinking he had accomplished that through an interpreter at the trading post, he returned to the hunting camp.

The hunting expedition then was completed, and the Sauk people returned to their home. There they discovered that the white families were still there and that more had actually arrived and were living in the Sauk lodges. Those lodges not being occupied by whites had been damaged or destroyed. Black Hawk instructed his people to repair the damaged lodges and build others as needed and proceed to do the spring planting. He then made extensive efforts to secure the help of federal agencies and territorial agencies to remove the white families who had intruded on the Sauk village.

The final response to Black Hawk's efforts was the arrival of federal troops of the regular army and the Illinois militia, the latter including Captain Abraham Lincoln. Instead of ordering the white intruders out of Black Hawk's village, the U.S. military under General Gaines ordered Black Hawk and his people to leave the village and the country and go west of the Mississippi River!

Black Hawk's response was a firm "*No.*" His efforts at achieving a peaceful solution failed, and he chose to make whatever defense he could. His people were now weakened from hunger, their supply of guns and ammunition not being adequate to provide them with a good hunt. But later he reflected on his refusal to leave his homeland.

When I called to mind the scenes of my youth, and those of later days—and reflected that the theatre on which these acted, had been so long the home of my fathers, who now slept on the hills around it, I could not bring my mind to consent to leave this country to the whites, for any earthly consideration.[70]

Had the colonists moved into vacant land and built their own homes, this particular confrontation might not have occurred. But they wanted the cultivated fields and the ready-built homes of the Sauk and Fox people.

> A final flurry of resistance was offered in 1832 by a band of Sauk and Foxes under the aged war chief, Black Hawk. A fiery rival of Keokuk another Sauk chief who was ceding tribal land wholesale, Black Hawk refused to evacuate his village at Rock Island, Illinois and move across the Mississippi to Iowa. Regular troops and militia finally chased him through northern Illinois and southern Wisconsin, and in a merciless massacre of his people at Bad Axe, Wisconsin, on the Mississippi River, August 3, 1832, ended what was called the Black Hawk War.[71]

The Black Hawk incident was extremely tragic when one considers that this group of people under Black Hawk's leadership had only returned to their homelands where their fields were lying fallow and began to plant their crops and resume their lives in peace. A federal court action that would take place far into the future would rule that there was nothing illegal in such movements (*Standing Bear vs. Crook*, 1879).

Most eyewitness accounts consulted describe the event as not a war but a massacre. The last moments were seen as a desperate effort of the few fighting troops available in the small Sauk band to form a protective barrier on the bank of the Mississippi River to fight off the Illinois militia and regular army troops, while some three hundred women and children and elderly men attempted to swim to safety on the west bank of the river.

In October 1832 Bishop Soule drew $3,175 for support of the "Shawnee, Delaware, Peoria, Ioway, and Sac [Sauk] missions." It is not clear whether there actually was missionary work among the tribes at this time. " 'There are four missionaries employed but with what success we have not learned.' Under conditions such as these it was now evident that the Missionary Society could take little responsibility for cultivation of missionary interest and support of new missions."[72]

THE FIRST WHITE FROST OF OCTOBER

Jackson sent the Secretary of War
to tell Indians of the law,
Walk oh jawbone, walk I say,
Walk oh jawbone, walk away.

—song composed and sung by a group of angry Choctaws as they plunged through the dense woodlands and swamps on their way to Indian Territory, west of the Mississippi (1832)

The forced removal of the Choctaw, Cherokee, Seminole, and Creek tribes from the southeastern section of the United States to Indian Territory (now Oklahoma) was a dark and tragic event in American history. The "Trail of Tears" cannot be spoken of without remembering that thousands of the people died on this perilous and cruel journey. Each tribe attempted to work through governmental processes, but found these processes inoperative. The U.S. government wanted their land, homes, and plantations and was willing to use all means, including military force, to plunder the tribes.

When it was clear that the Choctaws were not interested in removing to the West, Jackson sent troops into the area of the Choctaw towns in Mississippi to intimidate the people. It was only when the U.S. government, through its agents, began to threaten individuals and the whole Choctaw Nation that the Treaty of Dancing Rabbit Creek was signed.

Actually the Choctaws and other southeastern tribes had already participated in a treaty that compromised tribal sovereignty and did permanent damage to the prestige and powers of the tribal governments. The Treaty of Hopewell (1785-86) was decidedly one-sided when one considers that only the Native American people were expected to comply with its provisions. It features an article that withdraws protection from whites who encroach on tribal lands and refuse to withdraw when ordered to do so. It eliminates the practice of killing innocent people in retaliation for hostile attacks on either side. But the price for these concessions was high. Article III states, "The said Indians for themselves and their respective tribes and towns do acknowledge all the Choctaws to be under the protection of the United States of America, and of no other sovereign whosoever."

Article IV fixes the boundaries of the respective tribes, and Article IX agrees that

> for the benefit and comfort of the Indians, and for the prevention of injuries or oppressions on the part of the citizens or Indians, the United States in Congress assembled shall have the sole and exclusive right of regulating trade with the Indians, and managing all their affairs in such manner as they think proper.

When the signers of the Hopewell Treaty agreed to recognize the sovereignty of the United States, they did more than recognize the United States as a sovereign state. They recognized the U.S. government as sovereign with respect to the tribes, thus modifying the independent sovereign status of the Choctaw Nation. Article IX simply exemplifies the intent of power residing in the sovereignty article.

Perhaps the most odious of the agreements is Article XI, which requires tribal people to "give notice to the citizens of the United States, of any designs which they may know or suspect to be formed in any neighboring tribe, or by any person whosoever, against the peace, trade or interest of the United States."

The foregoing agreement could have far-reaching application, not necessarily limited to snitching on one's neighbor. The practical effect of the Hopewell Treaty was to give the U.S. government and its "citizens" the right to extend their influence and interests into the internal affairs of the Choctaw Nation. It appears that actions and decisions of the tribal leaders between 1785 and the Civil War, which seem incomprehensible to the present generation of Native American readers, would best be understood in relation to the Hopewell Treaty. Tribal leaders very seldom made treaties or agreements that they had no intention of keeping. Angie Deboe says about the Hopewell Treaty:

> In 1786 at Hopewell, on the Keowee River, in South Carolina, the United States and the Choctaws made the first of the many treaties that were to occupy such a conspicuous place in the relations of the two peoples. It established perpetual peace and friendship, a pledge which was never broken until the Choctaws joined the Confederacy in the Civil War.[1]

While it may have been the stated purpose of both sides to establish a "perpetual peace," the purpose of the United States was to eliminate the influence of France and Spain in the regions occupied by the tribes. It may be that only the southern tribes expected to provide the conditions for a peaceful coexistence.

A flood of "treaties" ushered in the nineteenth century for the Choctaws, all leading up to a deadly exodus. The Treaty of Fort Adams in 1801 affirmed the eastern boundary of Choctaw land based on an earlier treaty with the British. The Choctaws also granted permission to the United States to construct a road through Choctaw country from Natchez to Nashville, Tennessee. The treaty also secured to the United States 2,641,920 acres of prime Choctaw land.

The Treaty of Fort Confederation (1802) provided for marking the eastern boundary. It also secured for the United States a large block of land north of Mobile. Federal agents again showed up a year later and, employing a tactic recommended by Thomas Jefferson, stole 853,760 acres of land from the Choctaws. The tactic was to run the debt up for the Choctaw tribe in the trading houses located in Choctaw country and present the bill for payment. When, as expected, the Choctaws were unable to pay the full amount, since repayment was always predicated on farm production and receipt of annuities, the government agents would magnanimously offer to forgive the debt in return for a cession of land.

The Treaty of Hoe Buckintoopa (1803) was the first fraudulent treaty using that method. The United States used the tactic again in 1805, and with the Treaty at Mount Dexter, the Choctaws lost 4,142,720 acres of land for $50,400, of which $48,000 would go to the trading firm of Panton, Leslie, and Company.

In the meantime, several events took place that tested the Choctaw commitment to the Hopewell Treaty. In 1803 the Louisiana Purchase was concluded, and the United States and France negotiated a transaction over land that neither of these European nations owned.

Again in 1811, Tecumseh appealed to the Choctaws to join his confederation of tribes to liberate the Mississippi and Ohio valleys from white intrusion. In one of those incomprehensible decisions mentioned earlier, Pushmataha declined, as did most of the signers of the Hopewell Treaty. Only the Creeks, at least the party known as the "Red Sticks," saw the truth in Tecumseh's appeal and responded. Their military response was an attack on Fort Mims, which initiated the "Creek War."[2] The Choctaws, thinking they were on friendly terms with the United States, sent 750 Choctaw troops to assist General Clairborne against the Creeks.[3]

In 1814 the Choctaws supplied one thousand "warriors" to assist General Andrew Jackson in the Battle of New Orleans (January 1, 1815), a useless battle since it was fought after the War of 1812 had ended. Jackson thanked the Choctaws, as did the Mississippi territorial government.[4]

On October 24, 1816, the U.S. government took from the Choctaws a large chunk of prime land located east of the Tombigbee River, in the Treaty of Fort Stephens. In an act of arrogance, the Mississippi territorial government applied for and the United States granted the application for statehood for Mississippi. That state was admitted into the union in 1817, even while the Choctaw Nation controlled the largest portion of the interior of the territory. The same is true of Alabama, which was admitted in 1819.

In December 1816 General Andrew Jackson led a U.S. military expedition against the Seminoles in Florida. Failing in his campaign against the Seminoles, Jackson requested approval from President Monroe to do battle with the Spanish instead (January

6, 1818). Not waiting for answer, the "American" force began invading Spanish settlements.[5]

In 1819 Alexander Talley, a physician turned missionary, was appointed by the South Carolina Conference as a missionary to the white residents in Alabama. This placed him in the immediate vicinity of the Choctaw Nation. Later he would be appointed to be a missionary to the Choctaws.

The American Board of Commissioners were the first to send missionaries (Protestant) among the Choctaws. In 1818 the famous Presbyterian missionaries Cyrus Kingsbury and Cyrus Byington and their families, and helpers arrived in Choctaw country. The work of these missionaries was far-reaching and innovative.

The American Board of Commissioners for Foreign Missions was itself more innovative than the usual mission society of the time. The American Board required its missionaries to undergo training before they went into the field, and the supervising body monitored its workers in the field. Information derived from the field became data to be used in training future missionaries. Its initial goals may have been excessive, but they were inspiring:

"To make the whole tribe English in their language, civilized in their habits, and Christian in their religion" was the declared aim of the American Board for the Cherokees in its annual report for 1816. When the Board was founded in 1810 it had taken for its ambitious goal the evangelization of the whole world within a generation.[6]

Some education among the Choctaws had already taken place due to the presence of the first generation of half-blood Choctaws, notably the Folsoms, the Pitchlynns, and the Leflores. Building on this, the American Board missionaries established schools immediately. The first one established was the Eliot School, on the Yalobusha River; in 1821 the Mayhew school was opened. In 1821 the Newel station school was opened and began the Choctaw system of neighborhood schools.[7] The approach to education was to work first in the language of the students, then ultimately evolve into an English-oriented program. Scripture and religious tracts were translated into the Choctaw language, as were the hymns. By this means the Choctaw students became bilingual.

Eventually these learning experiences would provide a means for more effective treaty negotiating for the Choctaws, since they would not be dependent upon white interpreters on the U.S. government payroll for information about the content of the treaty documents.

> In 1830 it was reported that there were 11 schools in the Choctaw Nation, with a total of 29 teachers, and an enrollment of 260 children; and in addition, 250 adults had been taught to read their Native language. There were also 89 boys enrolled in the Choctaw Academy. Thus was established the educational system, that was to be the greatest pride of the Choctaws during all the rest of their tribal history.[8]

Methodist missions among the Choctaws began in 1824 when the Mississippi Conference appointed Wiley Ledbetter as missionary to the Choctaws. He was located (removed from active service) the following year because of unethical procedures used in his attempts to get established. Conference officials, trying to learn why the tribal leaders expelled him from their territory, learned that he had persuaded the Choctaw leaders to give to him a school that the American Board had built, so that he could establish a better school. This the Choctaws did, but Ledbetter couldn't deliver, so he was expelled.

In 1827 Alexander Talley was appointed as missionary to the Choctaws. He was oriented more toward evangelism than education, and by the end of his first year of tenure he had made some impact in Choctaw country.

> Few converts were made during the first ten years [of Christianity among the Choctaws], but in 1828 a great revival swept the country. The wealthy and prominent mixed bloods became active converts, and large numbers of the more humble citizens came into the church in a great wave of emotional excitement. This religious movement may have been due in part to the evangelistic efforts of the Methodists, who began their work in 1826, and who reported a thousand members in 1830.[9]

On the latter point there is some disagreement from one of the Methodist sources. Barclay states, "So rapidly did evangelization proceed by Talley's method that by 1830 approximately 4,000 church members were enrolled."[10] Talley also established schools. In that same report, there were "three missionaries, three inter-preters, and four school teachers."

Unfortunately, events had been unfolding that would eventu-ally undermine the work of the missionaries among the Choctaws. Up to 1820 the "treaties" were aimed at wresting land from the Choctaws. Events now were signaling to the Choctaws that their efforts to relate peaceably to their white neighbors were mostly in vain. The spectacle of Mississippi and Alabama being granted statehood before they owned the land should have been evidence enough that there was no intention on the part of the U.S. gov-ernment to provide the means for a permanent peace as long as the Choctaws owned and were on the land.

The Treaty of Doaks Stand in 1820 was the first overt attempt to force the Choctaws to move off their homelands so whites could have it. John C. Calhoun, who counseled just and humane treatment of Native American people, assigned Andrew Jackson to lead the delegation that would begin negotiations with the Choctaws. That appointment alone should be considered an act of violence against the Choctaws. The racism of Jackson and his colleagues, such as Thomas Hart Benton of Missouri, generally was very pronounced in their remarks. Both were vigorous advo-cates of removal without regard to humanity. Jackson had already stated in a letter that the Choctaws should be "removed by me for they are standing in the way of progress."[11]

The Choctaws were not interested in another treaty, however, and were not awed by the presence of Andrew Jackson on the negotiating team. The American Board missionaries urged the Choctaws to be cautious about negotiating with government offi-cials whose aim was primarily to dispossess them from their lands. Cyrus Kingsbury in particular strongly advised the Choctaws against taking part in the negotiation. The Choctaws respected Kingsbury, and it was not until government officials convinced Kingsbury that Calhoun's views of moderation and justice would guide the discussions that the Choctaws were willing to partici-pate. It would be almost comic relief, if it weren't so grim an occasion, when Jackson in his opening speech said to the five hundred or so Choctaws gathered at Doaks Stand; "It is stated to your father the President that a large proportion of his Choctaw children are in distressed condition, and require his friendly assistance."[12] Jackson continued and in his remarks completely misrepresented the condition of the Choctaw people:

> They live upon poor land and are unwilling to cultivate it. The game is destroyed and many of them are reduced to starvation. A few are to be found in Alabama, Louisiana, and Mississippi. A number are scattered over the country from Tennessee to New Orleans. Many have become beggars and drunkards and are dying in wretchedness and want. Humanity requires that something be done for them.[13]

DeRosier says generously, "This statement was not true, but the same theme was usually presented to all Indians as a general course of treaty procedure."[14] Actually, Jackson's remarks were an outright lie. A large number of the Choctaws he was addressing were operators of large plantations with extensive fields in cultivation. Their annual produce was adequate to supply all the needs of the tribe and leave a surplus for trade purposes. They had large herds of cattle: "Here again [the Choctaws] achieved noteworthy success and annually produced stock enough to sell many head not only to other Indian nations but to white settlers as well."[15]

Jackson continued his remarks by telling the Choctaws they were doomed anyway. They would be swept away by the waves of white people who would be filling the land throughout the nineteenth century.

The proposition was simple. The Choctaws should exchange their land in Mississippi for land west of the Mississippi. Those who wanted to move could move; those who wished to stay could do so and submit to the laws of Mississippi. The Choctaws withdrew to themselves to debate the issues. Later Jackson submitted the specific proposal that detailed the lands being discussed. Glowing description of the land being offered in exchange for Choctaw land were refuted by Pushmataha, who was very familiar with the area.

The real issue was not whether the land was good or bad but whether this treaty or any treaty would be honored. The Treaty of

Hopewell was useless to the Choctaws at this time because sovereignty resided in the United States. It may be that the overriding consideration was the survival of the Choctaw people. The majority of the Choctaws were prepared to leave the treaty site with no further discussion, but Pushmataha persuaded them to stay. The Treaty of Doaks Stand was signed on October 18, 1820. In this treaty the Choctaws lost 5,169,788 of prime land in Mississippi in exchange for 13,000,000 acres of unknown land in Arkansas territory.

As it turned out, the United States made a blunder in this transaction. White settlers had already squatted on Arkansas land involved in the transaction. The Choctaws made no effort to move to the West. In 1825 another treaty was negotiated with the Choctaws to correct the blunder, since the government wouldn't think of asking the squatters to leave.

The agenda for the meeting in Washington, D.C., was based on two requests of Calhoun: first, that the boundaries of the Arkansas territory be realigned, and, second, that the Choctaws give up more land in Mississippi. The twelve Choctaws in the negotiating team quickly dispatched the latter request, saying they would not give up any more land in Mississippi. The matter of the boundaries in Arkansas became the main issue. After Calhoun had made several proposals, only to have them vigorously refused, he told the Choctaws to present a list of demands and he would respond to them.

The Choctaw delegation already had a list prepared, and with this opening, they placed them before the secretary of war. They demanded freedom to remain in the Mississippi homeland if they so chose to, as the 1820 treaty stated. They also demanded additional compensation for lands taken, additional compensation to cover the costs of tribal-based educational systems and scholarships that would permit students to attend other colleges, and additional funds for education "beyond the Mississippi River."[16] The result of the ensuing negotiations, which lasted several weeks, was a five-point compromise:

1. A six thousand dollar annual annuity in perpetuity
2. An additional six thousand dollars a year for sixteen years
3. Government waiver on all back debts owed by the Choctaws

4. Government compensation for all Choctaws who fought in the War of 1812
5. Choctaw evacuation of Arkansas lands after a survey was completed [17]

This treaty was more favorable to the Choctaws, but unfortunately, Pushmataha died from croup and apparently the strain of the negotiations before it was completed.

The next several years would see the Choctaws remaining in their eastern homelands and working to resolve the leadership vacuum left by the death of Pushmataha. But it would not be long before efforts to force the Choctaws out of Mississippi would lead to further negotiations.

A public debate on the issue of Choctaw removal began to find expression in many newspapers in the South and the North. Whites in Mississippi who opposed removal called it unjust and immoral, as well as unlawful. According to DeRosier,

> a mass meeting was held in Natchez [Mississippi] on March 17 (1830) to gain support for the deprived Indians. . . . Furthermore according to the editor of the *Natchez*, "all attempts to accomplish the removal of the Indians by bribery and fraud, by intimidation or threats . . . are acts of oppression and therefore entirely unjustifiable." [18]

The debate and support for the Choctaws among white citizens of Mississippi were not adequate to quell the persistent demand for more Choctaw land, and the Choctaws began to gear themselves for the next assault on their remaining homelands. All of the worst features of fraudulent treaty making attended the negotiations at Dancing Rabbit Creek in 1830. The remaining lands of the Choctaws were lost, and the Choctaws were scheduled to be removed west of the Mississippi River.

The Choctaw Nation, numbering about twenty-one thousand, was mostly against removal; but the actors in the theater of decision were divided. The missionaries were on opposite sides; the Methodists generally supporting removal and the American Board missionaries being vigorously opposed. The Methodist appointments at this time were as follows:

1828–29 Yazoo, A. Talley Superintendent,
      Alexander Talley Pearl River,
      Robert D. Smith Old Queens School,
      Moses Perry Seneasher School, To be supplied
1829–30 Superintendent, Alexander Talley
      Tushkahemytta and Yockanukena, Robert D. Smith
        and Moses Perry
      Shenoahkehitto, To be supplied
      4 schools [unnamed], To be supplied
1830–31 Alexander Talley
      John Cotton
      Moses Perry [19]

During the days leading up to the Treaty of Dancing Rabbit Creek, the disruption in the Choctaw community was massive and often verged on open violence, as opposing parties of the Choctaw people confronted one another. Mosholatubbee led the most violent opposition, and during one confrontation, some of the opposition burned "two or three churches"[20] and a large number of books used in the mission schools. The Methodist appointments for the years 1828 to 1831 in Mississippi apparently reflect the effect of the violent confrontation on Methodist missions. The churches and ministries mentioned in the earlier years are not mentioned in the year of the "treaty." The Methodist missionaries were in favor of removal, naively believing that the Choctaws would be free of corrupting white influences west of the Mississippi.

The problem for the Methodists was that the one man who is credited with selling out the Choctaws was Greenwood Leflore, a half-blood and an active Methodist who vigorously pursued removal. Alexander Talley is frequently mentioned as being "in the service of Leflore."[21] There were 172 Choctaw leaders who signed the Treaty of Dancing Rabbit Creek on September 27, 1830. They were described as "Chiefs, Captains, and Headmen of the Choctaw Nation."[22]

Apart from the bribery of tribal officials in the treaty process was the attempt on the part of the Mississippi legislature to sabotage the position of the Choctaws. In February 1829 that body passed an act to extend the laws of the state to include Choctaw lands. This act was probably not enforceable without federal troops; but since there was the probability of persecution of individuals using this act as an excuse, Choctaw leaders who were as yet undecided were prompted to agree to removal.

The extensive livestock holdings of the Choctaws were possibly a source of graft during the initial days of the removal. Cattle were sold to white buyers at $4.00 a head; "a cow and a calf brought $6.04." The livestock and land belonging to the Choctaws were being sold "daily to the white people under the inspection of Col. Leflore, and he gives purchasers permission to come in and take possession."[23]

The removal itself took place over a period of time extending from 1831 to 1850 and on through the nineteenth century. The U.S. government was involved in some of the largest group movements, but many Choctaws made the move on their own, not wishing to have anything more to do with the U.S. government. One of the first groups to leave Mississippi was led by Alexander Talley. In that group was Thomas Myers, a white teacher who with his family made the hazardous trip. Moses Perry was the third missionary to accompany the advance party led by Dr. Talley. After much misery and loss of life, this party was among the first to arrive in Choctaw Territory West.

A larger movement, just under two thousand Choctaws, left Mississippi under Nail and Nitakechi, gathering at "the first white frost of October."[24] The size of the group changed from time to time as circumstances caused a fluctuation in the number of people who continued on the trip.

The U.S. government conducted three main movements, beginning in 1831 and ending in 1833. By the time of the end of the third movement, some two-thirds of the Choctaw Nation were in Indian Territory. Between six and seven thousand still remained in Mississippi. Many Choctaw lives were lost to cholera, starvation, and exposure.

The Methodist group that traveled with Talley, and the group of Methodist Choctaws among the company led by Joe Nail seemed to fare better in terms of morale on this hazardous trip. They formed the nucleus of the Methodist Church among the Choctaws of present-day Oklahoma.

The Cherokee Ordeal

The Cherokee people of the Iroquoian language group controlled some 10 million acres of land in the area now known as North Carolina, parts of Tennessee, Georgia, and Alabama. Besides being prime land, the Cherokee territory also contained gold and silver.

As they are today, they were then—a very industrious people. They made frequent adaptations to improve the quality of life of Cherokee citizens. As was true with most southeastern tribes, they were glad to meet people of other nations because it would provide another opportunity to expand their trading capabilities. When the encroachments of white colonists began, the Cherokees were patient; unless they were assaulted, they sought a measure of peaceful coexistence. When the encroachments turned to intrusions, the Cherokees served notice that they would defend their territory.

The Cherokees were signers of the Treaty of Hopewell on the Keowee (November 28, 1785). When, during the administration of George Washington, the colonists continued to intrude upon the lands of the Cherokees, the Treaty of Holston (1791) was signed, ceding land to the United States. Then, following another treaty (Tellico, 1798), came a succession of treaties in 1804— two in 1805 and 1806, three in 1816, 1817, and 1819. All of these treaties served to whittle away Cherokee land holdings.

Agriculture was a way of life for the Cherokees, and when better implements were available through trade, improvements were made in their crop production. Education was important, and they welcomed the early Christian groups, such as the Moravians in 1801, the Presbyterian missionary Gideon Blackburn in 1804, and Brainerd School in 1817, which was under Cyrus Kingsbury and the American Board. (All of these mission establishments featured schools as a part of their commitment to the Cherokees.

In the early years of the nineteenth century, Sequoyah created the Cherokee alphabet, which revolutionized the educational process among the Cherokees. Sequoyah spoke only the Cherokee language, never having learned the English language. He became interested in the fact that whites were able to communicate with one another by way of the "talking leaves." He spent numerous hours experimenting with symbols and words and then symbols and sounds until finally he had developed his alphabet, which featured a symbol for every sound in the Cherokee language.

When Sequoyah demonstrated the features of the alphabet to Cherokee officials who were about to conclude that he was possessed, he won over the officials and the young men present when he taught them to read the "talking leaf." In a short time, without the benefit of schools but using the method of having each person who learned the alphabet teach another, the system swept through the community until there was scarcely anyone who could not read or write the Cherokee language. *The Cherokee Phoenix,* a newspaper of the tribe, was eventually published in the Cherokee language using the new system.

The missionaries were not so friendly to the alphabet at first, with the exception of Dr. Worcester. "The missionary board was probably convinced, but objected to Sequoyah's alphabet because of its Indian origin."[25] Worcester had no such feeling about it and made good use of this phenomenal development in his missionary publications.

In the meantime Methodists were passing through Cherokee country on their way to circuits in the white settlements. Occasionally Cherokee families would offer their hospitality to travelers they knew to be clergy. In 1822 Richard Riley, a Cherokee, became acquainted with Richard C. Neeley, minister from the Tennessee Conference, and invited him to preach at his home.

Riley's house became a preaching point on the circuit, and this initiated Methodist missions among the Cherokees. By the end of the summer, a class of thirty-three was formed, and Richard Riley became the class leader. The first official appointment to the Cherokee Mission was Andrew Crawford. After receiving permission from the tribe, he opened a school that went into operation in the following December. In a short while the Cherokee people built a meeting house.

Following a campmeeting at the Riley home, the Methodist society among the Cherokees increased to over a hundred. The work was divided into two stations, "upper" and "lower." Two more missionaries were appointed along with Crawford, Richard Neely and Nicholas D. Scales. By 1827 the Cherokee Mission reported 675 church members in three circuits. Turtle Fields, the famous Cherokee minister, was under appointment at this time.

Richard Neely told the Conference of a community of Cherokees on the Caunasauga River near one of his preaching places. The Cherokee neighbors had all got together and built a meeting house and fitted it for worship—before they had even been contacted by a missionary—in the hope that it would attract a missionary, and he would come and preach to them.[26]

Then the trouble began. At a meeting called by William Haile, a congressman from Mississippi, representatives from North Carolina, Georgia, Florida, Tennessee, Alabama, and Mississippi discussed the matter of Native American presence in the South. They drafted a report calling for "total Indian removal."[27] This group recommended that the southern states, as a last resort, should enact laws extending their jurisdiction to include lands and territories controlled by the Native tribes and abolishing tribal governments.

When the federal government began to make its move toward "Indian removal," certain congressmen and territorial governors attempted to foster an image of Native American people as unrooted, wandering hunters. This was never true for any tribe in the Americas, much less the Cherokees. A much published survey made in 1826 is repeated here for emphasis:

> An 1826 survey which showed that the Cherokee people (somewhat more than 13,000) owned 22,000 head of cattle, 7600 horses, 46,000 pigs, 726 looms, 2488 spinning wheels, 172 wagons, 2943 plows, 10 sawmills, 31 grain mills, 62 blacksmith shops, 8 cotton machines, 18 schools, and 18 ferries. The next year after adoption of their constitution, Cherokee publishers started a bi-lingual newspaper, THE CHEROKEE PHOENIX.[28]

There would be little time left for hunting or wandering! Samuel Worcester, American Board missionary, in response to a request of the Cherokee delegation that was at the time presenting its case in Washington, spoke on that point:

> Agriculture is the principal employment and support of the people. It is the dependence of almost every family. As to the wandering part of the people, who live by the case, if they are to be found in

the nation, I certainly have not found them, nor ever heard of them, except from the floor of Congress, and other distant sources of information. I do not know of a single family who depend, in any considerable degree, on game for support.[29]

In that same correspondence he reported on the progress of the various Christian denominations then working among the Cherokees:

The whole number of Native members of the Presbyterian Churches is not far from 180. In the churches of the United Brethren, are about 50. In the Baptist Churches I do not know, probably as many as 50. The Methodists, I believe, reckon in their society more than 800; of whom I suppose the greater part are natives.[30]

In 1829 the state of Georgia passed an act extending its jurisdiction to include Cherokee territory and declaring null and void the government of the Cherokees, along with all of its laws. Civil and human rights of the Cherokees were abolished, and the Cherokees were forbidden to continue the operation of their gold mines.

The Cherokees fought back in court. The missionaries, angered at the arrogance of the act, sided with the Cherokees; eventually they would also suffer for their views. When Worcester was ordered to take an oath of allegiance or remove from Cherokee territory, he declined on the basis of conscience and loyalty to a view opposite that of the state of Georgia. In July 1831 Elizur Butler, Worcester, and other missionaries, refusing to take the oath of allegiance to Georgia, were arrested, chained to a wagon, and forced to walk twenty-one miles to jail. Methodist missionaries J. J. Trott and D. C. M'Leod (superintendent of Cherokee Methodist Missions) intervened in protest and were chained with the others. Worcester was convicted and sentenced to four years of hard labor.

The Cherokee National Council went to court. In an earlier court action attempting to prevent the state of Georgia from enforcement of the oppressive laws against the Cherokees, the Cherokee National Council was rebuffed by the Supreme Court, which refused jurisdiction. But in the *Worcester vs. Georgia* (1832) decision, the Court accepted jurisdiction and nullified the laws of the state of Georgia in Cherokee territory. The state of Georgia ignored the decision and refused to release Worcester. Steadfastly refusing to compromise his principles, Worcester was finally released.

As for the Methodist missionaries, they had to face an incomprehensible experience at the ensuing session of the Tennessee Annual Conference. Barclay notes, with some bitterness, "The Tennessee Conference was unwilling to defend its missionaries in their policy of civil disobedience."[31] They refused to hear resolutions supportive of the Cherokee people. Instead they attempted to distance themselves from the event: "As a body of Christian ministers, we do not feel at liberty, nor are we disposed, to depart from the principles uniformly maintained by members and ministers of our church in carefully refraining from all such interference in political affairs."[32]

Instead of praising the missionaries for their witness in the face of great personal danger and privation, the Conference passed a resolution scolding them for their actions: "Resolved, that however we may appreciate the purity of motive and intention by which our missionary brethren were actuated, yet we regret that they should have committed themselves and us so far as to render it impossible for us to omit with propriety to notice their proceedings in this public manner."[33]

Methodist missionary J. J. Trott would on another occasion be arrested for attempting to aid the Cherokees against the oppressive laws that now were illegal. He and several other men were on an assignment to inventory damage and losses sustained when whites entered Cherokee villages and looted and sought to take over Cherokee homes, on the strength of the Georgia annexation law. The data would be used by the Cherokees to try to collect damages from the federal government. Trott and his allies were in the process of collecting these data when they were arrested and made to walk sixty miles to a jail, built especially to hold Cherokees, where they were incarcerated. They were released, but their books and papers were never returned.[34]

Government agents John F. Schermerhorn, an American Board missionary, and Mr. Currey led the government attempts to secure a treaty of removal with the Cherokees. After several rebuffs by the

Cherokee leadership, Schermerhorn assembled a small number of
Cherokees (about three to five hundred), which did not include
the principal leaders of the Cherokees. He manipulated a "treaty"
and submitted it to Washington, claiming that it was ratified by the
Cherokees. Andrew Jackson, not caring whether it was legal or
not, pushed it through Congress. Efforts by the Cherokee National Council to have the illegal treaty set aside were angrily rejected by the Jackson administration.

Eventually General Winfield Scott was sent with seven thousand
regular army troops to forcibly remove the Cherokees to Indian
Territory, an act that would come to be the tragic symbol of Indian removal, in all its cruelty, for all southeastern tribes. It is reported that one-fourth of the entire Cherokee population died on
what was to become known as the Trail of Tears. At the time of
this forced removal of the Cherokees (1838), there were only
480 members of the Cherokee Methodist Church. A sad entry in
Barclay's account reads, "At the 1837 Holston Conference the
three Cherokee circuits of the Newtown District reported a
church membership of 480. The next year there was none."[35]

The Tennessee Conference had, in 1834, transferred the mission work among the Cherokees to the Holston Conference.
John F. Boot and Turtle Fields were the Cherokee pastors who
made the long journey with the exiles. The Tennessee Conference
notes their transfer to the Holston Conference. In turn the Holston Conference recorded their transfer to the Arkansas Conference.

The Muskogee Nation

The Creeks, or Muskogee Nation, occupied and possessed a
large portion of Georgia and Alabama. It was said that the Creek
Nation, numbering about twenty-four thousand in 1821, owned
some 5,200,000 acres of land in Alabama alone. "They were agri-
culturists, lived in log houses, many owning considerable property.
They cultivated tobacco, rice, corn, beans, potatoes, peas, cabbage,
melons, strawberries, grapes and grew orchards of peaches and
plums. . . . They raised cattle and hogs and an abundance of poultry."[36]

While the Creeks lived in settled communities, they were conscious of the need to control their territorial boundaries. Whites who moved into the vicinity were not of great concern to the Creeks until it was clear that the intent of the colonists was to secure the land for themselves.

The tradition of the Muskogee people provided the unifying spirit. As was the case with other nations, decision-making power was not limited to a single leader but was vested in the people of the various Creek towns. The Creeks had to be concerned with colonial encroachment long before the Choctaws did because Creek territory was on the so-called frontier. The 1763 line of demarcation drew the frontier line on the Georgia border.

Conflicts developed during the latter half of the eighteenth century. Creek leader McGillivray, it is said, "was thinking of a confederation of southern tribes comparable to that struggling for definition north of the Ohio."[37] Losing faith in the ability of the Spanish to provide the kind of strength needed in any ally, the Creeks began to firm up their own strength, both diplomatic and military.

In 1790 McGillivray headed a Creek delegation to meet with U.S. government representatives. After considerable food and drink, the Treaty of New York was signed. This treaty, it is said, established relations between the Creeks and the U.S. government and recognized Creek claims to lands in Georgia. Whites in Georgia, known by Creeks as "people-greedily-grasping-after-land," were angered by this treaty and began to put pressure on the Creeks.

After suffering heavy losses in the Battle of Horseshoe Bend, the Creeks were to suffer another loss. The Treaty of Fort Jackson took a portion of Creek lands, but the tribe still controlled most of Georgia. In 1825 a treaty, unauthorized by the Creek Nation, was drawn up, apparently instigated by Georgia Governor Troup and Creek leaders, notably William McIntosh. The effect of the treaty was to cede to Georgia the remaining Creek lands there, in violation of Creek law.

On May 1, 1825, William McIntosh and his son-in-law were executed for high treason by Creek soldiers. Menewa, a Creek patriot, went to Washington and negotiated a new treaty (1826), the McIntosh treaty being set aside as illegal. The Menewa treaty affirmed possession of remaining Creek lands in Georgia. But Governor Troup ignored the latter treaty, and over the next several years land speculators and other shysters were not only admitted but also encouraged to squat on Creek lands under the protection of the Georgia militia. The territory was out of control, and the people were in crisis.

The Creeks signed the treaty of 1832, obligating themselves to move in five years. During that five-year period, the United States promised to keep Creek lands clear of the crooks that were overrunning it at the time. The most damaging provision of the treaty called for partitioning the land and parceling out "reservations" to each tribal member, along with the right to sell it if he so chose, the sale requiring the approval of the president. This provision caused incredible suffering for the Creeks, as whites used every immoral and illegal device available to steal land from individual Creeks: "With good land to be obtained from Creeks for whiskey, five or ten dollars, fancy promises and the most flagrant confiscation—often with the Georgia militia casually standing by—white intruders overran the Creek country."[38]

Because of the rapid loss of homes, crops, and land, the Creeks sought refuge wherever they could. In desperation, they fought back. Eneah Emathla, Eneah Micco, and Jim Henry were resistance leaders who, after trying at length to persuade the U.S. government to live up to its treaty obligations and stop the outrage perpetrated on the Creeks, began a series of counterattacks against the colonists. The three Creek resistance leaders fought to preserve a measure of dignity, as well as to recover the means of subsistence for the starving and homeless Creeks.

Many whites who were not involved in the atrocities against the Creeks insisted that the U.S. government intervene. Governor Clay of Alabama told a presidential commission that "the frauds and forgeries practiced upon the Indians to deprive them of their lands, were amongst the principal causes that exited them to hostilities."[39]

The military resistance led by Eneah Emathla, Eneah Micco, and Jim Henry had its impact. The United States sent General Winfield Scott with several thousand regular army troops to put down the resistance. The Creek "war" was declared to be over when Jim Henry was captured. He was held in custody in Alabama, and when Georgia demanded that he be turned over to them, Alabama refused, saying that Jim Henry was an Alabama citizen. All three resistance leaders and their followers were shackled hand and foot and made to march ninety miles to Montgomery on the first leg of their exile. Eneah Emathla was at the time eighty-four years old: "Old Eneah Emathla marched all the way hand-cuffed and chained like the others, and I was informed by Capt. Page, the agent for moving the Indians, that he never uttered a complaint."[40]

Jim Henry became known as McHenry in Indian Territory. He was converted in a Methodist campmeeting in the Indian Mission Conference and became a very prominent pastor in that Conference. "The admission on trial of James McHenry was very pleasing to Bishop Pierce. He was known in Georgia and Alabama as Jim Henry, the hero of the Creek war. It will also be remembered that he attended the first Asbury Manual Labor School with Samuel Checote in the East."[41]

The Creek removal was now a military operation as well as one planned and executed by government agencies and private contractors. Hundreds of Creeks were chained and manacled; they had to walk through thick underbrush and uneven terrain until they arrived at waterways, which provided a brief respite from marching, as ancient, rotting vessels carried them upstream.

Some particularly tragic events took place during the Creek removal. One of these involved incompetence and negligence on the part of white contractors, which resulted in great loss of Creek life:

> The steamboat Monmouth, with 611 Indians on board, was proceeding up the Mississippi River, when through the negligent handling of the boat she was taken through Prophet Island Bend on a course forbidden to upbound vessels; in this place at night she collided with the ship Trenton, towed by the Warren: The Monmouth was cut in two, and sunk almost immediately with a loss of 311 Indians.[42]

Methodist work among the Creeks began in 1821 when William Capers was appointed by Bishop McKendree to begin work among the Creeks in Georgia. The Creeks at the time were not open to having the Christian religion preached in the nation, but concerned about the welfare of their children, they approved the establishment of a school, with written assurance that the children would be properly cared for. The Asbury Mission School was established, and a second one was planned. When Capers attempted to establish preaching services, the Creek Council objected. The second school was never opened. Later (1826), preaching services were allowed. The school was discontinued in 1830 when removal pressure brought about a major rupture in Creek-white relations.

Throughout the ordeal of the Creeks in their original homeland and the removal itself, a particular Creek leader and his family seem to have been very prominent. Jimboy is reported to have been in several circumstances in which he had to sacrifice ideals and risk his life and that of his family in the attempt to ease the suffering of his people.

When the Creeks had lost most of their holdings and were experiencing hunger, it is said that the U.S. government sought to persuade Creek leaders to provide fighting men to assist in the campaign against the Seminoles in Florida. For obvious reasons, they received no response. It is reported that the government then threatened to withhold annuities until they complied.

Jimboy, to prevent a further deepening of the famine, agreed to lead a contingent of Creek troops if the U.S. government would guarantee that their families would be kept safe in their absence. The United States agreed, and Jimboy led a force of 776 men into the Seminole campaign. Their families were placed in a concentration camp "under the supposed protection of federal officers."[43]

When the campaign ended, Jimboy and his regiment returned to find that they had been betrayed. White mobs had broken into the compound and had taken their families prisoner. The government agent had protested that these families were under the "protection" of the U.S. government while their men were aiding the United States in Florida. It was a useless protest. The situation that Jimboy found was told in a military report submitted by Lieutenant J. G. Reynolds and quoted by Foreman:

A fifteen year old girl was shot in the leg. She stated the men wished to ravish her: she refused and ran towards a thicket which was nearby where she was fired at. . . . Many of the women and whole families, under a state of alarm, ran to the swamp where the major part of them are still, and no doubt viewed as hostile.[44]

The families lost all of their belongings, which had been stored in the agent's quarters for safekeeping. These families were then hauled away on an enforced march to the West. The U.S. agent succeeded in retaining only Jimboy's family. Jimboy rejoined his family, and they made their way to Mobile, where they would board one of the rotting vessels supplied by the contractors. In the Monmouth disaster that took 311 Creek lives, four of Jimboy's twelve children perished.

One of Jimboy's sons is reported to have been involved in a heroic effort to rescue Creeks who had been incarcerated by white citizens in Alabama and enslaved on the pretense that they were indebted to these whites. Foreman's notes tell the story:

> Among a small number of Creeks yet remaining in Alabama was a son of Jimboy named Ward Co-Cha-My who did not remove west until 1845. Three years later he returned to Alabama to aid some of his people in emigrating to Indian territory. He arrived at Fort Smith June 24, 1848 with a party of sixty-five Indians, but despite his earnest efforts he was unable to secure a number who were held as slaves by white people. "I think" he said "there yet remains in Alabama not less than 100 Creeks, and most of them in a deplorable condition; a man by the name of Dickerson in Coosa County has one family, a woman and her children, 7 in number. A Mr. Floyd and a Rev. Mr. Hayes both of Autauga County have each a number of Creeks. I tried to get these but was prevented doing so by their would-be masters. I shall get them yet—but not this season; when the waters are in good boating order. Next season you will hear from me again."[45]

Later in the nineteenth century, the Jimboy family was associated with the Methodist Church. William Jimboy was acclaimed at the close of the century as one of the greatest evangelists of the time.

The Chickasaw Nation

The Chickasaw Nation occupied and controlled territory in the northeast corner of Mississippi, a portion of Alabama, and extensive lands in Tennessee. The population of the tribe was under six thousand. They were skillful defenders of their homelands and held the respect of neighboring tribes. They were probably the most affluent people among the area's various tribes. A spiritual people, the early Chickasaws associated the deity with "four beloved things above: the clouds, the sun, the clear sky, and He that lives in the clear sky."[46]

The Chickasaws were signers of the Hopewell Treaty, and so their political relationship with the United States dates from 1786. Other treaties by the Chickasaws dispossessed them of prime lands in Tennessee. Following the extension of state laws over tribal territories, though the state law was illegal, they became vulnerable to the avarice of state governments and land-hungry colonists.

On October 20, 1832, the Chickasaws signed the Treaty of Pontotoc, which ceded their remaining 6,422,400 acres of land. There was no new territory reserved for them in the West, so the next several years were spent in securing land for themselves. In 1837 they purchased land from the Choctaws and prepared to leave. In the meantime, whites, in a frenzy, were overrunning the Chickasaw Mississippi homes even before the ink had dried on the treaty.

A few of the Chickasaws traveled to the West under government escort and experienced the horrors of a trip under incompetent government agents and thieving contractors. About half of them refused government assistance and traveled at their own expense; all traveled by horseback. They refused to board the decaying boats provided by the contractors, preferring to travel overland. Once in Indian Territory, their suffering came in the year when the U.S. government defaulted on payments to the tribe, which were owed under the terms of the 1832 treaty. The Chickasaws reestablished their government out west and began to rebuild their tribal society, adapted to their current circumstances.

There was no mission established among the Chickasaws by the Methodist Church in the East, although a preaching point in Mississippi was designated Chickasaw Mission District. At least, there were no Chickasaws mentioned in the reported membership. However, there is no question that the appointment designated in 1844 Chickasaw Nation was among the Chickasaws. E. B. Duncan was the pastor appointed to that charge.

There were no specific missions among the Seminole Nation in the East provided by the Methodist church during the period prior to removal. Later, in Indian Territory, churches were established in the Seminole community, and they have provided excellent leadership in the work of the Conference.

The Seminoles are usually associated with Florida, where the eastern band of Seminoles still maintains the basic culture of the tribe. In Indian Territory they structured their lives with respect to the demands of tribal culture and human survival. More will be said later about their contribution to the historical ministry of the church.

C H A P T E R   6

FOR PEARLS OF EARTH

The story of Jason Lee and the Oregon Mission has been told many times, adorned with 99 percent embellishments. Nevertheless, it belongs to the limited body of evidence relating to the story of Methodism among Native American people. Therefore, it must be told one more time.

The story goes that four members of the Flathead tribe made their way to St. Louis in 1832 and made it known to General William Clark that they were in quest of the white man's Book of Heaven. Clark passed the information on to visiting Indian agent William Walker (himself a Wyandotte and a Methodist), and Walker publicized the incident in a letter to the *Christian Advocate* (March 9, 1833). Dr. William Fisk, president of Wesleyan University, was electrified by the idea and energetically raised money and urged the Methodist Church to send a missionary to the Flatheads. Fisk even named the man who should go: Jason Lee.

Barclay says that it is confirmed that four Native American persons from the far West came to St. Louis in 1831 (not 1832) and visited General Clark. Clark told Methodist and Catholic churchmen about it, and the story grew from there.

The mission was designated for the area now known as Oregon, although the Flathead (Salish) peopled lived in an area now known as western Montana. Consequently, when the Jason Lee party reached their destination, they did not find the Flathead tribe. Instead they found Dr. John McLoughlin, a white man and Chief Factor of the Hudson Bay Company. McLoughlin's greeting was cordial, and he went to great lengths to make the Methodist team welcome. But he surely was able to perceive that this was the beginning of something besides a Christian mission enterprise.

It was McLoughlin who persuaded Jason Lee to establish his headquarters in the Willamette Valley, where, it is claimed, no Native American tribes lived.[1] Lee's reasons were contained in a letter published in the *Christian Advocate.* He wished to establish a boarding and commuter system of education in a fertile farming area, and he was "laying the foundation for extensive future usefulness."[2]

Jason Lee spent a lot of his time defending his decisions and the mission itself and apparently did not take the time to understand the culture, history, and needs of the various tribal people he would ultimately encounter. In addition, he heard the damaging opinions of traders and others who had their own reasons for opposing the Christianizing of Native tribes. Even Captain Wyeth, who had piloted Lee's overland train, made an absurd remark to Lee as they completed their journey: "I have heard that the Indians threatened to give them missionaries hell . . . and advised us to say nothing to them on the subject of religion, for it was not possible to do them any good, and be careful not to give them the least reason, or excuse for abusing us."[3]

Not that Jason Lee couldn't see through their special interests. He did and said so, but remarks can have their effect. The beliefs of those unable to rise above their ethnocentrism are evidenced in their views of people of another culture. A Methodist writer in 1957 placed Native American people of Oregon in the 1830s "a half-step back of the mountain men." He described the mountain men as being intimately acquainted with the Bible, which "was well known to many trappers who were associated with regular Bible reading leaders like Jedediah Smith, or who made good use of the traders copy."[4] On the other hand, according to that author, the Native people spent their time "hunting, fishing, digging roots and gathering herbs and berries."[5]

In fact, as later missionaries discovered, the Native people welcomed the missionaries and responded to the gospel in much the same manner as any people. As for tribal economics, each group had developed its own way of coping with the needs of the people; most tribes had an economy based on trade; it was by barter and sale of goods that the people supplied their needs.

Jason Lee, after hearing the discouraging words of the special interest advisors, expressed an important insight: "It is my opinion that it is easier converting a tribe of Indians at a missionary meeting, than in the wilderness."[6] It may be that Lee was of the opinion that it made no difference what the background of the objects of mission was, since the purpose of the mission was to fashion a means, both educational and mechanical, to culturally reorient their lives anyway.

When the living quarters and other necessities of the mission staff were in place, the school was opened. Problems began almost immediately. By the end of 1835, fourteen children were enrolled. By the end of the next year, four of them had died from diseases brought by whites, against which they had no immunity. One had been expelled. However, it appears that the Native people continued to bring their children in spite of the deaths:

> During the summer of 1837, the enrollment in the school totaled 40. Being taught were Indians, half-breeds, orphans, even adults. Those who received daily instruction were trained to aid the missionaries in teaching their own people. Unfortunately, by the end of the second year, only two of the original wards were left. The rest had died or fled for fear of dying.[7]

When Lee called for enforcements from the Mission Board, he raised some eyebrows with his list of personnel—it was literally a small colony. But at least one of the requests was for doctors.

Lee's *other* mission was beginning to become evident. He had, on one of his eastern trips, taken a petition from the Oregon Mission staff that effectively called for U.S. occupation of the Oregon country and its subsequent annexation to the United States. It is difficult not to conclude that Jason Lee was intimately involved in the political annexation intrigues of the government.

> There are rumors in the history books that government money from a secret fund subsidized the Methodist Mission in Oregon. These rumors, with their modern CIA overtones, are probably

true. Those patriotic missionaries would have seen no conflict in encouraging the rule of law through American influence concurrent with spreading the word of Christ.[8]

Missionizing of the Native people was not being accomplished, and the discontent of mission personnel sent the Oregon Methodist Mission spiraling downward. The Mission Board was lately reluctant in its support of Lee's mission, particularly when his demands for reinforcements began to be somewhat spectacular; on the basis of the widespread discontent in the mission staff and their own perception that things weren't going as originally planned, the Mission Board decided to discontinue Jason Lee as superintendent. Lee successfully cleared himself in a meeting with the Mission Board, but while he was stating his defense, his replacement arrived in Oregon and closed down the mission.

The colonizing process had been done. If the Flathead tribal emissaries really did ask for the white man's Book of Heaven, they only got part of their request—and it wasn't the Book of Heaven, because with the sale of the last of the mission property to the American Board of Commissioners for Foreign Missions, Methodist missions to Native tribes of Oregon ceased (1847) and waited for another day.

There were other responses to the story of the Flathead request. One of these was not a Methodist response but a response of the American Board. Marcus Whitman, a physician and ordained minister, established a mission with headquarters located in the Cayuse territory in 1836. Almost every reference to Whitman's Mission in Oregon is focused on its violent ending in 1847. The indexes consistently inform you of the page where you can find the "Whitman Massacre." Also, most church historians who comment on this tragedy ignore the precipitating circumstances by being somewhat oversolicitous with regard to his role as a missionary in Oregon.

It is said that when Marcus Whitman and his mission team arrived in the vicinity of Nez Perce and Cayuse territory, the Nez Perce people with whom he had become well acquainted during the trip invited him to establish his mission in their territory. Whitman declined, indicating that he would look for a site in the

Waiilatpuan area (although Whitman made no such distinction). The Nez Perce walked off, shaking their heads.

The Cayuse people were a very distinct and proud people, and they had a very clear understanding of their territorial boundaries. These boundaries were respected by other tribes, since they also were very clear about their territorial boundaries. The Cayuse were "a small, but powerful, Plateau tribe occupying the headquarters of the Walla Walla, Umatilla and Grand Ronde rivers in Oregon and Washington in the 18th Century when they numbered about 500. They were very powerful for the size of the tribe, possessing great numbers of horses and dominating lesser tribes."[9]

They belonged to the same language division as the Nez Perce, and during the nineteenth century conversed in the particular dialect of the Nez Perce. Their spiritual lives revolved around the Great Creator Spirit and their own concept of creation in the vicinity of the Palouse River. Ceremonies included fasting, the sweat lodge, and the ceremonial pipe. Social life included oratory, dancing, and equestrian feats.

In the nineteenth century their economy was based almost entirely on trade with other tribes and traders (European) coming up and down the river. The horse was their most important acquisition and gave a great boost to their expansion of their area of trade. Many of the Cayuse became very proficient in horse breeding, and the Cayuse pony was sought after in a fairly wide trade area as the horse became an important trade commodity for the tribe. Later, cowboys would refer to their mounts as "cayuses," as the name of the tribe that bred them became associated with the pony itself. Other items traded by the Cayuse were beaver and otter furs and their own manufactured items, such as ornate saddles, bridles, and stirrups. They were also noted for their basketry.[10] Trade was the only means by which the Cayuse supported themselves.

When Jason Lee and his party arrived in Oregon territory, Lee committed a blunder that may have been a contributing factor in the failure of both his and the Whitman Mission. He records: "Two Indians [Cayuse] came and presented me with two beautiful w[h]ite horses. Surely the hand of providence must be in it for they presented them because we are missionaries and at a time when two of our horses are nearly worn out."[11]

Actually, the Cayuse were offering them for sale or trade; Lee took them but didn't pay for them. Many years later in 1843, three hundred Cayuse and Walla Walla tribesmen showed up on the Whitman Mission grounds with some grievances, one of which was Jason Lee's failure to pay for the horses he took. "The Indians were given a cow for each horse that Jason Lee had taken and so an old score was settled."[12]

Marcus Whitman looked around until he decided on a site for the mission station. When he was approached by the Cayuse people as he was looking things over, he told them through an interpreter that he was going to build a mission on that site. He didn't ask if he could; he just told them he was going to.

The site Whitman chose happened to be an area reserved for one of the headmen. The headman accepted the Whitman remark. A mission house was eventually built, as were living quarters for the mission staff. Narcissa Whitman opened a school, and crops were planted. Things seemed to be going along fairly well.

Narcissa turned out to be the real missionary. She gave direction to the school and guidance to the young people under her care. As the mission staff grew in size and white immigrants would make their way to the mission station, the school's administration took on an ominous racist overtone. There were separate schools, one for the Cayuse children and one for the white children of the mission staff. The Cayuse children worked the fields along with a few Cayuse adults. White mission staff acted as supervisors. A somewhat distasteful practice is revealed in a letter written by Jason Lee to his nephew after visiting the Whitmans and Spauldings at their mission stations (1838):

> I visited Mr. Whitman and Mr. Spaulding and find them getting along well with their Indians. . . . both the Kioose [Cayuse] and the Nez Perce are doing a great deal in cultivation, the former with wooden plows with a little iron nailed to them, and hoes, the latter with hoes alone. . . . Both Mr. Whitman and Mr. Spaulding use high handed measures with their people, and when they deserve it let them feel the lash.[13]

Using the whip on the Cayuse and Nez Perce people would hardly serve to create good Christian relationships.

Occasionally the old headman on whose property the mission was built would show up on the mission grounds and notify Whitman that he (Whitman) had not yet paid for the use of the land on which the mission was built. Whitman ignored the Cayuse headman, but Narcissa would feel dread each time it happened.

Trouble began for the Whitman Mission when the Native people began to distrust the motives of Dr. Whitman, who himself openly declared to Narcissa that he had come to a conclusion regarding his mission:

> Suddenly Marcus realized that something more than saving the Mission was in his mind. Here was his opportunity to help gain Oregon. Here was the answer. He would go to Washington, see the politicians, the president, tell them about Oregon. Show them that now was the time to act to claim the land for the United States before it was too late. It had all been leading up to this, all he had been and done prepared him for this moment. This was his wider mission and larger purpose.[14]

The coming of huge caravans of white immigrants began to make the people of the Native tribes in the vicinity of the Whitman Mission uneasy. Whitman seemed abrasive to the Native people. The mission was being transformed into something other than a mission to the northwest tribes. "The mission was now a way station to the Oregon Trail. That spring [1844] the plows again turned the good earth, and every foot of soil was planted with crops and gardens. They must be ready for the immigrants who would be arriving in the fall."[15]

Whitman was sending letters to the East, extolling the wonders of Oregon: "He urged that strong New England families come to this land of plenty, where every man was given one square mile (640 acres) of land wherever he might choose."[16]

As the immigrants came, they intruded on clearly accepted lands of the Native tribes in the territory. Clashes occurred when overbearing immigrants arrogantly tried to push their way into Indian lands. White immigrants also began to steal cattle belonging to the Cayuse people in the Umatilla and Walla Walla valleys. Whitman's activities were observed more closely, and even the

Mission Board was uneasy about how Whitman was managing the mission. Mr. Green of the board wrote and expressed his objections to Whitman: "We are not quite sure that you ought to devote so much time and thought to feeding the immigrants, and thus make your station a great restaurant for the weary pilgrims on their way to the promised land."[17]

In particular, concern should have been expressed because of the fact that the food used to feed the immigrants was being raised using the labor of the Cayuse people, who were tilling the fields in the belief that their own people would be benefited thereby.

The white immigrants also were a source of diseases against which the Native people had no immunities. Tribal populations were devastated by plagues, especially the Cayuse. Out of a population of five hundred, the Cayuse lost two hundred to these diseases—mostly measles.

During the winter of 1844, Elijah Hedding, the son of Peo Peo Max Max (a Cayuse headman), was killed by an immigrant at Sutter's Fort. Elijah Hedding had gone on a trading mission to California to purchase cattle for the Cayuse, the Walla Walla, and other interior tribes. On their return trip, they were confronted by a band of horse thieves. Elijah's party soundly defeated the horse thieves, drove them off, and captured several of the horses. They continued their journey toward home, reaching Sutter's Fort on the sabbath.

Elijah Hedding was a Christian, having attended the mission school, and so he decided that he would attend church services at Sutter's Fort. He and several young men from the trading mission entered the church. One of the white immigrants came over to Elijah and accused him of stealing his horse. Elijah denied it, explaining that what he had was purchased, except for those animals that were captured from the band of horse thieves. The immigrant became belligerent and demanded that one of the horses be turned over to him. Elijah said he would talk with him about the matter, but first he wanted to pray. He knelt on the floor to pray. The immigrant stepped behind him and shot him in the back of the head. In the days and weeks following, Peo Peo Max Max would be hearing angry young men of the Cayuse telling him he should seek blood revenge.

The Whitman Mission was destroyed in 1847. At the time of the destruction, there were about seventy-two persons present at the mission, of whom forty-two were children. Only twelve were killed in all. Most references claim fourteen were killed, but this is because they were counting two sick children: Louise Sager and Helen Meek were not killed in the raid but died two weeks later of measles.

All of those killed were men, except for Narcissa Whitman. The only child killed in the raid was a teenage boy who pointed a gun at one of the attackers and was himself shot. Thus ended the Whitman Mission.

For a time, mission work among the Native tribes in the Pacific Northwest was not to be found except that carried on by the Jesuits. The Catholic Mission had been established among the Flatheads in 1840 or 1841 by the priest Pierre Jean DeSmet. He spent most of the remainder of his life among the Flatheads and Nez Perce. Another Jesuit, Joseph M. Cataldo, came later (1867) and is credited with reviving and strengthening the mission. He is said to have spent some sixty-three years as a missionary to the Native people. He died in 1928.

The mission in Oregon for Protestant Christianity in general was on hold for a while. Not that the church didn't try, but its relations with the Native peoples had developed into conditions of confused policies on the part of the church and distrust on the part of Native peoples.

The reason for Native people's distrust was not without foundation. In 1841 Captain Charles Wilkes of the U.S. Navy reached the Columbia River on a fact-finding trip for the U.S. government. His observations are published in *The Centennial History of Oregon*. His report on the work of the Protestant and Catholic missionaries is as follows:

> "As to the missionaries, Wilkes reports that little had been effected by them in Christianizing the Indians. They [the missionaries] are principally engaged in the cultivation of the mission farms, and in the care of their own stock in order to obtain flocks and herds for themselves, most of them having selected lands . . . in the part of the country where the missionaries reside, there are very few Indians, and they [the missionaries] seem more occupied with the settlement of the country and in agricultural pursuits than mis-

sionary labors." This is the testimony of an impartial observer as to both Protestant and Catholic, and it is probably true and just.[18]

When the Whitman Mission was destroyed, panic swept throughout the territory among the immigrants. Immigrants in the Willamette Valley were called upon to arm themselves and wage a punitive war against the Natives peoples and to rescue the other missionaries. The provisional government could not provide weapons and ammunition. The Hudson Bay Company refused to supply them with weapons. The immigrant government then appealed to the Methodist Mission for help.

> William Roberts, in his capacity as Superintendent of the Mission, advanced $1,000.00 of mission funds for the purpose. He was very reluctant to do so without the authorization of the Board of Missions, but there was no time to get such authorization. The missionaries of the American Board and all the white inhabitants of the region east of the Cascades were in mortal peril. So, without waiting for any authorization save that of moral responsibility, he acted to do what he could to save them.[19]

This was an overreaction since only a small number of Cayuse were involved in the attack on the Whitman Mission. As for the American Board missionaries, the Hudson Bay Company had already acted to ensure their safety. The "loan" was repaid by the immigrant provisional government, but this dangerous precedent stands in the records of historic Methodism.

The Status of Native American Missions after Twenty-Five Years

Barclay sums up Methodist Missions among Native Americans from 1819 to 1841:

> The Methodist Episcopal Church established missions among some thirty-five Indian tribes in sixteen states and territories. . . . Altogether fifteen Annual Conferences sponsored missionary work among the Indians . . . and not less than 214 preachers were given Indian Mission appointments. This number does not include 15 or

more Indians who were received into conference membership and given missionary assignments among their own people.

. . . There had been gathered into . . . [the] several domestic missions . . . two thousand three hundred and forty-one Indians as church members. The General minutes for 1844 give the total membership of the Societies in the Indian Mission Conference alone as 2,992.

There were Indian members also in . . . other conferences . . . Oneida, 80; Rock River, 130; North Ohio, 5; Michigan, 338; Mississippi, 115; Holston, 109. A grand total of 3,769.[20]

In 1844 the tragedy of Indian removal was still in process. Only the Seminoles made the United States pay dearly for the few hundred Seminoles who finally came to Indian Territory, as they held their ground in Florida. In the Carolinas a major southeastern tribe, the Lumbees, which was not affected by the Indian Removal Act, was nevertheless engaged in a number of skirmishes as they challenged oppressive laws designed to control nonwhites.

In the case of the *State vs. Oxendine* (1837) the North Carolina Supreme Court ruled on the validity of a law that stated if a free, nonwhite person convicted of an offense couldn't pay his fine, the sheriff could sell the offender's services to anyone who would pay the fine. Oxendine had challenged this practice, saying it violated his rights. Oxendine had pleaded guilty to the offense with which he was charged.

The North Carolina Supreme Court ruled that since the law in question applied to persons convicted of crime, the question should revolve around whether Oxendine was convicted. He pleaded guilty, said the court; therefore a conviction had not occurred. Adolph Dial, in whose book this account is found, pointed out that the Supreme Court in North Carolina ignored the basic question, which was whether the law was valid with respect to the Constitution.[21] Other oppressive laws that applied only to "free non-whites" were in effect and were occasionally challenged by individuals of the Lumbee people.

West of the Mississippi the Choctaws, Cherokees, Creeks, Chickasaws, and Seminoles were attempting to reconstruct their national lives. After some twelve years, they had achieved a great deal. The churches that had been working among the tribes in the

East had to start all over again. Alexander Talley wrote that shortly after they arrived, the Methodist Choctaws divided into two
churches because of their settling in various locations.

The Continuing Evolution of the Methodist Church

The issue of slavery was coming to a head in the church, and
eventually it would force an intranational confrontation. The
Methodist Church would have to deal with the issue in 1844 and
would have to face the sad consequences.

The General Conference met in New York on May 1, 1844,
and the slavery issue became the order of the day when the antislavery forces showed their strength and influenced the agenda.
The outcome of the hotly debated issue was a plan of separation
that would establish the ground rules for division of the Methodist
Church into two distinct ecclesiastical bodies, if the southern
Conferences chose to separate. The southern Conferences' delegates met at General Conference and agreed to call a meeting of
the southern Conference in Louisville, Kentucky, on May 1, 1845.

Another action taken by the 1844 General Conference was to
create the Indian Mission Conference:

> Resolved, that there be established an Indian Mission Confer-
> ence to be bounded as follows, viz; on the North by the Missouri
> River: East by the states of Missouri and Arkansas: South by Red
> River: and West by Rocky Mountains.
> Resolved, that the Indian Mission Conference be entitled to all
> the rights and privileges of other Annual Conferences.[22]

Administratively, the Indian Mission Conference would be in
the same episcopal area as the Missouri and Arkansas Annual
Conferences, and Bishop Thomas A. Morris would have its supervision. The organizational meeting was scheduled for October
23, 1844, at Riley's Chapel, Cherokee Nation. The site was two
miles away from Tahlequah, the historic center of Cherokee tribal administration.

An account of Bishop Morris's trip to the Indian Mission Con-
ference appears in Bryce and Babcock's *History of Methodism in
Oklahoma*. It is said that Bishop Morris took a boat from St.
Louis and, along with about twelve other ministers, rode the long

distance to the vicinity of present-day Kansas City. By the time he arrived at his destination, all of the other ministers had left the boat at points along the river to go to their appointments.

Bishop Morris stood on the riverbank, completely alone in the evening. Fortunately, he saw a light in the distance and found a haven for the night in the home of Colonel Chick.[23] The next day he went by horseback to inspect the Indian Manual Labor School in the Shawnee Nation. Two days later, he and three missionaries started the long trip to Riley's Chapel. They rode in an open buggy through driving rains and snow.

At one point on their trip, they arrived at the home of Mrs. Daniel Adams. It must be remembered that she was the former Electa Quiney (Housatannuck tribe), who developed the first school among the Oneidas in Wisconsin. She married the famous Mohawk evangelist Daniel Adams; when they left Wisconsin, they took an assignment among the Senecas of Indian Territory. She was a widow at the time of Bishop Morris's visit. She gladly hosted the travelers, and on the sabbath day she arranged services in her house. Attending were Senecas, Stockbridges, Shawnees, Cherokees, blacks, and several white persons.

On October 22 the bishop and his traveling companions arrived in Tahlequah and prepared for the organizational conference.

At 9:00 A.M. on October 23, 1844, Bishop Morris presided over the first Methodist Annual Conference to be held in Indian Territory. Charter members of the Indian Mission Conference were Thomas E. Ruhls, David B. Cumming, J. C. Berryman, Edward T. Perry, Nathaniel M. Talbott, William H. Goode, Johnson Fields, Thomas Berthoff, James Essex, Samuel G. Patterson, John M. Steel, Erastus B. Duncan, Isaac F. Collins, William McIntosh, Learner B. Stateler, William Okchiah, and John Fletcher Boot.

Three of these charter members were Native Americans. William McIntosh was a Cherokee, as was John F. Boot. Both of these ministers were among other Cherokee clergy who came on the tragic Trail of Tears. William Okchiah was a Choctaw ordained in the Mississippi Conference and came with the Choctaw movement.

In addition, Tussawalita, who was admitted on trial in the Arkansas Conference, was a Cherokee. He was continued on trial in the Indian Mission Conference. John Page, a Choctaw, was received into full connection at this Conference. Page was college educated, having received his degree with honors from an eastern college.

> He was a trusted, popular leader among his people, was for some-time treasurer of the Choctaw National Council. He was one of the Indian Commissioners selected to negotiate the terms of peace between the Choctaw-Chickasaw Nations and the United States. Being an educated man, of native ability, and well versed in Indi-an customs, laws and history, he was an influential member of the Commission.[24]

Page had "considerable business acumen." He also had considerable wealth. He owned a large home near present-day Fort Smith, Arkansas. Page loaned three thousand dollars to Dr. E. W. Sehorn, the missionary secretary of the Methodist Episcopal Church, South, when the latter was visiting in the Indian Mission Conference. The loan was never repaid. Page spent almost his entire ministry (taking time out to serve as a major during the war) in the Mashulatubbee District—twelve years in the same charge. His sermons represented advanced views, and "his manner in the pulpit was quiet and dignified."

Another Choctaw, the Reverend Isaac Chuckmubbee, was elected a deacon.

William Okchiah, the Choctaw circuit rider, died on his way to his appointment.

> He was found by strangers on the streets of Fort Smith in a dying condition. In his saddle pockets were found a Bible, a hymn book, a few hickory nut kernels and a few grains of parched corn. These were all of his earthly possessions. He was taken to the home of a Christian family and put to bed. His host heard him leave his room early the next morning. He followed him out, only to see him fall in the yard, his hands extended toward heaven and heard him breathe his last prayer.[25]

In spite of the presence of Native Americans in the charter membership, and others present, such as Page, when the Conference committees were chosen, no Native Americans were named to serve on them. Even when the Conference voted to send delegates to the Conference of southern Annual Conferences in Louisville, Kentucky, no Native Americans were included to represent the Indian Mission Conference. Instead, white missionaries E. T. Perry and David Cumming were chosen to represent the Conference.

The statistics for that first Conference represented twelve years of reconstruction by Native American Christians since being exiled from their native homes: "27 local preachers, 85 white members, 133 negro members, 2992 Indian members."[26]

There were twenty-eight pastors appointed to serve the various charges of the Oklahoma Indian Mission. Jerome C. Berryman was appointed superintendent of missions, an office that was discontinued in 1847 as an "economy measure."

The official boundary of the Indian Mission Conference on the north was the Missouri River, which extended well into the northern part of Montana. The Indian Mission Conference ministry did not extend beyond Kansas.

Babcock and Bryce, in the *History of Methodism in Oklahoma* estimate that there were about ninety thousand Native American people in the territory in 1845, most of whom were of the "civilized tribes." That figure may be too small and most likely should be one and a half times that many. The tribes of the Great Plains, called "wild tribes" by whites, were present in the territory. These tribes were well organized units that functioned with precision and self-discipline. They were not pleased with the sudden presence of large numbers of other tribal people in their familiar territory. Consequently, territorial conflicts occurred.

In addition, in the case of the Choctaws and Chickasaws, the Chickasaws had been coexisting with the Choctaw National Council. Believing that they would best serve their interests by self-government, they reconstituted the Chickasaw National Council and designated the principal leader as "governor" of the Chickasaw Nation. These nations, as well as the Creeks and Cherokees, had to deal with the moral as well as the political issue of slavery, since many of them owned slaves.

It is not known whether their contribution to the proceedings of the Louisville Conference would have been any different from those of the white clergy if Native clergy were included in the delegation, but it is known that there was an organized antislavery movement building up among the tribes, especially among the Cherokees. The Cherokee abolitionists were the Keetoowah Society (the Night Hawks). The followers of Opothleyahola (Creek) were opposed to joining the South in the Civil War. Forced into Kansas, they "formed the nucleus for the Indian regiments who fought on the union side during the war."[27]

It may be noticed that there were no Creek clergy among the charter members of the Indian Mission Conference. There was work assigned that was designated "Creek Mission," but at this time the Creeks did not permit preaching within the Creek Nation.

There is what appears to be an absurd action on the part of this first Annual Conference, which resulted in their failure to admit on trial an experienced and popular Creek preacher. The Creek Mission submitted a recommendation to the 1844 Indian Mission Conference that Daniel Asbury, a Creek, be admitted on trial. The Conference failed to act on the recommendation for reasons unknown, and it was not until the following year that Asbury was received on trial. Daniel Asbury was the first Creek to become a clergyman in the Indian Mission Conference. He came west with the Creeks during the forced removal.

> He with Samuel Checote signed the petition to have the Scriptures translated into the Creek language that was introduced into the first Conference which met in 1844. He was admitted on trial in 1845 and served among the Creek Indians until his death. As a local and traveling preacher he served at least twenty years. He patiently endured the Creek opposition to the Christian religion and by his firm stand and preaching in season and out of season he helped to overcome the opposition and pave the way for Asbury Manual Labor College and the meeting of the Conference there. He lived and died in the faith.[28]

Also it must be noticed that the Kansas Mission was represented in the person of Presiding Elder N. M. Talbot. This mission, called the Kansas River District, included the Indian Manual Labor School, Delawares and Kickapoos, Shawnees and Wyandottes, Potawatomis and Chippewas, and Peorias and Weas. In 1845 three Native American preachers appear on the appointment list in the Kansas River District: Charles Ketcham, Paschal

Fish, and Macinaw Boashman. Macinaw Boashman was the young Potawatomi man who joined Bishop Morris and became an interpreter for him.

The Native American pastors do not appear on the 1848 appointment list for the Kansas River District, mainly because Charles Ketcham was discontinued in 1847, Macinaw Boashman died in 1848, and Paschal Fish was discontinued in 1848.[29] The Kansas River District itself does not appear on the appointment list in 1850. One of the reasons is that the slavery issue raised in the church in 1844 was then destroying the peace in Missouri and Kansas. But the main reason for the Kansas River District's not appearing on the Indian Mission Conference appointment list is because that district was transferred to the St. Louis Conference in 1850. The reason for the transfer was because of the distance ministers had to travel to the seat of the Conference (250 miles).

A struggle occurred in the Wyandotte church over the issue of the split church. The northern church attempted to work with the Wyandottes, as did the southern church. The Wyandottes, divided on the question of northern or southern administration, split in two and met in separate church buildings. In 1857 both churches were burned to the ground.[30] Bishop Holter, in his book *Fire on the Prairie,* says that the northern branch of the Wyandotte church became present-day Trinity United Methodist Church, and the southern branch became present-day Seventh Street United Methodist Church, both in Kansas City, Kansas.

The Conference took another action related to a clergy appointment that on reflection seems asburd. In 1848 Tussawalita was recommended for admission on trial, but the Conference did not admit him because it "had preachers sufficient to fill all of these charges and there was no place suitable to which he might be appointed."[31]

In 1849 there were seven appointments in Cherokee stations. Five of those stations did not have Cherokee pastors. Reassignment of one of the white missionaries would have provided a suitable appointment.

In 1849 a Creek District appears on the appointment list of the Oklahoma Indian Mission. The work of several dedicated Creek workers, such as Samuel Checote and Daniel Asbury, had some good results. James Essex, a white missionary, also rendered devoted service that ultimately cost him his life. E. B. Duncan, the district superintendent of the Creek District, reported "12 societies besides four other places." He reported also that the Nation had built meeting houses that presumably were made available to the church.

The 1851 statistics reflected the absence of the Kansas River District by showing a drastic drop in membership. Powerful social forces were at work that no doubt contributed to the decline in membership. There was considerable unrest due to the North-South struggle, which broke the church in two and created further internal stress.

Samuel Checote was admitted on trial in 1852 and began a long and distinguished career: "Samuel Checote was a growing influence in the Creek political affairs as well as the church. It was through his influence that the laws forbidding the Christian religion being taught in the nation were abrogated."[32] The tenth Annual Conference (1853) met at the Creek agency on the invitation of Samuel Checote. The presence of the Annual Conference in Creek Territory was symbolic of the hospitality of the Creeks and also of the patient work of Checote, Asbury, and Essex.

At this session William McIntosh was granted a superannuate relationship. Dixon Lewis was not appointed, so he could work on the project of translating the Scriptures and other worship aids into the Native languages.

John F. Boot died this year. He united with the church in 1824 in Alabama. He received his license to preach and "was an ordained elder before coming to the Indian Territory."[33] He came to Indian Territory during the forced removal of the Cherokees. His sermons were centered on his personal testimony and were gladly received by those fortunate enough to hear him.

In 1855 the Annual Conference was convened at the Asbury Manual Labor School. Bishop Pierce presided and apparently was very impressed when Jim McHenry—or Jim Henry, as he had been known in Alabama and Georgia, the feared and respected leader of the Creek resistance movement in the eastern Creek Territory—was recommended for admission on trial. His appointment in 1855 was to North Fork.

In 1856 Bishop George F. Pierce found his life in jeopardy from roving bands of both abolitionist and pro-slavery vigilantes, when he attempted to hold a session of the Kansas Conference, which grew out of the former Kansas River District and was constituted by the General Conference of 1854.[34] Bishop Pierce succeeded in holding the Conference and later called for more "young men for regular circuits in Kansas": "We want no land hunters, but strangers and Pilgrims, who declare plainly that they seek a country, even a heavenly."[35]

Bishop Pierce, on a later occasion, expressed in writing a prevailing error of his time regarding Native peoples, and one that persists to this day:

> The desire to learn the English language is almost universal among them. They seem to regard the knowledge of it as one of the chief agents of their elevation, and as a security against the relapse into their former ignorance and superstition. This is a powerful motive with them in patronizing the schools, and they avow they wish that their language may perish with the old and adult population.[36]

That was grossly untrue, particularly among the tribes Pierce had contact with. Instead, several prominent Native American clergy were waging a political battle to persuade the Methodist Church to translate the Bible and other Christian literature into Native languages. Included among these were Samuel Checote, Daniel Asbury, and Dixon Lewis. The initial Conference of 1844 authorized such a project, but Dixon Lewis, who was designated to head up the project, found all of his efforts thwarted by bigotry among the Methodist publishers and other non-Indian church officials, who fostered views like those held by Bishop Pierce. Pierce's recommendation regarding translation of literature in other Native languages was apparently accepted: "The necessity to learn our language ought to be thrown upon them by refusing to translate our laws or to print a paper in their mother tongue."[37] Dixon Lewis died after thirteen frustrating years of trying to make the Scriptures readable to the Native American masses.

Skullyville, the location of which was near present-day Spiro, Oklahoma, was an important center of Choctaw life in the early days of Indian Territory. The name was derived from the Choctaw word *iskuli*, whose English equivalent is "money." The town was originally the Choctaw agency, and it was here that Choctaw annuities were received. The money, in gold coins, was shipped by steamboat up the river and then overland to Skullyville.

> The money was usually brought to Fort Coffee by steam boat from Fort Smith, and from there hauled in wagons to the Agency, a distance of about sixteen miles. The money was placed in kegs. Sometimes there would be as many as six wagon loads of money in one caravan. There would be one driver and one guard to each wagon. Hold ups or robberies of the wagon train were unknown in Indian Territory in that day.[38]

It was said that the kegs of gold coin "were often left in the yard or on the front porch of the agency, day and night without guard."[39]

It was in Skullyville that Bishop Early convened the fifteenth Annual Conference on October 7, 1858. Willis Folsom and Jim McHenry were ordained deacons.

The following year (1859) William McIntosh, a Cherokee and a charter member of the Indian Mission Conference, died. (Babcock and Bryce incorrectly designate him a Creek, probably confusing him with William McIntosh, Creek signer of the treaty, for which he was executed by the Creeks.) The announcement was made at the sixteenth session of the Indian Mission Conference, which was convened by Bishop Paine at the Creek agency. Standing Man was admitted into full connection. Samuel Checote and Jim McHenry were ordained traveling elders. Robert Jackson and Bolin Perry were ordained local elders.

The Dark Clouds of War

The next year was a prelude of things to come, as the American nation drifted into the War between the States. A drought in Indian Territory brought on a crop failure and a serious famine. Food supplies that were brought in gave some relief. In other parts of the nation, events were occurring that began to set the stage for the war. In 1859 John Brown had been hung under the official sentence of treason. Henry David Thoreau launched a defense of John Brown, declaring the high purpose of Brown's activities:

> I have no doubt that the time will come when they will begin to see him as he was. They have got to conceive of a man of faith, and of religious principle, and not a politician or an Indian; of a man who did not wait till he was personally interfered with or thwarted in some harmless business before he gave his life to the cause of the oppressed.[40]

Ralph Waldo Emerson "hailed Brown as that new saint who will make the gallows glorious like the cross."[41]

The U.S. population in 1860 was 31,443,321 (excluding Native Americans, who are not counted as citizens). The Pony Express experiment began, only to fail. In December South Carolina seceded from the union. It was reported that William H. Seward, in a speech in Chicago, remarked, "The Indian territory, also, South of Kansas, must be vacated by the Indians,"[42] thus providing the South with a motivating device for recruiting the five major southeastern tribes for the Confederacy.

In the old Southeast, a number of young Lumbee men volunteered to fight in the Confederate Army. Most found themselves being drafted not to fight with southern forces but to work in labor camps "building batteries and making salt."[43] The blatant oppression of the Lumbee people by the racist leaders of the Confederacy led to events that produced one of the most feared resistance movements in the Southeast. Centered in the person and spirit of Henry Berry Lowrie, the movement would span the Civil War and beyond.

In Indian Territory, both Union and Confederacy forces sought to enlist the tribes. The Confederacy was the most successful, at least partially, some suggest, due to William Seward's remark about vacating the Indians from Indian Territory south of Kansas. But economics and social circumstances such as the presence of slaves among the five southeastern tribes moved the tribes to a defensive stance in alliance with the Confederacy.

The Cherokee Night Hawks were active and sought to promote the abolitionist course by direct and forceful action among their own people and whites as well.

There was no bishop present at the 1861 Annual Conference, which met at Chickasaw Manual Labor School. "Samuel Checote and James McHenry requested to be located in order that they might join the combat forces on the Confederate side."[44]

The American Board abandoned their missionaries in Indian Territory because of the board's opposition to slavery. The missionaries themselves, including the famous Cyrus Kingsbury, stayed at their posts. Others of the team included Dr. Elizur Butler, Cyrus Byington, Ebenezer Hotchkin, and C. C. Copeland. A brief respite from abandonment was provided by the Southern Presbyterian Church, but eventually the work was interrupted.

Principal military leaders among the Indian Territory tribes were General Stand Watie (Cherokee), Lieutenant Colonel Samuel Checote (Creek), Major Jim McHenry (Creek), and Major John Page (Choctaw).

Meanwhile, a steady stream of whites was encroaching in the West, causing disruptions among the tribes settled in those areas. Many of the tribes were reacting and attempting to protect their homes. John M. Chivington is first noticed for his action against the Confederate forces in New Mexico. But his name will forever be associated with the maniacal slaughter of old men, women, and children at Sand Creek, Colorado.

> John M. Chivington was born in Ohio in 1821. Taking up the Methodist ministry in 1844, he preached in Ohio, Illinois, Missouri, Kansas and Nebraska prior to his arrival in Denver on May 19, 1860, as presiding elder of the First Methodist Church.[45]

Incredibly, John M. Chivington was a Methodist missionary to the Wyandotte people in Kansas City, Kansas, in 1853. Apparently he preached to the northern division of the split Wyandotte church. From the Wyandotte Mission, he went to Nebraska and became the district superintendent of the Omaha District of the Kansas-Nebraska Conference. In 1860 Chivington was appointed by Bishop Baker as district superintendent of the Rocky Mountain District of the Conference.[46]

When he was offered a commission as a chaplain, he declined and insisted on a "fighting commission." When the Civil War started, he was among those military leaders called out of the northern plains to prosecute the Union side of the war in the South.

Tribal life on the Plains during this period was in great turmoil because of the increasing population of whites who arrogantly located themselves on tribal lands. Wars against the Native tribes were started on the slightest pretenses. A typical incident was the story of the white soldier who entered a Native tribal encampment and attempted to buy a woman with a bottle of whiskey. One of the tribesmen took the bottle but refused to produce the woman. The soldier shot him and made his escape.[47]

Annuities paid to the Native tribes as a result of a treaty also provided grounds for conflict. Many times, the tribes would require the government to provide their annuities in goods rather than currency. The operators of trading posts who somehow were able to intercept the deliveries often were caught trading or selling the annuities to both whites and Native people. Skirmishes, it can be seen, were bound to happen.

Chivington, an overbearing man, was not popular and on one occasion had a complaint lodged against him by a colleague over the distribution of troops in the territory. The concern was based on the troubles related to some tribes' anxiety over fraudulent treaties that they did not understand to mean the loss of their land. Governor Evans asked for a council with the "chiefs" of the Cheyenne and Arapaho tribes (May 1863). When they responded, he threatened "a war of extermination"; if the tribes wanted war, they should "pass the word around."

There was desperation among the tribes because of widespread hunger, precipitated by the intrusions by whites in areas that were their primary source of food supplies. The tribes became dependent on their government annuities and trade with unscrupulous white traders.

The hostile attitudes of military and civilian whites are expressed in the following quotation of remarks made by Major Scott Anthony, who was in command of Fort Lyon:

> Major Anthony was less compassionate about the welfare of the tribes. He wrote, "The Indians are all very destitute this season, and the government will be compelled to subsist them to a great extent, or to allow them to starve to death, which would probably be much the easier way of disposing of them."[48]

Some of the military leaders, as well as the governor of Colorado Territory, were promoting a "war of extermination" against the Plains tribes. It is said that their favorite fabrication was of a tribal confederation that was planning an all-out attack. Stan Hoig states, however, that the Cheyenne "war" started over two reports of cattle theft, not an attack by an intertribal confederation. There seemed to be considerable absurdity about the confrontation, which ultimately led to a number of atrocities; U.S. troops and territorial militias were being continually dispatched to investigate reports of cattle thefts, and in the process the U.S. soldiers would themselves steal horses and cattle from the Cheyennes and Arapahos.[49]

In April 1864 Lieutenant George S. Eayre was sent with a detachment of men to pursue and kill Cheyennes who allegedly had stolen 175 head of cattle from government contractors. After a lengthy absence, Eayre reported to Chivington that he was attacked by four hundred Cheyennes and "after a persistent fight . . . succeeded in driving them from the field. They lost 3 chiefs and 25 warriors killed. My own loss is 4 men killed and 3 wounded."[50]

Chivington praised Eayre and promised to give a good report to their superiors. A later investigation showed that Eayre had misrepresented the encounter and had himself been forced into a retreat:

> Alfred Gay and John W. Smith were dispatched from Fort Cottonwood on June 2 to investigate into Cheyenne country. They reported that the Indians—1,200 lodges of Cheyennes, Arapahoes, Commanches, Kiowas—were still in the vicinity, fifty miles north of Larned and it was Eayre who had retreated from the field. . . . Only 2 Cheyenne chiefs and one brave were killed.[51]

Chivington's continuous dispatches of troops on search and kill expeditions began to yield their consequences. The tribes began to retaliate, and the number of skirmishes increased. Governor Evans was a source of many of the untrue rumors that kept tensions high. He created an atmosphere of paranoia, fear, and hatred among the whites living in the area.

Panic occurred in Denver when a man came riding into town shouting that the "Indians" are coming to "town to burn and massacre." Following him was a group of frightened whites in wagons and on foot who had been warned about the impending Indian attack. People in Denver stayed in hiding all night, and nothing happened. When the man's story was checked out, it was discovered that all he had seen was "a group of shapes" moving around. In the paranoid atmosphere of the day, he imagined them to be Indians, but it turned out that they were a group of drunken "drivers of a freight train camped for the night."[52]

Chivington himself prepared an expedition against the Cheyennes, which was opposed by a number of military men and some civilians. They told Chivington that it would be a crime "to attack Indians who were considered to be prisoners." Chivington's reply was "Damn any man who is in sympathy with an Indian!"

He led an attack on Black Kettle's encampment of Cheyennes on November 29, 1864. Black Kettle and White Antelope had, on September 26, been in a conference with Governor Evans and military officials, including Chivington, in which they accepted a covenant of friendship and made a pact that virtually rendered Black Kettle's band of Cheyenne prisoners. Having pledged themselves to peace, they had no fear of being attacked. When Chivington's volunteers attacked, several attempts were made by Black Kettle's people to identify themselves as parties to the peace conference. When the white flag was presented, the bearer was fired on. Black Kettle hoisted an American flag and a white flag on his lodge and called out to his panic-stricken people not to be frightened, that the camp was under protection. White Antelope also tried to identify the camp as one of those under a covenant of peace. White Antelope "stood in the middle of Sand Creek with his arms folded over his chest, hoping to signify by the gesture that the Cheyennes did not wish to fight the whites. The heroic act was wasted on the soldiers, and he was shot down in the bed of the creek."[53]

The women and children ran up the creekbed in desperation and tried to hide themselves in the crevices along the banks. Mothers frantically tried to dig holes in the sand in which to hide their children—a futile attempt. The soldiers chased them and chopped them down and picked off the others with gunfire. When the carnage was over, the soldiers in a frenzy began to mutilate the bodies of the people, cutting souvenirs from their bodies.

Over five hundred elderly men, women, and children were massacred at Sand Creek. Major Edward Wynkoop was enraged over Chivington's actions and immediately traveled from Fort Riley, Kansas, to Fort Lyon, where he immediately conducted an investigation. In a seething report to Washington, he called Chivington an "inhuman monster."

Captain Cree of the Colorado Third (which participated in the massacre) wrote the following remark, the latter part of which is true—but not in the way he intended: "All I can say for the officers and men is, that they all behaved well, and won for themselves a name that will be remembered for ages to come."[54]

Three investigations, two by congressional committees and one by the army, were conducted. The congressional committees were clear in their criticism of Governor Evans and Chivington. The army investigation was a fact-finding inquiry and made no recommendations. No official action was taken against Chivington by the U.S. government. He resigned his commission on January 4, 1865.

> For John Chivington there would remain a long and empty life, leaving Colorado for California, thence to Cincinnati, returning to Denver in 1883, where he made a speech at a celebration of the Denver Pikes Peak Pioneers and impassionately justified the Sand Creek attack. The account of the one white scalp which Chivington found in the Sand Creek village had again grown with the years. "What of that Indian blanket," he asked, "that was captured fringed with white women's scalps?"[55]

Chivington's attempts to fabricate evidence in his later years is perhaps indicative of the isolation that characterized his relationships in the social and political circles where he sought acceptance. He did show up at the Kansas Conference annual meeting of the Methodist Church and was cordially received, but "the great prestige he had once enjoyed and which had promised so much for him was gone. Chivington's page in history . . . was nullified by the Massacre at Sand Creek."[56]

In another part of the country, the Sioux in Minnesota were reacting to "ten years of rapes, beatings, and murders" of Sioux families, by "Indian agents and citizens of Minnesota." They launched retaliatory attacks in 1862 on those responsible. Calling it an "uprising," the army eventually regained control, and in a hastily convened Army court, convicted 303 Sioux men and sentenced them to death. The army permitted no defense for the prisoners. "The court did not permit the Indians to submit evidence against the Indian agents and citizens who for ten years had committed brutal deeds."[57]

Abraham Lincoln, who at this time had his hands full with the Civil War, intervened because of the large number of those convicted. He ordered that court documents be sent to him so he could review the evidence. Lincoln determined that only 39 of them should be executed, and in a letter dated December 6, 1862, designated which of the 303 Sioux prisoners should be executed. One was reprieved at the last minute, and the remaining 38 were hanged.

Those who were to be executed were allowed a visit by a Sioux-speaking priest. Father Rauoux attempted to convince them of the impending condition of their souls and the need to rely on "the Great Spirit before whom they were to appear." The Sioux were already involved in their own ceremony of preparation. "Old Tazoo broke out in a death wail, in which one after another joined, until the prison room was filled with a wild unearthly plaint which was neither of despair nor grief."[58]

They would then sit quietly until one of the leaders would once again begin to chant. The effect on the Sioux men was a calmness, as if they had come to terms with the event that would sacrifice them and remove them from human activity. "It seemed as if during their passionate wailing, they had passed in spirit through the valley of the shadow of death, and already had their eyes fixed on the . . . beyond."[59]

When the appointed time for the execution arrived, it was the priest who had the terrible task of telling the prisoners, since he could speak their language. The men arose and followed the provost marshall with not the slightest expression of fear. They sang as they proceeded to the scaffold. Once on the scaffold they offered no resistance as a noose was put about the neck of each of the men. The scene that followed was described in an account appearing in the *St. Paul Pioneer,* December 28, 1862:

> Then ensued a scene that can hardly be described, and which can never be forgotten. All joined in shouting and singing, as it appeared to those who were ignorant of the language. The tones seemed somewhat discordant, and yet there was harmony in it. Save the moment of cutting the rope, it was the most thrilling moment of the awful scene. And it was not their voices alone. Their bodies swayed to and fro, and their every limb seemed to be keeping time. The drop trembled and shook as if all were dancing. The most touching scene on the drop was their attempts to grasp each other's hands, fettered as they were. They were very close to each other, and many succeeded. Three or four in a row were hand in hand, and all hands swaying up and down with the rise and fall of their voices. One old man reached out each side, but could not grasp a hand. His struggles were piteous and affected many beholders.
>
> We were informed by those who understood the language, that their singing and shouting was only to sustain each other. . . . Each one shouted his own name, and called on the name of his friend, saying in substance, "I'm here! I'm here!"[60]

The newspaper praised the soldiers for their military efficiency and declined to describe further details, pleading: "Imagination will readily supplie what we refrain from describing."[61]

The People of the Plains would have many occasions to call upon the inner spiritual strengths of their native faith, as their homelands began to be coveted and stolen.

The Civil War Affects Indian Territory

The Methodist Church in Indian Territory had cause to call upon its spiritual resources too. Most of the civil war traffic hit the Creeks and Cherokees, but occasionally Choctaw and Chickasaw territory felt the impact. Many refugees from the tribes hardest hit came into Choctaw territory, and some made their way to Kansas. Elsewhere, the Methodist Mission Board (South) was located in Nashville, and its operation was disrupted when federal troops invaded Nashville. The publishing house was partially destroyed, and the work of the church was paralyzed. No funds would be forthcoming into the mission field. Workers would be on their own.

Most missionaries fled to safety when the civil war broke out, but a significant number of them remained at their posts. All of the Native American clergy who were not conscripted for the tribal armed forces remained on the job and worked to keep the church alive in those destructive years. White missionaries Dick Hider and E. G. Smith died in Cherokee country. James Essex remained on his post at the Creek agency and carried on his ministry until Union troops captured him and held him captive until his death in 1864. Essex was the Methodist clergyman who worked alongside Samuel Checote in the patient ministry that finally saw the gospel introduced among the Creeks. John H. Carr remained, along with his family and teachers, in the empty buildings of Bloomfield Academy in Chickasaw country. Eventually the buildings were occupied by Confederate troops. Refugees also made their way to the academy. Carr and his staff remained and raised food to help feed refugees and soldiers and also to provide care for wounded and dying soldiers.

Through all of this, the Cherokee District continued operation, with Native clergy and white missionaries continuing to work. Young Ewing, W. A. Duncan, D. B. Cumming, Elijah Butler, Isaac Sanders, and Walker Carey were still at their posts during the years 1863 to 1864.

Willis Folsom, Choctaw, was "the brightest star of them all." He rendered service far exceeding anyone's expectation, given the times. He remained at his post but redefined it to include all of Choctaw territory. He was only seven years old when he came on the forced removal from Mississippi to Indian Territory. His conversion came after a struggle for understanding, as he tried to identify the spiritual forces working in him. He finally declared, "Suddenly, my whole soul was filled with light and joy. Immediately I felt that I must learn what was in the Bible that I might tell my people."[62]

He worked, as did many young Native American Christians, as an interpreter for white missionaries, but his own style probably embellished that of the missionaries, as he also exhorted during the services. He was twenty-six or twenty-seven when he received his license to preach in 1851. His name doesn't appear on the appointment list until 1868, but Folsom was an energetic worker. He preached almost constantly, whenever he could gather people around him. He was ordained a local deacon in 1858. "During the entire period of the war, he remained with his people preaching, traveling and visiting. Even after white missionaries had fled, he remained."[63]

He kept a diary of his work during the war years. He traveled long distances, often by foot. During the opening days of the war, soldiers burned his home and confiscated his livestock. His main complaint in 1862 was "I have only preached one hundred and thirty one times this year. Been poorly all the year. Very few saved." And then this entry: "Today I returned home to find my little girl dead."

Folsom kept the church alive and created the remnant that would provide the nucleus for rebuilding the church.

The Civil War laid waste the church in Indian Territory, except for that faithful remnant. The appointment list for 1864 may illustrate the pain and nature of ministry in Indian Territory during the war:

Army missions: John Harrell, Superintendent
Choctaw-Chickasaw District: John H. Carr, P. E.
Bloomfield Academy: John H. Carr
Chickasaw Circuit: J. C. Robinson
Chickasaw Academy: J. C. Robinson, Superintendent
Boggy Circuit: J. H. Walker
Doaksville: I. S. Newman, S. P. Willis
Refugee Cherokees: W. Carey, Standing Man, Isaac Sanders
Creek District: Thomas Bertholf, Presiding Elder
Asbury Manual Labor School: Thomas Bertholf, Superintendent[64]

THE TARES AND THE WHEAT

The war theaters were in shambles in 1865. President Lincoln was assassinated, and Andrew Johnson succeeded him. The debate was still going on among the southern tribes on the matter of whether they should have aligned themselves with the Confederacy or remained neutral. The Choctaws, Chickasaws, Cherokees, Seminoles, and Creeks were quickly reminded that from the standpoint of the U.S. government, all treaties and agreements formerly made between the tribes and the government were null and void because of the tribes' alignment with the South during the Civil War.

On October 30, 1865, a presidential commission convened a conference in Fort Smith, Arkansas, with the "Indian Tribes of the Territory" to reconstitute relationships between the tribes and the U.S. government. The Southern Treaty Commission, headed by Indian Commissioner Dennis N. Cooley, set forth the terms of the new treaty proposal. The new treaties must include the provision that slaves be freed and granted all the rights and benefits of tribal citizenship, including a share in annuities and the land base. They should include a cession of tribal land to be used for the "settling" of other tribes in Indian Territory. For its part, the United States would pursue a policy of amnesty for those who fought on the side of the South and would reinstate all provisions of the treaties previous to the Civil War.

In the specific treaties negotiated with individual tribes, other provisions included a railroad right of way (a strip of land six miles wide) and a military occupation of Indian Territory, ostensibly to protect the interest of the Creeks (in this case). In their version of the treaty (eventually signed in 1866), the Creeks lost one-half of all their land in Indian Territory. The Choctaws didn't lose their primary land base but lost an area of leased land on their western border.

Particularly troublesome was the provision relating to the settlement of emancipated former slaves (freedmen) in tribal territories. In the case of the Choctaws, their bargaining chip was the leased district. The final treaty called for the cession of the leased land to be compensated for if the tribe agreed to accept freedmen citizens in its territory, but it was to be used for the colonization of former slaves if the Choctaws and Chickasaws, acting jointly in this treaty of 1865–66, did not agree with the provision, thereby requiring the United States to remove and resettle the former slaves in the leased district. The Choctaws and Chickasaws had two years to declare their intentions. The two tribes chose to allow that time to lapse, thereby obligating the U.S. government to act on behalf of the freedmen. After two years, the Choctaws and Chickasaws waited in vain for the United States to fulfill its obligation and remove the former slaves. They didn't. Eventually the Choctaws and Chickasaws provided for the well-being of the freedmen in tribal territory.

The treaty negotiated by the Choctaw-Chickasaw delegation, which included Methodist clergyman John Page (Choctaw), provided for continuation of tribal sovereignty and almost complete control of immigration of nontribal people within their territory, a provision that would prove to be very important later on. The treaty further provided that the Native American nations through which the railroad would pass would have "the right to subscribe to railroad stock and pay for it by land grants."[1]

So the nations of Indian territory began the Reconstruction period with considerably less land, tribal sovereignty with modifications, and more troubles looming in the future. It has never been explained why punitive measures were taken against the Native tribes of Indian Territory, while the southern states that seceded and initiated the war were allowed to resume their lives under an unconditional policy of amnesty. President Johnson proclaimed unconditional amnesty with reservations for those accused of treason against the Union during the Civil War.

The federal government was busy on the Great Plains too, as pressure from many sources mounted for a new federal Indian policy.

A joint special committee of Congress "appointed under a joint resolution of March 3, 1865, and chaired by Senator James Doolittle of Wisconsin"[2] was dispatched to investigate the state of Indian affairs in the United States. The reason for congressional concern was the sudden serious decline in the population of Native American people, to below 250,000.[3]

The committee's report, filed in January 1867, drew less than surprising conclusions. The Plains tribes were being decimated by diseases brought by the immigrants, warfare, starvation due to white intrusion in traditional Native homelands, and the lawlessness of whites on the so-called frontier. Chivington's massacre of Cheyennes and Arapahos at Sand Creek, Colorado, was singled out as an example of this lawlessness. Wars against the Native people on the Plains were wars of extermination.

During this time there was a question of whether to move the Bureau of Indian Affairs to the War Department where it once was lodged or to retain it in the Interior Department. The committee argued in favor of the Interior Department, stating that "military posts have frequently become centres of demoralization and destruction to the Indian tribes."[4]

Another commission was created in 1867. In its report (1868) this commission also cited abuses by whites on the frontier, but also blamed indifference on the part of Congress for continued hostilities on the Plains. The commission proposed that "civilization" of Native people was preferable to extermination. It called for a reorganization of government bureaucracy relating to Indian affairs, including a revision of the intercourse laws, since they were geared for military implementation instead of civilian administration. The commission simplified the criteria for deciding the question of whether the Bureau of Indian Affairs should be lodged in the Interior Department or the War Department: "If we intend to have war with them the Bureau should go to the Secretary of War. If we intend to have peace it should be in the civil department."[5]

There was corruption in both the military and civilian sections, but at least the civilian department would be more likely to carry out programs of education and acculturation of the people. "The records are abundant to show that agents have pocketed the funds appropriated by the government and driven the Indians to starvation. It cannot be doubted that Indian wars have originated from this cause. The Sioux war in Minnesota is supposed to have been produced in this way."[6]

The commission recommended an act of Congress to vacate all government Indian Affairs offices so that those who were proved to be honest could be rehired and the corrupt could be barred from being hired. They recommended that instead of lodging the Bureau of Indian Affairs in any existing department, it should be made an independent department, perhaps with cabinet status. This commission also recommended that governors or legislatures of states or territories not be allowed to form state militias because of their having been the cause rather than the cure of hostilities on the Plains; the "butchery at Sand Creek" under Chivington was cited as evidence of the incompetence of such state militias.[7]

Simultaneously with the closing days of the Civil War, violence was erupting in North Carolina as the Lumbee people rose up to resist a power system whose brutality was not unlike that of the Plains militias. The Home Guard in the South was a quasi-military organization of local white citizens whose purpose was stated as being to maintain law and order while the war was being prosecuted by those best suited for military duty. But like the state militias, they were more likely to be initiating atrocities than preventing them.

In this case the Home Guard turned its attention to the Lowrie family, accusing them of killing one James Brantly Harris, described as "a 230 pound swaggering, cursing, red-faced bully."[8] Harris was an officer in the Home Guard, and it was known that he had murdered three of the Lowrie sons, one in a dispute over a young woman, the other two in a senseless killing that was as irrational as it was brutal. When he was gunned down by unknown persons on January 15, 1865, the Robeson County War was on.

Conscription of young Lumbee men to work in the labor camps so angered the Lumbees, who at first were willing to fight for the

Confederacy, that desertions from the camps became common. In the swamps and other hideouts, some of these men came together under the leadership of Henry Berry Lowrie to form a resistance movement that continued until his mysterious disappearance in 1872. The Henry Berry Lowrie band launched raids in retaliation for past injustices.

For a while, no one was hurt since the raids were to secure food and supplies. But as the conflict deepened, there were deaths. Lowrie was jailed twice and twice escaped. Official reaction to the band widened. The state of North Carolina placed a twelve thousand dollar bounty on Henry Berry Lowrie's head. Eventually a Boston undercover agent tried to trick the Lowrie band into exposing themselves to arrest, but that and other attempts to trap the band failed. After years of terror and retaliation, of oppression and vengeance, Henry Berry Lowrie vanished as if he had never been there. It may be that amid the tales told in the evening, the legends and endless speculation, there is an unperceived clue to whatever became of him, yet to be found.

An assessment of the impact of Henry Berry Lowrie on Robeson County and the state of North Carolina appears in a work quoted by Adolph Dial, to whom this writer is indebted for the story:

> With the triumph of a frankly racist party during Reconstruction, it appeared that nothing could stop the winners from putting the Lumbee River Indians into the same half-free "place" in which they generally succeeded in putting the Blacks. But this effort failed. It appears to have failed, furthermore, to a great extent because of the bold deeds of the Lowrys, which filled the Lumber River Indians with a new pride of race, and a new confidence that despite generations of defeat, revitalized their will to survive as a people.[9]

Dial wrote that although there were still many rough years ahead as the nation experienced Reconstruction, with new patterns of discrimination developing, the Lumbees did well. They built an educational system that was as comprehensive as any in the country. It included a college, now known as Pembroke State University.

The Lumbees have contributed educators, attorneys, physicians, clergy, and qualified personnel in every profession and occu-

174

pation. They have a substantial land base and seek to maintain a competitive foothold in their economic activities.

It would appear that the early years of Reconstruction might be a less than fertile season for planting the gospel. The emergence of hate groups caused considerable turmoil, especially in the South but also in Indian Territory. In March 1867, the Pulaski, Tennessee, newspaper *The Citizen* published a news story telling about a new organization called the "Kuklux Klan [*sic*]." The group promoted the notion of white supremacy and launched an attack on proponents of radical reconstruction in the South. But it turns out that several Native American Methodist churches were established during this time. For example, a Methodist Board of Home Missions report dated 1931 states that the work in White Swan, Washington, among the Yakima tribe was organized in 1865. The missionary was James A. Wilbur. The White Swan Mission, named after a Yakima tribal leader, produced two preachers, Thomas H. Pearne and George Watters. Watters was instrumental in spreading the gospel in other parts of Washington and Idaho.

During the presidency of Ulysses S. Grant following the Civil War, a number of landmark events took place that marked the beginning of modern efforts to bring to realization the ideals of the Constitution. Unfortunately, confused policies and bigotry frustrated many of those efforts.

The Fifteenth Amendment to the Constitution was passed, and the four states not yet readmitted to the Union were required to ratify the Fourteenth and Fifteenth Amendments before they could qualify for readmission. Military force was provided by Congress to enforce the voting provisions for black males in state and local elections.[10]

Women's suffrage was a major issue during this time. The first National Women's Suffrage Convention met in Washington, D.C. Former Civil War nurse Clara Barton appealed to Civil War veterans at their convention for support in gaining the vote for women, but in vain; only Wyoming Territory provided a measure of political recognition for women at this stage. When the immigrant nation (United States) celebrated its centennial in Philadelphia (1876), Susan B. Anthony disrupted the proceedings and "presented a declaration of Women's Rights."[11]

Women's suffrage became an issue in the Methodist Church in 1877. Several denominations at this time had women preachers, but the Methodist Church would not ordain women for the ministry. In 1877 a Miss Oliver was invited to speak at a minister's meeting in New York. Her speech was canceled because the Methodist ministers objected strenuously, saying, "there is no power in the Methodist Church by which a woman can be licensed to preach."[12] When Miss Oliver petitioned the General Conference meeting in Cincinnati in May 1880 for the privilege of ordination, the General Conference declined and stated in a resolution, "Women have already all the rights and privileges in the Methodist Church that are good for them."[13]

On April 10, 1877, newly elected president Rutherford Hayes ended the Reconstruction period—at least technically—by withdrawing federal troops from the South.[14] As for the Native American tribes, the nation resumed its established practice of using every devious means of wresting the land base from its original owners, but by this time in history, it was casting its covetous eye to the West.

The Medicine Lodge Treaty of 1867 created two large reservations in Indian Territory. The tribes involved in the treaty were the Kiowas, Commanches, Cheyennes, and Arapahos. The success of the peace commission in negotiating this treaty apparently had Congress fantasizing that all Indians could be eventually stuffed into Indian Territory. But the treaty at Fort Laramie was decidedly of a different sort. It was signed on Red Cloud's terms, following the Sioux fighting forces' defeat of U.S. troops protecting the Bozeman Trail. This treaty of 1868 is still an important document to the great Sioux Nation, as many of the Sioux do not accept the contention of the whites who hold that the treaty was displaced by the Sioux Agreement of 1889. It was the latter that shrunk Sioux land holdings to the minimal acreage held today.

Warfare proliferated between the United States and Native American tribes on the Plains and in the far West, as the military attempted to protect intruding whites from Native tribes who were defending their homelands. When warfare became too expensive in terms of money and human lives, the United States began to look for other ways to achieve the goal of taking Indian lands.

Various kinds of treaties were negotiated. Some were intended to guarantee safe passage for wagon trains passing through tribal territories, while others were pledges of peace in a noncombative atmosphere. The most damaging treaties were those defining the boundaries of tribal territories, the effect of which was not understood by the tribal representative who signed for his people. Often U.S. agents would lie about the written contents of the documents, claiming certain provisions were there when there were no such provisions stated. Red Cloud complained of that practice in a speech he made in Cooperstown, New York, in 1870:

> In 1868 men [U.S. agents] came out and brought papers. We are ignorant and do not read papers, and they did not tell us right what was in the papers. We wanted them to take away their forts, leave our country, would not make war, and give our traders something. They said we had bound ourselves to trade on the Missouri, and we said no, we did not want that. The interpreter deceived us.[15]

Many times the treaties themselves precipitated the desire for warfare, when tribal leaders realized they had been lied to. The reservation system grew out of this kind of one-sided negotiation. When gold was discovered on Indian land in the West, white immigrants in a piranha-like frenzy sped into the Western lands. Attempts were made to exclude from treaty provisions those portions of reservation lands containing gold and other mineral deposits. But legal or not, whites who imagined themselves becoming millionaires by digging gold trespassed on Indian lands.

In the Far West a number of smaller tribes were experiencing the incomprehensible style of treaty negotiations, where the agent would say one thing and mean another. The Modocs had agreed in a treaty at Council Grove to move into Klamath Territory north and east of Upper Klamath Lake in Oregon. The Modocs, led by Kintpuash (Captain Jack), complied even though the treaty was not ratified until 1870. Later realizing that the government had lied to them and had no intention of keeping its part of the agreement, the Modocs returned to their homelands along the eastern base of the Cascade Mountains on the southern edge of Oregon. In 1872 the Bureau of Indian Affairs obtained consent to use the army to force the Modocs back into Klamath Territory. The "Modoc War" started on November 29, 1872, when federal troops made their appearance at Captain Jack's camp. The Modocs established their defense in the lava beds, "the land of the burnt out fires." "It was an almost impregnable fortress. Scarcely more than fifty fighting men manned it against a besieging force that ultimately numbered a thousand regulars and militiamen."[16]

On January 16, 1873, the federal troops attempted an assault on the Modoc stronghold, but the fifty Modoc defenders, using the lava beds to great advantage and combining that with accurate rifle fire, forced the U.S. troops to retreat.

The United States decided on diplomacy instead of war. A peace commission headed by General Canby approached the Modocs midway between the lines. The Modocs proposed that a territory reserved for them be located in their homelands. Canby demanded nothing short of unconditional surrender. In the confusion that followed, Captain Jack is said to have shot General Canby in the chest.

The Modocs won other encounters with the federal troops, but they (the Modocs) were weakened by internal strife. They were eventually exiled to Indian Territory, and Captain Jack was executed. Many years later, the small band of Modocs returned to Oregon.

Conflicts accompanied treaty negotiations involving other tribes of the great Northwest, as tribal leaders became divided on the issue of whether they should sign away their ancestral homes. The Nez Perce agreed to a treaty at Walla Walla, but the discovery of gold on the reservation land brought government agents back to the Nez Perce doorstep. Land was guaranteed to the Nez Perce and then taken away by no less than President Ulysses S. Grant, who yielded to white pressure and opened Nez Perce land for settlement by whites in 1875. The subsequent resistance of the Nez Perce symbolized in the person of Chief Joseph is well known.

In 1871 a brief rider on a minor congressional bill brought a closure to the government practice of treaty making with Native tribes. On June 26, 1876, the Sioux and Cheyennes defeated three military forces joined in a campaign to eliminate those tribes in an area known as the Little Big Horn. Leaders of those federal troops were Major Reno, Captain Benteen, and General George Armstrong Custer. Earlier the tribal forces had defeated General Crook and forced him into retreat. Native American leaders were Crazy Horse, Gall, Sitting Bull, and Two Moon. Most accounts mention only that Custer's command was defeated during this encounter.

In 1869 the Quakers had recommended that religious denominations would be better equipped morally and otherwise to manage agencies among the tribes on behalf of the federal government. In 1872 President Grant agreed, and the annual report of the Indian commissioner, dated November 1, 1872, stated the rationale and the assignments to the various denominations. In population, the Methodist Church received the largest allocation. Agencies for which the Methodist Church would provide personnel were as follows:

California:
Hoopa Valley	Population	725
Round Valley		1,700
Tule River		374

Washington Territory:
Yakima	3,000
Skokomish	919
Quinault	520

Oregon:
Warm Springs	626
Siletz	2,500
Klamath	4,000

Montana Territory:
Black Feet	7,500
Crow	2,700
Milk River	19,755

Idaho Territory:
Fort Hall	1,037
Michigan:	9,117
Total	54,473

To some extent this historical event explains why some denominations are where they are today with respect to Native American ministries. This did not limit the denominations to these areas, because most denominations were active among tribes listed as assigned to another church.

There were some harshly opposing views in government circles regarding the treatment of Native American people in the years following the Civil War. Military actions on the Great Plains were intended to be wars of extermination. But when the population of Native people was reported to have fallen to 250,000,[17] government spokesmen began to emphasize education and acculturation as the proper way of relating to the nation's original people.

The matter of citizenship for Native people became a persistent issue in the remarks of Indian commissioners and other governmental spokesmen. As early as 1862, William P. Dole, Indian commissioner under Lincoln, promoted the confinement of Native people on reservations pending their orientation toward becoming U.S. citizens. The treaty at Fort Laramie in 1868 included a provision whereby an individual Sioux male could choose 320 acres or 80 acres, depending on whether he was the head of a family or not, and as a land owner "shall thereby and from thenceforth become and be a citizen of the United States, and be entitled to all the privileges and immunities of such citizens."[18]

In his annual report of 1874, Commissioner Edward P. Smith depicted the Native American people as a lawless people living outside of civilized restraint.[19] His recommended solution was to pass new legislation to extend criminal law to include reservations, making Native American people amenable to state and territorial laws and providing "a way into citizenship for such as desire it."[20]

In 1876 those sentiments were echoed by John Q. Smith, commissioner of Indian affairs. He believed that concentrating all "Indians on a few reservations," the allotment of lands, and the extension of United States law over them would result in the eventual acculturation of the people. In his report he cited as an example the work of Methodist missionary (and government agent) "Father Wilbur" on the Yakima Reservation.[21]

Unfortunately, these views were more optimistic than the reality of contemporary human relations demonstrated. The case of *Standing Bear vs. Crook* attests to both the good and the ugly in immigrant American society as regards Native American presence. In 1868 a treaty negotiated with the Sioux resulted in land belonging to the Ponca tribe on the South Dakota-Nebraska border being inadvertently assigned to the Sioux. Instead of seeking redress for the Ponca tribe, the U.S. government used military power to force the Ponca tribe to go to Indian Territory. The following year Standing Bear, seeking to honor his dying son's final request, took his son's body and a party of sixty family members and set out to bury him in the tribal homeland in the vicinity of Niobrara, Nebraska. The party was intercepted by U.S. troops at the Omaha reservation and placed in the Fort Omaha stockade.

General Crook, who received orders to place them under arrest, opposed the action but carried out his orders anyway. He expressed his displeasure to the local newspaper, which reported the incident to its readers. Local citizens protested the arrest of the Poncas, and "two white attorneys . . . persuaded Judge Dundy to issue a writ of habeas corpus to the Army General."[22] The army was required to appear in court to show cause for the arrest and detention of Standing Bear and his family. The army declared that the Poncas had no right to a writ of habeas corpus because "they were not persons within the meaning of the law."[23] The intent of the army then was to return the Poncas to Indian Territory at gunpoint.

Judge Dundy said, "I have never been called on to hear or decide a case that appealed so strongly to my sympathy as the one now under consideration."[24] He praised General Crook for forcing the issue and expressing his own revulsion for having arrested the Poncas. Judge Dundy's ruling concluded

> 1. That an Indian is a "person" within the meaning of the laws of the United States, and has, therefore, the right to sue out a writ of habeas corpus in a federal court, or before a federal judge, in all cases where he may be confined or in custody under color of authority of the United States, or where he is restrained of liberty in violation of the Constitution or laws of the United States.[25]

He stated that the arrest and detention were illegal and that no "rightful authority exists" for forcibly returning the Poncas to Indian Territory:

4. That the Indians possess the inherent right of expatriation, as well as the more fortunate white race and have the inalienable right to "life, liberty, and the pursuit of happiness" so long as they obey the laws and do not trespass on forbidden ground.[26]

They were ordered released from custody, and the Poncas completed their journey to Niobrara.

Clearly, the Standing Bear issue demonstrates the confusion that existed in regard to the legal status (under U.S. law) of Native American people.

Carl Schurtz became secretary of the interior and is credited with eliminating "corruption and abuses within the Indian Office." He also instituted changes in policy as regarded the removal of tribal people from their homelands for purposes of the reservation system. In his report of November 1, 1880, he declared the removal and concentration of Indian peoples as

a mistaken policy; that it would be vastly better for the Indians and more in accordance with justice as well as wise expediency to respect their home attachments, to leave them upon the land they occupied . . . and to begin and follow up the practice of introducing among them the habits and occupations of civilized life on the ground they inhabited.[27]

Schurtz also indicated that full citizenship was the logical goal of U.S. Indian policy.

Indian Commissioner Hiram Price, described as a "prominent Methodist layman,"[28] pursued this line of thinking in a report dated October 24, 1881, in which he said, "It is claimed and admitted by all that the great object of the Government is to civilize the Indians and render them such assistance in kind and degree as will make them self-supporting."[29] Price followed that remark by criticizing the then-current practice of paying annuities and providing goods and supplies to Native people on reservations. He depicted the U.S. government as a benevolent body of humanitarians bestowing gratuities upon the Native tribes.

He stated his view of the choices Native Americans had, "to wit, either civilization or extermination of the Indian. Savage and civilized life cannot live and prosper on the same ground."[30] Price's solution was an echo of previous government spokesmen. He would break up tribal property into individual parcels, provide draft animals and tools so the Native American male could become a farmer, and then "compel him to depend upon his own exertions for a livelihood. Let the laws that govern a white man, govern the Indian. The Indian must be made to understand that if he expects to live and prosper in this country, he must learn the English language and learn to work."[31]

Price, himself a churchman, praised the missionary work of the various denominations, saying, "One very important auxiliary in transforming men from savage to civilized life is the influence brought to bear upon them through the labors of Christian men and women as educators and missionaries."[32]

It must not escape the careful reader that a different trend of thinking is in process at this time. Price's remarks indicate that the nature of treaties and the Native American-white confrontation had been forgotten. The "American Indian" was now thought of as an alien, being ministered to by a benevolent U.S. government, which now can say, "If the Indian expects to live and prosper in this country" and then lay down any conditions it wishes to. In contrast to that view, Andrew Rolle wrote in his introduction to Helen Hunt Jackson's book *A Century of Dishonor,* "By the 1880's the United States approached the end of its thirty-seven Indian wars. A time for healing the wound inflicted on the Indians by the nation had arrived."[33]

Price did make use of a report on the condition of the Mission Indians, a large contingent of Native American people living on the southern California coast. He suggests that they probably were "entitled to all the rights and immunities of citizens of the United States by virtue of the Treaty of Guadalupe-Hidalgo," but being unfamiliar with legal processes, they failed to secure title to their land. Most other references indicate that the land was stolen from them by force. Regardless of how it happened, they were landless and destitute. Based on the recommendation of Helen Hunt Jackson and Abbot Kinney, Price asked for legislation to bring relief to the suffering coastal people, saying, "With the measures already taken and with those herein recommended, it is believed that these poor and persecuted people may be protected from further encroachments, and enjoy in some measure the prosperity to which their peaceful conduct under all their wrongs entitles them."[34] Congress didn't act until 1891, when a land base was established and allotments in severalty were authorized.

The theorizing about citizenship for Native Americans was more rhetorical than sincere, in spite of high-level speculation. In 1884 John Elk, a Native who had expatriated himself from his tribe and was living among whites, had his day with the Supreme Court. He had been denied the right to vote in Omaha, Nebraska (the site of the *Standing Bear vs. Crook* case), on the ground that he was not a citizen. His attorney sought redress for him on the grounds that the Fourteenth Amendment guarantees citizenship to Indians, as it does to all groups. The Supreme Court ruled against Elk, saying that since the Constitution and the amendment had an exclusion clause for "Indians not taxed," they were not counted in the state population. Since they weren't included in the count—"the basis of representation"—they could not be considered citizens.[35]

Nevertheless, influential forces continued to press for a policy that would result in altering the land base of Native Americans and the extension of laws to bring Native American individuals within the jurisdiction of white America. These influential forces were government spokesmen, social reformers, land speculators, and one group that met annually for thirty-three years "to discuss Indian matters and to make recommendations," the Lake Mohonk Conference of Friends of the Indians.

This latter group is said to have had "tremendous impact on the formulation of Indian policy."[36] Many of the recommendations of the Conference are positive and compelling. But the 1884 second annual address to the public of the Lake Mohonk Conference contained the basis for the destruction of the Native American community. Basically the conference called for the abolition of tribal governments and structures, and the break-up of reservation land bases. They called for allotment of land to Indians in severalty to be inalienable for a maximum of twenty-five years and the enfranchising of all adult Indian males following a test for "intellectual and moral qualifications."[37] The positive tone and substance of the report belie the potential disaster resident within its context.

The writings of Felix Cohen came too late to help the true reformers and Native American leaders know what was actually taking place, but in retrospect the modern reader may find a measure of understanding for themselves in his words. In an article appearing in *Indian Truth,* March–April 1948, Felix Cohen wrote,

> Of course no assault on Indian lands can succeed if it is formulated as a barefaced steal. To be successful on a large scale, plunder must always wear the mask of national interest and high moral purpose. The national interest in impoverishing the Indian is generally cast on the assumption "that Indians do not know how to develop their own resources, which must be turned over to enterprising corporations in order to ensure full production of commodities needed for war or peace."[38]

Cohen proceeded to refute the latter assumption by citing Native American successes in specific timber and mineral resource management. But his main point, that theft of land and resources from Native tribes had to be couched in language that pretended to be in the best interests of the people, revealed the hidden agenda of both the government and reformers. No doubt there were true reformers who genuinely sought change to promote the best interests of the tribal people. But at this period of time, it was difficult to distinguish between those who wished to destroy the Native American people and those who truly wanted a better life for them—because both sides were saying the same thing.

The decade of the 1880s was the period when the government and reformers made far-reaching decisions that affected Indian policy for more than fifty years.

The work of Christian missionaries among Native American people was indistinguishable from the political and social developments being inflicted upon them, except in some of the practical accomplishments of mission work. New churches established among Native American tribes during the period beginning with the close of the Civil War and the end of the decade of the 1980s were mostly in the West.

New churches in the East included the Prospect Methodist Church among the Lumbees of North Carolina. This church, established in 1874, was reported in 1931 as still existing as a one-room frame building located on a quarter-acre tract of land.[39] By 1988 it was the largest Native American Methodist church in the world, with over seven-hundred members worshiping in a huge structure that includes an educational unit and a fellowship hall, all of which was built and paid for by the Lumbee people.

While the question of what was the first local church established among Native Americans by the Methodist Church may be, in the long run, unanswerable, the Lumbees probably can boast that Saddletree Meeting House (or Hammonds) "located five miles north of Lumberton dated in 1792" was the first.[40] This church was served by the Reverend W. S. Chaffin from 1865 to 1884, and it was through his grandson, also a Methodist minister in Robeson County, that this information is preserved.

Churches were also established among several tribes in Michigan, east of the Mississippi River. Earlier, a flurry of mission activity took place, which resulted in the establishment of Hermansville (Potawatomi) Methodist Mission (1850). This mission church was in the Marquette District of the Detroit Conference in 1931. It was on a circuit with three white churches and was served by a white pastor. He only held services once a month at the Potawatomi church. On other Sundays "a local preacher and two exhorters, all Indians," conducted services in the morning, afternoon, and evening.[41]

The name of Simon Greensky, a Native American Methodist pastor and a popular and prolific worker, is associated with several churches. Beginning his work in 1896, he had been at work over thirty-five years at the time of the Board of Home Missions Report in 1931. Assisted by his wife, Simon Greensky served Pinconiny Methodist Mission (1860), Saganing (1872), Oscodo (1879), and Hubbard Lake (1919). All except one of these churches helped pay the pastor's salary. The Board of Home Missions report of 1931 says this about Greensky: "If it were not for the whole hearted consecration of our Indian missionary at this place we could not continue this important work without furnishing a much more adequate support." The report says this of the Native American congregation: "They have no trades and own no property, yet they are liberal and give to their church when able."

Kewadin was established in about 1871 on about forty acres of land. By 1931 it was also on a circuit with a white church and being served by a white pastor. In Wisconsin the DePere Mission was established in 1867, "but no church was built until 1892." The mission was located on thirty-seven acres of land, and in 1931 reported two hundred members.

During the same period in the West, churches were established among Native Americans in Washington, Nevada, Oregon, California, Idaho, and Montana.

In 1865 James Wilbur began work on the Yakima reservation, whose first church building was constructed in 1879. At first James Wilbur was actually appointed by the Oregon Conference. Two of the reservations assigned by the federal government to the Methodist church, although they were in Washington Territory, were under the superintendency of the Oregon Conference: the Klamath and the Siletz reservations.

There was considerable hostility between the northwestern Native tribes and the whites who were brazenly moving in on their territory. In 1850 Congress had passed the Oregon Donation Act, which allowed, at least from the white point of view, for so-called settlers to receive 320 acres of land per adult person free. The U.S. government had not bothered to tell the Native tribes about the legislation, so when white persons moved in to claim land that tribal people were living on already, the Native people were reluctant to move out of the way. Feelings were not good between the whites who wanted the land and the Native people who had it: "In 1851 Anson Dart was appointed to negotiate with the Indians of the Willamette Valley—with all too familiar results. The government wanted the Indians to give up their lands altogether; the Indians would not agree."[42]

Thomas Yarnes, a Methodist historian in Oregon, expressed the white point of view when he wrote, "It is a remarkable thing that, in a time of such turmoil and savagery, the Church would even think of special service to the Natives."[43] Perhaps Mr. Yarnes could not rise above the racism of his time, for he was born in 1883; otherwise he might have seen the other side of the matter. It was just as remarkable that Native people responded to missionary efforts in the light of the turmoil and savagery of the colonists entering tribal homelands.

Apparently it was important that a man like James Wilbur should come along at this time in history. He bridged the great rift in western missions created by the prostituted ministries of Jason

Lee and Marcus Whitman. It was better for Wilbur and the Oregon Conference to develop new missions, to exist in their own right to serve purposes relevant to the needs of the Native people and true to the intent of the gospel, than to develop missions subservient to colonial causes hostile to Native people.

By most reports James Wilbur was well liked by the Yakima people. They responded generously to his ministry by providing 160 acres of land to be used for mission purposes. When the "old church" was built, the Yakima people also provided the labor to complete the project. The Board of Home Missions report of 1931, states, "We have gone to work here with the idea of Indian workers for Indian people. We feel that we have won their confidence somewhat and that the old Pom Pom religion is breaking down and we can look for an increase from that group." Therein is an illustration of good intent founded on a false premise. Any method of spreading the gospel that is based on prejudice is self-destructive. The gospel is good for people because it is good for people, not because something else is bad for people. The spiritual principles resident in Native religions are not at enmity with those of Christianity.

Two outstanding leaders came out of the early efforts of the Yakima Mission: Thomas Pearne and George Watters. From 1869 to 1873 these ministers served at one or the other of the Klamath or Siletz reservations. They were also active in other parts of Washington Territory. Pearne and Watters were ordained deacons in 1871.

The planting of Christianity in Oregon apparently grew out of the persistent efforts of the Oregon Conference to reinstate its mission efforts among the Native tribes. The New York Missionary Society was not interested in Oregon missions following the Jason Lee failure. In the organizing Conference of the Oregon Annual Conference (1853), however, Josiah Parrish, formerly a blacksmith in the Jason Lee Mission, was received on trial and "appointed full-time missionary to the Indians."[44] Unfortunately, his contribution was to assist the U.S. government in the formation of reservations and to use his influence to persuade Native peoples to accept the reservation system. *A History of Oregon Methodism* contains this quotation: "In this work, as it proceeded and in leading the Indians to understand the obligations they had assumed, they [the government agents] were greatly assisted by J. L. Parrish: without whom progress seemed at one time to be well-nigh balked altogether."[45]

Five reservations were placed in Oregon. Eighteen were placed in Washington Territory. In 1856 Parrish was assigned to the Grand Ronde and Tillamook reservations and also the Neah Bay and Quinault reservations in Washington Territory. Apparently these appointments were unsuccessful.

In 1859 the Oregon Conference sought to consolidate all Indian missions under its care under the supervision of one man. That was not accomplished until 1872, six years after James Wilbur was appointed pastor of the new work on the Yakima reservation. In 1872 he was appointed presiding elder of the Indian Mission District.[46] The idea of an Indian mission district was innovative for the time. It was of brief duration, however. The appointment list for the Oregon Conference shows the Klamath and Siletz missions appearing in the Indian Mission District only in the years 1872 and 1873. After that they show up in the Eugene (or Eugene City) District for several years, and James Wilbur does not appear on the appointment list after 1873.

The Siletz Mission was established in 1872, with John Howard appointed as the first pastor. It continued until 1966 and was then abandoned by the Conference. The Board of Home Missions report of 1931 deplores the lack of community development on the part of the Conference appointees:

> On our first visit to this Mission we found the work in a deplorable condition. The whites were assuming the responsibility and the Indians were almost wholly neglected. We finally refused to permit any more money to go into the Mission until better leadership had been secured and a worthwhile program for the Indians had been advanced.

Two months later they resumed payments to the mission. The work of the Siletz Mission was apparently undermined by another influence in the community—the "Shaker" church. This was not the Shaker church known in the East but an accommodation to a number of religious influences that found expression in spectacular ritual. It was perhaps this influence plus the lack of aggressive ministry on the part of the Conference appointees that led to the closing of the Siletz Mission in 1966.

The Yainax Mission was established in 1873, with James Harrar as its first appointed pastor. This mission appears on the Oregon Conference appointment list until 1922. After that it no longer appears. The Board of Home Missions report (1931) explains:

> In 1908, resident workers came to live at Yainax. They found a church building already under construction at Whiskey Creek. This they finished, and the next year built the parsonage on ground held by the church at what later became known as Beatty, about four miles from the church building.
>
> In 1922 a church building was erected on our property at Beatty [named after Methodist missionary J. L. Beatty] by Rev. and Mrs. Belknap who were the missionaries serving at that time. This building was dedicated in 1923, the first year of Rev. Mackintosh's administration [as pastor] by Bishop William O. Shepard. . . .
>
> This mission serves Klamath, Modoc and Paiute Indians. Following the Modoc War, followers of Captain Jack—their war leader who was hanged—established themselves at Yainax and surrounding country. Our Modocs of today are the descendants of those who fought in that bloody war.

Thus Yainax evolved into the Beatty Mission and continued to be a center of community activity. The confusion over the founding date of the Beatty Mission may be partially explained by the fact that J. L. Beatty, the pastor whose name was given to the village, served the Yainax Mission last in 1913. Between 1910 and 1923, work was carried on at both places, that is, at Whiskey Creek, where the original church building was located, and at the parsonage location about four miles from the church at Whiskey Creek.

The Methodist work among the Nooksacks was founded by William George and Jimmy Adams in 1875, both Native Americans, although white missionary C. M. Tate is usually credited with formalizing the work. The story as it is told in the *Board of Home Missions* 1931 report goes as follows. William George and Jimmy Adams had been attending a campmeeting in Chillinack (Canada), where they were converted. "On their return they stopped at Lynden and held services in the home of Lynden Jim, Chief of the Nooksack tribe, one of the first converts on the Nooksack River. Some white persons fearing the Indians did not know what they were doing, sent for C. M. Tate, who found a revival in progress."[47]

Earliest appointments were made by the Oregon Conference and the Women's Home Missionary Society. Barclay notes that in 1880 they were left "to be supplied" by the Oregon Conference, but in 1884 appropriated three hundred dollars "to establish a mission among the Nootsach [sic]."[48]

In 1884 the Oregon Conference was divided, and the Puget Sound Conference was organized. The latter, a newly formed Annual Conference, inherited the work among the Nooksack. The Women's Home Missionary Society brought a woman medical missionary and established the Stickney Home and Industrial School on twenty-five acres of land given by Nooksack Lynden Jim. The school and farm, operating in the last decade of the nineteenth century, served young people between the ages of five and eighteen years.

According to Barclay, work was attempted by the Oregon Conference among the Nez Perce in the 1870s, and again in 1890 by the Columbia River Conference, with no success.[49]

Of the three California reservations assigned to the Methodist Church by the Grant administration—the Hoopa Valley, Tule River, and the Round Valley reservations—only the Round Valley reservation was permanently established as a local church site. The Hoopa Valley work appeared on the California appointment list in 1871, 1872, 1874, and 1875. In 1894 the Conference Committee on Indian Missions reported that the "Hoopa Valley Indians, among whom we once had a mission, have been lost to us through our own neglect."[50]

The Tule River agency (population 280) had preaching services, a Sunday school, and a day school, and was served by the Methodist Church from 1874 to 1887, after which the Tule River Mission disappears from the Conference records.[51]

The Methodist mission at Schurz, Nevada, is said to have been started in 1875. It is on the Walker River reservation and serves the Paiute people. The Board of Home Missions report of 1931 states that there were about four hundred Native American people living on the reservation. At the time of that report there were two day schools, one for Indians (with forty-one students enrolled) and one for white children (with twenty-one enrolled). The membership of the Schurz Mission was thirty, and of its Sunday school, sixty. A hospital had just been completed.

In Minnesota there was a rather large gap in time from 1851 when Peter Marksman was appointed to "Fond du Lac," which apparently was immediately abandoned by the Conference until 1893, when "it [was] reported that a log church 'has been erected at the Vermillion Indian Mission.' John Clark, an educated Chippewa Indian, had been appointed as supply. In 1894 the District Superintendent had assured the Conference that the 'good work . . . [had] continued throughout the year and the moral effect [had been] noticed by all.' "[52]

Apparently that report was overly optimistic, as mission reports tend to be. According to other sources, the missionary effort among the Sioux and Chippewas of Minnesota has been a continuous experience of mission initiative and failure in the field. The fact that each initiative left a faithful remnant among the tribal people has provided the basis for continued effort. The tribal people in the great northern plains were understandably suspicious of white missionaries who seemed oblivious to the atrocities being committed against the tribes occupying Minnesota, the Dakotas, Nebraska, and adjacent territories. Is it possible that the missionaries did not know about the army court-ordered mass murder by official hanging of thirty-eight Sioux men in 1862? In 1890 the Seventh Cavalry slaughtered and butchered over three hundred men, women, and children at Wounded Knee, South Dakota, on the pretense that as followers of the Ghost Dance religion, they were a threat to white settlers. Were the missionaries ignorant of that atrocity?

It appears that Methodist missions remained in Minnesota because of the nurturing ministry of Duane Porter, a Chippewa clergyman. Porter was converted after being challenged by S. G. Wright, a Presbyterian missionary on the La Courtervilles reservation in Wisconsin. He immediately sought ways to take the gospel to other peoples in the upper Midwest.

In the summer of 1888, leaving the family at the mission, with a pack on my back, I struck out over Indian trails through the then wilderness a distance of 200 miles to Tower, Minnesota. There I bought a birchbark canoe and a few supplies and paddled 30 miles to the Indian village at the head of Lake Vermillion, at Wakimup Bay. Among the first to greet the new arrival was the old Indian chief, a very crafty man, who when he learned that I wished to come and live in his village and teach and preach Jesus to the Indians, gave me a ready welcome.[53]

Duane Porter tirelessly preached and counseled among the Chippewas, and many people were led into Christianity. Unfortunately Porter, as did many early Native clergy, believed that acceptance of Christianity meant giving up the ancient religions. A touching if frustrating scene is described in Porter's autobiography:

I spoke to the people about helping to build a tabernacle of poles and cedar bark. They were willing to help. Then the medicine man said "You can have the grand medicine lodge which belongs to me, if you will clean it out and fix it up to suit yourself." On the morning of July 4, 1891, we gathered together a company of converts and went inside the lodge, took down all the wooden images of birds and animals, carried out the drum and threw all these things in a pile. Soon many of the old pagan Indians came up the hill with their little drums, medicine bags, skins of small animals used in the medicine lodge ceremony and threw them also on the pile. We then walked around the lodge hall singing, "Nearer my God to Thee." Some young brave touched a match to the pile of pagan relics and a great fire consumed them as we stood and watched.[54]

So even the most traditional of Natives are willing to make great sacrifices to demonstrate the integrity of their commitment. Porter was at this time not a member of any Christian church denomination. When he chose to become a member of a Christian denomination, he chose the Methodist Church.

Soon after the close of this meeting I made up my mind to join the Methodist church. So on Sunday I went by canoe to Tower and from there to Sudan, arriving at the close of the service. I arose and said I wanted to join the church. After questioning me I was accepted and made a member of the Church. A few days later Reverend McCausland gave me an exhorters license. So with the knowledge I was a member of a great church body and backed by their license to teach and preach to my people, I went back to the village filled with renewed courage. A few weeks later I had finished with the help of my people a rough tabernacle built of trees and bark.[55]

Porter continued to minister in the upper Midwest. He traveled hundreds of miles by canoe and built several churches and tabernacles, as well as "minister's homes." He gathered congregations wherever he went. He suffered incredible hardships, never receiving more than six hundred dollars a year in salary. On one occasion a jealous missionary sought to discredit his work and caused further hardships for Porter. Seeing that it was better to support the mission work than to defend himself against the missionary's false remarks, Porter ignored the attacks and continued his work of building and planting the gospel. Through all these hardships, he remained loyal to the Methodist Church.

On one occasion an Episcopal missionary, a Mr. Gilfillan, seeing his suffering, sought to persuade Porter to join the Episcopal Church and serve the Leech Lake Episcopal Mission. Gilfillan said, "You have been working among your people for 14 years now, and the Methodist Church does not back you up in your work. I will give you a good home to live in, all furnished, and a good salary." Duane Porter replied, "I cannot go back on the church to which I belong even if they never give me any help in my work. Brother, that doesn't make any difference with me, and doesn't discourage me. I have built my house on that foundation rock and I can't pull off my house for little things like these."[56]

Duane Porter's name will always be associated with historical Methodism in Minnesota. Many other Native leaders shared in this nurturing ministry, such as Ah-be-dad-sung, the traditional spiritual leader; Joe Baptiste, "who built a church at Sawyer, Minnesota";[57] Frank Pequette (D. 1937),[58] Chippewa clergyman and a member of the Northern Minnesota Conference; and others whose names are not recorded on earth.

In Kansas there were no new developments in Indian missions, but in 1880 the General Missionary Committee of the Methodist

Episcopal Church reinstated the Wyandotte Mission on the Wyandotte land in Indian Territory. The Wyandotte tribe gave three
acres of land on which a church and parsonage were located in
1882 and 1883, respectively.

In 1860 the Kansas and Nebraska Conference appointed
Richard Duvall as missionary to the Sauks and Fox. He left this
assignment to resume his work as a missionary, because of lack of
support. When the Annual Conference convened in 1866, the
government agent showed up with Keokuk (headman of the
tribe), and a few tribesmen made "an urgent request for a missionary." The Conference declined their request.[59]

Indian Mission Conference in Indian Territory, 1866–1892, 1905

It is not possible to know how many local churches there were
in the Indian Mission Conference of Indian Territory in the nineteenth century. It is only possible to state how many appointive
charges there were at a given time and how many ministers there
were to serve them. Appendix A contains a table of the available
statistical information on the Indian Mission Conference of Indian Territory.

It can be seen that there is considerable difficulty in the attempt
to reconcile many of the statistical figures from one year to the
next. The lowest number of Native American members of the
Indian Mission Conference (1,795) was recorded in the Conference minutes of 1867. The highest number of Native American
members was recorded in the Conference minutes just four years
later, at 4,320. The Indian Mission Conference was never able to
provide a ministry to the vast territory assigned to it, having been
forced by the Civil War, the shortage of leadership, and other
factors to limit the Conference's outreach to the Wyandotte Mission in Kansas and to the area occupied by the five civilized tribes.

Another complicating factor was the division of the Methodist
Church in 1844 over the slavery issue. All of the work of the
Indian Mission Conference at this time, immediately following the
Civil War, was concentrated among the so-called five civilized
tribes. Thus following the division of the Methodist Church, this

Conference fell within the jurisdiction of the Methodist Episcopal Church (MEC) South.

Work Done by the Methodist Episcopal Church (North), 1889–1892

It would be the MEC (North) that would establish new work in the West and Northwest. From 1889 to 1892 the MEC also had an "Indian Mission Conference" operating simultaneously in the same area. Among the missions supervised by the MEC North Indian Mission Conference were the following:

1. *The Ponca reservation,* where mission work had originally been established by the Women's National Indian Association in conjunction with the Plymouth Congregational Church of Brooklyn, New York (1884). H. W. Beecher was the pastor. In 1897 the Women's Home Mission Society, with the support of the Troy Conference, took charge of the Ponca Mission. The Ponca Mission was located on twenty acres of land, and their first Methodist missionary was S. C. Bundy.

2. *The Osage reservation,* which the Women's Home Mission Society opened in 1886 in Pawhuska. Adelaide Springer was the missionary, and she began her work in 1888.

3. *The Pawnee Mission* was also received by the Women's Home Mission Society from the Women's National Indian Association. In spite of Pawnee opposition to women missionaries, Mrs. Francis Gaddis began her work in 1885. In 1892 the Indian Mission Conference (MEC) became the Oklahoma Annual Conference (MEC). This must not be confused with the turn of events occurring with the Indian Mission Conference (MEC South) later (1905). The Oklahoma Annual Conference (MEC) developed the Arapaho and Cheyenne missions in El Reno, Oklahoma, territory in 1891, with Mrs. J. E. Roberts serving as the missionary.

4. *The Wyandotte Mission* was also founded by the Indian Mission Conference (MEC). That mission had split into two divisions in Kansas City when the Wyandotte people divided over the slavery issue, and about one-half of the Wyandottes refused to associate with the MEC South.

5. The dates for the establishing of mission work among the Blackfoot people at the North Montana Indian Missions vary depending on the writer. The dates used here are from Barclay's *History of Methodist Missions,* volume 3.[60] In turn, Barclay drew his information from the seventy-sixth annual report of the Methodist Missionary Society of the North Montana Mission (1894):[61] "On April 3, 1893, Eugene S. Dutcher, of the West Nebraska Conference, and Mrs. Dutcher, under contract with [the Women's National Indian Association] arrived at Blackfoot as missionaries to the Piegan who at that time numbered about two thousand. Dutcher was transferred from West Nebraska to the North Montana Mission."[62]

Dutcher is said to have built the first parsonage and chapel on the 160 acres of land provided by the Blackfoot tribe for the mission. Originally under the auspices of the Women's National Indian Association, in July 1894 the mission was transferred to the MEC. Fort Browning was established one mile east of the mission site, resulting in the growth of a small community centered around the fort.[63]

Work Done by the Methodist Episcopal Church, South: The Indian Mission Conference, Oklahoma and Indian Territory, 1844–1906

During the Civil War, the Native members of the Indian Mission Conference made efforts to keep the work alive. Willis Folsom spent most of his time traveling from community to community preaching and counseling. While most white missionaries fled to safer territories, some remained in the field. James Essex was one of those who stayed. Essex was imprisoned by Union soldiers and died in captivity (1864).

Bloomfield Academy was one of the few schools kept open during the war. It was located in Chickasaw territory, which was not invaded by the federals. The appointment list in 1861 showed twenty-seven appointments. In 1864 the ministers in the field divided the work among themselves, with John Harrell functioning as a presiding superintendent. The appointment list showed ten appointments, including one for army missions and one for "refugee Cherokees."

Methodist mission work in the Indian Mission Conference was devastated.

> As the winter of 1865 approached, the people of the Indian Territory were face to face with conditions of unspeakable horror. The whole country had been laid waste. Crops of every description had been destroyed. There was little food and no time to plant and grow another crop. Famine was inevitable.[64]

Complicating matters ever further, the Native peoples who had sided with the North and those who had sided with the South were still in bitter confrontation with one another. In spite of heroic efforts to keep the spiritual fires burning, the church was suffering.

> Religiously the patient toil of more than a quarter of a century had nearly all been swept away. Churches were destroyed, membership killed or scattered, schools closed. The humble firesides, where missionaries held family prayer and occasionally gathered the family around for a sermon, were put out.[65]

When it was finally possible for a bishop to be present in Indian Territory, Bishop Enoch M. Marvin presided over the Indian Mission Annual Conference in September 1866 at Bloomfield Academy. According to Babcock and Bryce, this was the first Annual Conference he ever held, and it was almost the last one held by the Indian Mission Conference.[66] It was reported at this Conference that no money had been appropriated by the church for home missions, since all available money had been used for the support of foreign missions. There was no means of supporting the missionaries in the work of the Conference. There is no official indication that the missionaries were willing to abandon the field, but an article in *Chronicles of Oklahoma* states that was a clear possibility: "The records show that the preachers were about ready to give up the struggle and abandon the field, but the Bishop stepped into the breach and guaranteed funds sufficient to carry on the work for a year."[67]

Bishop Marvin guaranteed five thousand dollars to continue the operation of the Indian Mission Conference. That amount was paid in full. It is speculated that most of that amount came from the bishop's own pocket.

After about three years, the Indian Mission Conference was well on the way to its own reconstruction. It must be remembered that the church was seeking to retrieve its members and churches at a time when tribal governments were being redefined, lands were being lost, and the federal government was seeking ways to punish the tribes for their role in the Civil War.

Appointments in the Indian Mission Conference were still, to a large extent, to large, loosely defined territories rather than to established stations. Preachers held services wherever they could— in homes, public buildings, brush arbors, and the like. Travel was by horseback, foot, or wagon. They depended on the hospitality of people they met and preached to, and perhaps more often than we know, they slept out under the stars.

Eventually the loosely defined territories would become identifiable communities of converts, with designated preaching places, a home, a public building, or even a brush arbor. Then when the preacher had cultivated several such communities and served them all, it would become the preacher's circuit.

Native clergy who provided effective leadership during these difficult times were Samuel Checote (Creek), James McHenry (Creek), Willis Folsom (Choctaw), and John Page (Choctaw).

Samuel Checote was influential in persuading the Creek tribal headman to eliminate the law prohibiting missionaries from coming among the Creeks and prohibiting Creeks from hearing or preaching the gospel. He assisted in the translation of English hymns into the Creek language and campaigned to persuade the Methodist Church to translate the Bible and other Christian literature into the Creek language. In 1868 he became the first Native clergyman to be appointed a district superintendent when he was appointed presiding elder of the Creek District. He was a respected tribal leader and served as the head of the Creek Nation for a number of years.

James McHenry had been resistance fighter in the East. When he came to Indian Territory, he became a member of the Methodist Church and responded to the call to preach. In a letter to the Conference newsletter *Our Brother in Red,* Samuel Checote spoke of McHenry: "He was always at his post working for his Master's cause. He has always been regarded as a prominent man among his people, served a number of years in the upper House of our National Council and four years as President of the Senate and was Judge of the Coweta District."[68] McHenry was credited with starting the Indian Mission churches at Broken Arrow, Okmulgee, Muskogee, and Coweta. He was pastor at Coweta at the time he was district judge.[69]

Willis Folsom worked continuously during the Civil War to keep the church alive and to minister to the Choctaw people. He was the kind of legendary personality that inspired superlative descriptions of his life and times.

> Not only people, but even animals knew his kindly spirit. . . . The wild beasts roamed beyond the boundaries but they never harmed a righteous man. Through all of Brother Folsom's long weary journeys through the lonely woods he never feared harm from a wild beast. . . .
> The wild birds would fly into his dining room, light on his shoulder and feed from his hand.[70]

Most of his ministry was served as a local preacher. In his old age, the Conference admitted him into full connection as an act of love and honor.

John Page was a highly intelligent man. With good business sense, he served as the tribal treasurer and was a prominent member of negotiating teams of the Choctaws. His sermons were scholarly and delivered in a calm, deliberate style. He served twelve years in the same charge in the Moshulatubbee District. He began his ministry in the Missouri Conference, where he was admitted on trial. He was admitted to the Indian Mission Conference in full connection at its organizing conference in 1844.

The Indian Mission Conference would lose these great men during the Reconstruction. James McHenry died in 1883 at the age of sixty-four or sixty-five. Samuel Checote died in 1884 at sixty-five years of age, and Willis Folsom died in 1897 at the age of seventy-three. Those were the prominent clergy whose names are familiar to those who are aware of the history of the Indian Mission Conference. Their lives and ministries spanned the mid-

dle two-thirds of the nineteenth century, and that includes reset-
tlement in Indian Territory, the Civil War, and the desperate years
of recovery following the Civil War.

A tribute to Samuel Checote may be found in Paul Mitchell's
From Teepees to Towers:

> The Creek Nation made it a penal offense between 1845 and
> 1848 to profess the Christian Religion, the penalty being thirty-
> nine lashes with a cowhide whip. Samuel Checote suffered penal-
> ty, being less than twenty years of age. While blood flowed to his
> ankles, he was asked "Will you give up Christ?" He replied "You
> may kill me but you cannot separate me from my Lord Christ."
> . . . He received his license to preach in 1852. . . . He served as
> Chief of the Creek Nation in 1867, 1872, and 1879 . . . He was a
> pastor at Okmulgee the same time he was chief and preached in a
> large arbor near the Council House . . . He was elected a dele-
> gate to the Ecumenical Conference of Methodism which met in
> London, England in 1882, but because of age and illness was
> unable to go.[71]

(Samuel Checote never confirmed that he suffered at the whipping
post because of his Christian faith, perhaps out of respect for the
people of the Creek Nation.)

There are others whose names are not so well known but who
stood firm when everything seemed to be crumbling around
them. Those described below, and many unnamed laymen and
women, preserved the work of the Indian Mission Conference
through some very traumatic experiences. Standing Man, a
Cherokee Methodist clergyman, was one of those. His name first
appears on the appointment list in 1857, and it appears every
year appointments were made until he died at his post in 1869.
During the Civil War he remained at his post and was one of four
Native American clergy present when an Annual Conference was
finally held in 1864.

Isaac Sanders (Cherokee) was a contemporary of Standing
Man. His career started in 1850 and continued until he was granted the superannuated relationship in 1879. When he died in 1882
at the age of eighty, the newspaper *The Cherokee Advocate* identified him as "Isaac Sanders [Methodist] . . . an itinerant preacher
of the Gospel. . . . [He] was a man of gentle disposition in his

intercourse with his fellows but full of zeal in the pulpit or when otherwise engaged in the Master's work. He had no enemies; his friends were legion."[72]

Isaac Chuckmubbee (Choctaw) began his ministry in 1848. In his entire career he served only one charge. For nine years he served Kiamichi, changing it from a broadly defined mission territory into an established circuit. Chuckmubbee was not listed after 1857.

According to Babcock and Bryce, the year 1858 saw the first appointments of local preachers to "regular works."[73] Thus Willis Folsom heard his name read as being appointed to Skullyville. Also, many previous mission territories were being designated as circuits. Meeting houses were being built by the Native American people and other "preaching places" designated.

Social and political circumstances began to affect the work of the church and veer it away from the direction intended by the Native people. More whites were entering Indian Territory because of the railroads and because of the government seizure of tribal lands following the Civil War and the "opening" of these lands for "settlement" by whites. The attitude of white Methodists was beginning to find expression, and it signaled bad times for Native American Methodists in the Indian Mission Conference. Babcock and Bryce probably expressed that attitude as they reflected in their writing that

> from 1870 on, the Church was no longer a missionary church to the Indians. It must now lay a foundation for work in what soon was to become a great cosmopolitan state. The Indian nations must gradually lose their identity as Nations, and the Great Father, as the Indians called the government at Washington, must become the Father of all.[74]

But the Indians had no such intent in mind. The Five Tribes were secure in their identity as nations with a land base, court systems, educational institutions, and churches. A few white church leaders saw value in pursuing social and religious development within the framework of Native American interests and purpose. One of those wrote anonymously to *Our Brother in Red* the following encouragement to develop Native American leadership in the church:

Now while I am fully in sympathy with our noble band of work-ers in our Indian field—which my labors while with them will evince—I do respectfully suggest that more attention be given to the rearing up of competent teachers and preachers from among the Natives. I believe much of this tardiness [in developing native leadership] has been owing to a mistaken policy in our white lead-ers. It is with great pleasure that I have noticed a few natives received into the traveling connection and ordained, who met with distrust and even opposition on making application for admis-sion a few years ago.

No doubt there slumbers among the Native converts in our church of six thousand souls the very gifts which under the direc-tion of the Spirit and the encouragement of the Church would speedily set the cause upon a self-sustaining basis and add this one more conference to our great effectual force for saving the world. Surely the Indian Christian is not an exception to the well estab-lished principle "Go, or die."[75]

The establishment of an Indian-administered Annual Confer-ence may have seemed good to the anonymous writer, but most white Methodists were thinking along other lines. As the Indian Mission Conference entered the last quarter of the nineteenth century, the Native church population began to be overwhelmed by the growing white population. The Native Methodist com-munities that would preserve Methodism among Native Ameri-cans in Indian Territory were in place. Most of the efforts of the church were concentrated among the Five Civilized Tribes and other eastern tribes. The western tribes, ushered in by way of the Treaty of Medicine Lodge and other postwar treaties, were not as yet objects of evangelism by the Indian Mission Conference.

In 1887 a peculiar event took place in the Annual Conference. Previous to this Conference, it was decided to consider mission-ary efforts among the western Plains tribes (the Kiowas, Com-manches, Arapahos, etc.), and recommendations were sought. It must be remembered that at this time there were over five thou-sand Native American members in the Conference. The records indicate that Native American Methodists were not requested to participate in plans to develop work among the western tribes.

When Bishop Galloway read the appointments in the 1887 Annual Conference, J. J. Methvin, a white missionary, was assigned the task of carrying the gospel to the western tribes. Church historians tell about the hardships and dangers he faced as a missionary to the Plains tribes. It may well be that the western tribes were justifiably suspicious of a conference called the Indian Mission Conference, with five thousand Native members, which sent a white missionary to convert them.

Thus the church began to serve the Kiowas, Commanches, Arapahos, Cheyennes, Caddos, Apaches, Wichitas, and other western tribes. Eventually preaching places around Anadarko were cultivated, and a school, not so surprisingly called the J. J. Methvin Institute, was established. The preaching places later evolved into churches, but the school was eventually closed because of lack of support.

The work among the western tribes appeared on the appointment list as "Anadarko" or "Anadarko Circuit" from 1888 to 1895. J. J. Methvin's name appeared as the person assigned to that charge. But in 1895 Methvin's name did not appear on the appointment list (in Babcock and Bryce's book), and Anadarko was left "to be supplied."[76] In 1896 Methvin once more appears as appointed to Anadarko. In 1897 he is listed as president of Methvin Institute, which was closed soon after its last report to the Conference in 1904.

In 1901 a new appointment appears in the Duncan District, called "Indian work." B. F. Gassoway is shown as the minister appointed to that work. In 1903 Gassoway and Kickingbird are listed. Most probably Kickingbird was an interpreter at this time. In 1904 M. A. Clark and Kickingbird were teamed up under the appointment listed as "Indian work." In 1906 Kickingbird was the lone appointee as a supply pastor for "Indian work." Kickingbird had been ordained a deacon in 1905.

Charges among Native people that would emerge in the twentieth century and that were listed in 1906 are the Atoka Circuit, Bethel, Chickasaw Circuit, Kullituklo, Owl, Rufe, Sans Bois, Sugarloaf, Broken Arrow Circuit, Okmulgee Circuit, Sapulpa Circuit, Seminole Circuit, Wewoka Circuit, Bokchito Circuit, Canadian Circuit, Washita Circuit, and Honeycreek. Native clergy appearing on the 1906 appointment list were A. H. Homer (Choctaw), A. S. Williams (Choctaw), Louis Colbert (Chickasaw), James W. Frazier (Choctaw), W. F. Tobley (Choctaw), Lincoln W. Ishcomer (Choctaw), Elvin McCurtain (Choctaw), Griggs Durant (Choctaw), Harrison E. Nahio (Choctaw), Kickingbird (Kiowa), Moti Tiger (Creek), M. L. Checote (Creek), D. L. Berryhill (Creek), William Hill (tribe unknown), Thomas Long (Creek), Johnson Tiger (Creek), and R. C. Alexander (Choctaw). The loss of the Cherokee work must be regarded as a serious failure, but it is not mentioned in Babcock and Bryce's *History of Methodism in Oklahoma*.

The sixty-first Annual Conference of the Indian Mission Conference was held in 1906 in Tulsa. It was this Conference that changed the direction for Native American Methodism in present-day Oklahoma. A committee was formed to decide on a new name for the Conference since "the Indian and missionary character of the Conference had changed."[77] The committee members were N. L. Linebaugh, T. F. Brewer, P. F. Eaglebarger, J. F. Thompson, and J. J. Methvin. The committee proposed the name "the Oklahoma Conference." It was adopted, and the work of the historic Indian Mission Conference came to an end. That was true in more than a technical sense. The effect of this action was an abandonment of Methodist work among Native Americans. Work among the Cherokees had already gone into a serious decline. Anti-Indian sentiment among whites in Indian Territory had motivated the move for statehood and the elimination of tribal governments, whose systems of law whites living in tribal boundaries had to abide by.

At the time of this event, the Indian Mission Conference had about five thousand Native people as church members. About seventeen clergy could be identified as Native. It is not known how many Native American local churches there were, since some of these were served by white pastors, and a good portion of the work was still being served in the manner of broad mission territories.

By abandoning the mission among Native Americans, the Oklahoma Conference lost about half of its Native American membership. As they did during the Civil War, faithful Native American clergy worked hard to keep the Native Methodist communities together, but it would be several decades before the damage would be overcome.

TWENTIETH-CENTURY
BEGINNINGS

It is written "but do good and to communicate forget not; for with such sacrifice God is well pleased." Surely God must be well pleased with my people . . . for they surely do sacrifice much.

—*the Reverend Byars Columbus (Choctaw), report of the district superintendent to the Annual Conference, Indian Mission Conference Minutes, 1944*

From the viewpoint of Native American people and other peoples who were objects of mission activity, things were very confusing most of the time. Generally they were not involved in the preliminary discussions and planning sessions that took place prior to the deployment of missionaries to mission assignments. Their lot was to respond to the implementation of strategies that they had nothing to do with in the planning stages. They were not party to the assessments of their needs and the consequent decision making about how to go about meeting those needs. They were not involved in interdenominational field agreements about who could work among which people. It is no wonder that they often became incredulous spectators of events that drastically affected their lives and reflected on their status as intelligent human beings.

From the very beginning of the major missionary movements, when the American Board of Commissioners for Foreign Missions debated heatedly on the subject of whether to "civilize" the Indian first and then "Christianize him," or vice versa, to Reconstruction Era top-to-bottom mission deployment that resulted in the abandonment of the Native American emphasis by the Oklahoma Conference, Native people have generally been unwilling spectators of the frustrating results.

The church itself was not administratively stable enough to perform its mission task. Only the Woman's Home Missionary Society and other missionary organizations run by women seemed consistent. The three major divisions of the Methodist Church struggled with similar problems, but for our purposes here, only the evolution of the mission program of the Methodist Episcopal Church (North) will be sketched.

The Civil War disrupted the structural evolution of the Methodist Church and delayed its development by at least the number of years representing the duration of the war. Consequently, the Methodist Church did not develop administratively for mission work, from its initial beginning with the organization of the Methodist Missionary Society in 1820 to the end of the nineteenth century. Annual Conferences were, for all practical purposes, responsible for initiating and supporting mission work within their boundaries, with some financial support coming from the General Board. By the end of the nineteenth century, Methodist Church leadership saw the need to organize the national administrative body of the church in order to bring into better focus the basic thrusts of its ministry. The Methodist Church administration also began to aggressively involve itself in new mission initiatives, such as increasing its foreign mission program and domestic work in Alaska, the lower forty-eight states, and Puerto Rico.

In 1900 the Methodist Missionary Society was reorganized to change from three corresponding secretaries related to the churches' work patterns to an administrative plan that featured one top executive and one assistant. In 1907 the General Conference formed the Board of Foreign Missions and the Board of Home Missions and Church Extension. The Women's Foreign Mission Society and the Women's Home Mission were auxiliary to those boards, respectively. Another aspect of the evolution of the Methodist Church mission program was the key role of bishops in the various foreign fields. From 1900 to 1920 the church followed the practice of appointing bishops to be resident administrators in foreign mission territories. The General Conference abolished the missionary episcopacy in 1920.[1]

In 1916 another reorganization took place, and familiar patterns of administration began to emerge. Five departments were put in place: Church Extension, City Work, Rural Work, Evangelism, and Frontier Work.[2] "Indian Activities" were lodged in the Department of Rural Work at first and then in the Department of Frontier Work. Edward Laird Mills, superintendent of the Department of Frontier Work, was pessimistic about the church's ability to do mission work among Native Americans: "Indian activities did not constitute a major element in the Board's work. . . . When it was assigned to the Dept. of Frontier Work in 1916, Superintendent Mills bluntly declared that the Board had spent a hundred thousand dollars in Indian Missions, but with unsatisfactory results."[3]

In 1920 the General Conference ordered renewed efforts in Native American missions. The Board of Missions responded by forming a seven-member Joint Committee on Indian Work. The joint committee was eventually discontinued. In 1926 "Indian Activities" were assigned to the Department of Evangelism. That same year the Department of Frontier Work was merged with the Department of Rural Work. The Department of Evangelism transferred "Indian work" to that merged department in 1932. In 1939 the uniting Conference of the Methodist Episcopal Church, the Methodist Episcopal Church South, and the Methodist Protestant Church established the organizational plan that would dominate the twentieth century. The Board of Missions at that Conference was subdivided into its two major patterns of ministry: the Division of Foreign Missions (later World Division) and the Division of Home Missions (later National Division). Native American ministries would be a programmatic component of the Division of Home Missions.

Preceding the establishment of the General Board mission components was the work of the women's organizations, which were geared solely for mission work. While these organizations were principally engaged in social service and educational ministries, the effect of what they did was evangelistic. New congregations and indigenous leadership most frequently grew out of the work of organizations such as the Women's National Indian Association and the Women's Home Missionary Societies of the Methodist Churches. This necessitated a response from the Methodist Church, as well as Annual Conferences, to provide for the ministry initiated by the women's missionary organizations.

In summary, the question of who did Native American Ministries in the Methodist Church on the national church level is answered as follows:

1820   Methodist Missionary Society
1844   Methodist Missionary Society, North and South
1900   Methodist Missionary Society (MEC) reorganized
1907   Board of Missions
          Board of Foreign Missions
          Board of Home Missions ("Indian Work" assigned here)
1916   Board of Missions reorganized by General Conference into five departments:
          Church Extension
          City Work
          Rural Work ("Indian Activities" assigned here)
          Evangelism
          Frontier Work ("Indian Activities" later assigned here)
1920   Board of Missions ordered by General Conference to renew efforts in ministry to Native Americans. Board of Missions, with Women's Home Missionary Society, organized a seven-member joint committee on Indian Work. The joint committee ceased functioning prematurely.
1926   Department of Evangelism assigned "Indian Work"
1932   Department of Rural Work (having been merged with Department of Frontier Work) assigned "Indian Work"
1939   Division of Home Missions (of General Board of Missions) assigned programmatic and administrative responsibility for Native American ministries

Throughout the entire history of Methodist missions among Native Americans, the Women's Home Missionary societies and other women's groups that later evolved into the present Women's Division were key participants.

Native American Church Development Through 1939

Alaska missions began due to the initiative of the Women's Home Missionary Society (WHMS). In 1886 the Society opened work at Unalaska, which along with the work of John Carr (at this time a local preacher) evolved into the Jesse Lee Home. By 1904 it "was a home and industrial school staffed by a physician-super-intendent, Dr. Q. W. Newhall and by three W. H. M. S. women missionaries."[4]

In 1897 the Methodist Missionary Society initiated the Alaska Mission by Bishop McCabe's appointing C. J. Larsen as superintendent of the new work.[5] The work was formally recognized in November of that year.

J. J. Walter, who succeeded Larsen in 1899, opened new missions among the settlers and received repeated requests from the Tlingit tribe to establish a Methodist mission among them. Walter responded by sending Milo Sellon, a dynamic young convert from Skagway. Sellon established a church among the Tlingit and learned to teach and preach in the Tlingit language. By 1902 Sellon had developed a congregation of 175 Tlingit people and added them to the roles of the Methodist Church. Walter was replaced as superintendent by W. H. Selleck. Selleck received the bad news of a pact that granted the Presbyterians an exclusive right to establish missions among the Natives in that territory. "W. H. Selleck then was compelled regretfully to transfer the Indian Mission to the Presbyterians because of a longstanding Missionary Society compact granting the former exclusive right to evangelize the tribes of Southeastern Alaska."[6]

The new bishop Earl Cranston annulled the agreement for future projects. The Tlingit people were the incredulous spectators to this arbitrary, nonsensical arrangement on the part of jealous denominations, which eliminated their choice of Christian association. This form of ecclesiastical serfdom existed for a time under the Grant administration (Peace Policy) and no doubt in other places at one time or another. It is good that comity agreements were never an authorized policy of the Methodist Church.

The Alaska Mission was formally organized as a separate connectional unit in 1904. The first Annual Conference of the Alaska Mission was held that year. As for Milo Sellon, he and his wife became missionaries in a new work among Alaska Natives at Sinuk, near Nome, which was opened by the Women's Home Missionary Society in 1905.

In North Carolina several Lumbee churches were organized between 1906 and 1912. According to a work edited by R. Pierce Beaver, churches organized among the Lumbees during that period were Pembroke First Methodist (1906), Ashpole Center (1906), Sandy Plain (1908), Hickory Grove (1910), Fairview (1912), and Pleasant Grove (1912).[7]

The 1900 Lumbee Methodists found themselves divided over an issue that resulted in the formation of a separate and independent Annual Conference of Lumbee churches. After ignoring an order from the Methodist Episcopal Church authorities to cease and desist their activities, which led to the division of Lumbee Methodists, the Lowry brothers, both clergy, were expelled from the church and denied their rights to administer the sacraments. The Lowrys and their followers proceeded to form the Lumbee Methodist Conference on September 20, 1902.[8] It is said that the issue centered around the perception of the Lowrys and their followers that Lumbee people should be the principal decision makers in their own churches.

Those of the Lumbee people who chose to remain in the Methodist Episcopal Church were the nucleus of the present-day system of Lumbee churches in The United Methodist Church. Other churches among the Lumbee people are Philadelphus (1958), Collins Chapel (1960), Branch Street (1962), Coharrie (1963), and Lighthouse (1979).

Prominent Methodist leaders among the Lumbee include Henry H. Lowry, Calvin C. Lowry, French R. Lowry (leaders of the independent Lumbee Methodist Conference), and William Luther Moore (who opposed the split). The Reverend Jerry

Lowry identifies the following as prominent leaders in the historic Lumbee Methodist Church:

French R. Lowry (1869–1971)
James Walter Smith (1885–1955)
R. W. Woodell (1873– ?)
D. F. Lowry (1881–1977)
Jakie Locklear (1912–1973)
P. M. Locklear (1868–1933)
Harvey Lowry (1928–1978)[9]

In 1916 the Salem Methodist Church in Michigan was organized, first as a Sunday school. Henry Medawis donated land for a church building in 1919, and the first structure was started in 1920.

The Hubbard Lake Methodist Mission in Michigan was organized in 1919 and was still active in 1931. At that time, however, there were only twenty-five people in the community, of whom twelve were members of the church.[10]

In Minnesota the Nett Lake Mission was organized in 1917. It appears that this church was still operating in 1949. A booklet by Charles Purdham cites "a 1949 report" that tells of a constituency of fifty families, worship attendance of forty to fifty persons, an organized Woman's Society of Christian Service, and two youth groups.[11]

In northern California the Board of Missions (MEC) stated they had worked among the Pomo tribal people for forty years before a "definite organization was attempted [in the] spring of 1929." The church was organized, and a church building was constructed at a cost of about $650. The Pomo people did most of the work, and the Board of Home Missions contributed $250. The district contributed $100. The remaining cost was absorbed by the Pomo people and local white Methodists. Apparently a prior agreement allowed exclusive missionary rights to the Methodist Church in this area. A Presbyterian church found operating a mission in the area was required to "make adjustments": "In 1931 an adjustment was made with the Presbyterians by which they will not hold further services there and will as rapidly as possible transfer their property and good will to the Methodists."[12]

Oklahoma Indian Mission 1918–39

Powerful social forces were operating in Oklahoma in the first quarter of the twentieth century. Havoc caused by the General Allotment Act (1887) for the reservation dwellers was being repeated in Oklahoma among the Five Civilized Tribes as a result of the Curtis Act (1898). The unilateral legislation was enacted by Congress after the Dawes Commission failed to persuade the Five Tribes to voluntarily accept the terms of the Dawes Act (General Allotment Act) for themselves.

The Curtis Act called for the finalizing of the tribal roles and the dissolving of tribal governments and court systems and the allotting of tribal lands to individual ownership based on the tribal roles. The clear intent was to create a means by which lands could be stolen from individual tribal members easily and quickly. As expected, white citizens seized the opportunity to take Native lands by fraud, intimidation, and outright theft or squatting. An extremely odious development was the "guardianship" system, which was used to loot Indian lands, especially in eastern Oklahoma. John Collier comments: "In Oklahoma, individualized Indian estates were looted through a system of local white 'guardians' named by the Oklahoma courts pursuant to Congressional grants of power."[13] Collier reports as an example that following 1915, two thousand Osages were paid in cash (received by their guardians) $265,000,000 in royalties from Osage oil. "Ninety per cent of this total went 'down the wind' of ruined Osages and corrupted and corrupting whites."[14]

The tragedy of the oppressive climate was expressed in human casualties as well. The story of seven-year-old Ledcie Stechi, a Choctaw minor, will serve to illustrate the incredible number of horror stories occurring during this period of time.

Ledcie Stechi lived with her grandmother about two and a half miles from Smithville in southeastern Oklahoma. Ledcie was heir to land formerly owned by her mother, who had died. Twenty acres of that land was found to contain valuable oil deposits. In spite of that, Ledcie lived in poverty because the local judge allowed only ten dollars a month for her support, coming from a sale of land made and deposited by her uncle.

When the twenty acres of land began to produce oil, Mr. Jordan Whiteman, "owner of the First National Bank of Idabel," worked through his attorney to get himself assigned as Ledcie Stechi's guardian. He allowed fifteen dollars per month for Ledcie's support, from a court-allowed two hundred dollars per month from oil royalties. When a medical examination showed Ledcie to be undernourished and ill from malaria, she was provided medical treatment, and when her health improved, she was "placed by an employee of the Indian service in the Wheelock Academy." Mr. Whiteman, apparently wishing to retain control of the rich little girl, demanded that she be returned to his custody. She was, and the grandmother never saw Ledcie Stechi alive again.

On the fourteenth of August, word came to the grandmother that Ledcie was dead. This was a profound shock for the old woman, because she had heard nothing of Ledcie being sick.

Even before the little girl's body was brought to the grandmother, "grafters" showed up at her back door, hoping to persuade the old woman to sell Ledcie's inheritance to them.

> Greed for the girl's lands and rich oil property activated the grafters and made them like beasts surrounding their prey, insensible to the grief and anguish of the whitehaired grandmother. Feebly, hopelessly she wailed over the little dead body—its baby mouth turned black, little fingernails turned black, and even the little breast all turned black! In vain she asked for an examination of the little body, believing Ledcie had been poisoned. "No use. Bury the body," commanded the legal guardian.[15]

Reconstituting the Indian Mission

Methodist missions had not done well in Oklahoma since the beginning of the century. In 1918 Bishop Edwin Mouzon decided that a change of approach was needed. He separated "Indian Work" from the East Oklahoma Conference and established the Indian Mission of Oklahoma, first known as the Brewer Indian Mission. In 1919 when the Brewer Indian Mission met at Newtown, it reported two districts, 82 churches, 18 charges, 8 licensed ministers, 116 local preachers, and 2,702 members.

When the Indian Mission Conference was organized in 1844 at Riley's Chapel, the conference reported 3 districts, 18 charges, 27 local preachers, and 2,992 members.

Because of unclear records, we can only estimate, based on available figures and a letter to *Our Brother in Red* [16] stating that in 1883–84 there were "six thousand souls" in the church, that there were four to five thousand Native members in the Indian Mission Conference at the close of the century. The Indian Mission Conference in 1918 was starting over with 290 fewer members than the organizing Conference of the former Indian Mission Conference in 1844. The former Indian Mission Conference (1844–1905) lasted sixty-one years. In 1979 the Indian Mission Conference (at that time known as the Oklahoma Indian Missionary Conference) had been in existence sixty-one years. That year the Oklahoma Indian Missionary Conference reported 8,678 members. So numerically at least the twentieth-century work seems to be experiencing successful returns for mission workers' efforts. It is difficult to make a fair comparison between twentieth-century work and work done earlier, since the twentieth century has not been interrupted by a Civil War, but there are nevertheless some distinct differences.

Native American leaders seemed to be asserting themselves in the opening years of the Brewer Indian Mission (although when it came time to choose a superintendent for the new Conference, Bishop Mouzon appointed a non-Indian, Dr. R. T. Blackburn).

The new Brewer Indian Mission gave greater freedom to Native pastors to perform their ministerial calling. No longer merely assistants and/or interpreters for white missionaries, as many of them were during the nineteenth century, Native preachers could preach their own sermons in their own language—the language of the people.

Bishops also played an important role in the early years of the twentieth century. They took personal interest in the Brewer Indian Mission as a distinct ministry. Their efforts to visit local Native churches and their advocacy on behalf of Native churches to the general boards of the Methodist Church did not go unnoticed in the Native American community. During a fairly long period of time prior to the merger of the Methodist Church and the Evangelical United Brethren church, fieldworkers from the General Board and the Women's Society of Christian Service were present in the various fields of mission activity. In addition, Board of Missions chairpersons of Annual Conferences often were personally involved in direct ministries.

After 1921 the Indian Mission was no longer called the Brewer Indian Mission; under Bishop John Moore, the work was called simply Indian Mission (of Oklahoma). It was known by that name until 1944, when under Bishop Angie Smith the work was formally known as the Oklahoma Indian Mission Conference. It did not have the status of an Annual Conference, however, and was said to function administratively as a district. Ordination of Native American clergy of the Oklahoma Indian Mission Conference was accommodated by the Oklahoma Annual Conference, which also provided pension and other benefits that accrued to white clergy members of the Oklahoma Annual Conference, except for salary.

Membership growth in the Oklahoma Indian Mission Conference doesn't seem to have moved along well in the early years of the twentieth century. It stayed at around 2,700, more or less, until 1936 when it first exceeded 3,000 under the administration of Bishop A. Frank Smith. After that the Mission Conference experienced a steady rate of growth that lasted until it peaked at about 12,000 in 1968 under Bishop Angie Smith, the brother of Bishop A. Frank Smith. In the 1970s the membership began to decline and continued to decline until it reached 7,752 in 1976 under Bishop Paul Milhouse. A brief recovery brought the membership to just over 8,500, where it remains at this writing. The dynamics (cultural, political, social) that influenced membership levels are not easily evident and require a closer examination. The people endured many hardships but survived through them all.

The faith of the people may have best been expressed by William Jimboy, the noted Creek-Muskogee evangelist and pastor of the Oklahoma Indian Mission. "Samuel N. Jones and William Jimboy had died during the year [1906]. The latter a fullblooded Creek Indian, ranked among the best Creek preachers. His last hours were full of pain, but he died singing 'What wondrous love is this, oh my soul!' "[17]

During the first quarter of the century, the Methodist Church funded the Willis Fulsom Training School. The school, which was located in Smithville, Oklahoma, reportedly served students of the Choctaw, Creek, Cherokee, and Sioux tribes. It also served the white population, and in its newsletter *The Fulsom Forum* promoted the idea of whites and Indians learning together. However, the unfortunate way in which this notion was discussed in the newsletter is instructive of the real underlying attitudes of the times. For example, a letter from Orlando Shay to *The Fulsom Forum* dated July 14, 1923, carries this remark: "Of all the Indians I have known (since coming to the Indian Territory in 1886) who have been most successful in all callings have had the personal contact of the whites in their school life."

Call it white arrogance or racism, this was apparently the philosophical principle that guided the Fulsom Training School. More surprising is the apparent support for the notion coming from Native students. Johnson Bobb, a 1924 graduate of Fulsom, wrote the following in a letter to *The Fulsom Forum:*

> One of the chief purposes of this institution is to educate the Indians and whites together. It has been heretofore the Indians who have had separate schools—the tribal schools. It has been drawback [*sic*] of the Indians as well as the Whites. In the government Indian schools there have been questions arose why the Indian boys and girls who have graduated from these schools go back to the blanket. For instance among some of the Western tribes. There is only one way to educate them to be loyal citizens, that is with the Whites.[18]

Perhaps the best way to understand Johnson Bobb's letter is to perceive that its meaning and intent were different from those of the previous letter. His family was and still is prominent in Oklahoma Native American Methodism. His name adorns The United Methodist Church at the Southeastern District Center: the Bobb-Meyers Memorial United Methodist Church of the Oklahoma Indian Missionary Conference. Johnson Bobb's wife, Mae Wesley, was a dedicated worker in the district and Conference Women's Society of Christian Service. She was under appointment by the Women's Division as a contract worker in the Eastern District in 1946. Her specialty was Christian education.

The Fulsom Training School was discontinued when the Department of Home Missions, which listed among the "types of work" that it does "Indians, Negroes and Lumber Camps," withdrew its funds.

When the Indian Mission was organized in 1918, the number of churches was seventy-four. These were not merely preaching places but church buildings valued at a total of $56,747. The mission also had nine parsonages valued at a total of $4,603. Native American Methodists had not been idle. In 1944 the Indian Mission reported eighty-five churches in three districts. There were thirty-one charges. Significant growth had taken place in the Western District among the Plains tribes. That district reported fourteen appointments in 1944 (Conference minutes). The largest number of churches was in the Eastern District, among the Choctaws and Chickasaws. Byars Columbus, a powerful preacher and outstanding leader, was serving as the Southeastern District superintendent in 1944. In his report to the Annual Conference, he said:

> There are fifty churches and ten circuits in the District [Eastern] located in ten counties in the Southeastern part of Oklahoma. Your District Superintendent has visited each charge in the District four times during this Conference year.
>
> There are only two of the ten pastors who have cars but they do not fare any better than those who do not because of gas rationing.
>
> In all of these and other difficulties the pastors and their local preachers and other helpers strive on with their work doing all they can with much sacrifice to carry on their work. It is written "But do good and to communicate forget not; for with such sacrifice God is well pleased." Surely God must be well pleased with my people of the Choctaw District for they surely do sacrifice much.[19]

These were the war years. Persons who know southeastern Oklahoma are familiar with the rugged, mountainous terrain and dense woodlands that characterize the area. The pastors and helpers would go from place to place by foot, horseback, or hitchhiking. In McCurtain Circuit it is said that an early-day Choctaw pastor would catch a freight train after walking several miles to get to the railroad tracks and ride to one of his appointments on Friday. He would visit in the community, conduct services on Sunday morning, Sunday afternoon, and Sunday night, and on Monday would catch a freight train and return home. Local preachers helped to fill all preaching assignments. The local preacher system was a great advantage to the Oklahoma Indian Mission; these were tireless workers as well, who helped to maintain that communication Byars Columbus spoke of in his report. When the local preacher system was discontinued, it was a great loss to the Oklahoma Indian Mission Conference.

Women preachers reporting to the Annual Conference included Mrs. Willa Crowe (Osage) from Fairfax and Carolina Campbell, a Euchee from Stroud. Lay delegates who became very prominent in the church included Mrs. Harry Dunn of the Oklahoma City Mission and Alice Premeaux of the Ponca Mission.

McKinley Billy (Choctaw), who was a licensed preacher until the 1944 Annual Conference, later left an important legacy to the church. He owned substantial oil properties that provided him personal wealth uncommon among the Choctaws. When he died, his will provided a scholarship for every Choctaw and Chickasaw person enrolled full-time in Oklahoma City University.

The Indian Mission Conference at this time entered the period of its greatest growth so far. Bishop Angie Smith was beginning his tenure in the Oklahoma Episcopal area. During his tenure Bishop Smith had the reputation of being heavy handed and tyrannical, but he can't be faulted on one point—loyalty to his charge. He was a strong advocate for the Indian Mission Conference, both in Oklahoma and the general boards and agencies of the Methodist Church. He was willing to appoint Native American pastors to non-Indian churches if Native pastors so desired such an appointment. If there was a leadership weakness, it would have to be his extreme paternalism with respect to Native American pastors. His appointment of D. D. Etchison as general superintendent of missions for the Oklahoma Indian Mission Conference symbolized the prevalent belief among non-Indian church leaders that there were no Native leaders in Oklahoma capable of holding executive positions.

A number of significant things happened this year and the next. The Conference began to open new churches in the cities. The Oklahoma City Mission (Angie Smith Memorial) was represented at the Annual Conference of 1945. In Tulsa the Tulsa Mission was meeting in a Sunday school classroom in the Boston Avenue Methodist Church, where Bascom Watts was pastor. The Tulsa Mission would become Witt Memorial Methodist Church in 1946 (according to John H. Lowe, Methodist pastor now retired). Fred Skeeter, an ordained deacon, was one of the principal organizers of this new mission.

W. U. Witt reported that twenty years prior to 1945, the Conference was serving six tribes in Oklahoma; they were at this time serving fourteen tribes. Work among the Cherokees still was not succeeding. The Reverend Oliver Neal, a young Chickasaw clergyman, organized a church in Muskogee—Fife Memorial—to serve the large Native population there. Lee Chupco, David Long, Sr., and Hampton W. Anderson, all destined to become district superintendents, were licensed to preach in 1946. Hampton Anderson was appointed to Muskogee Mission, and Dave Long, Sr., went to Concharty. In 1948 several other persons who would become prominent were licensed to preach: Woodrow Haney, Isaac James Sockey, and Presley Ware.

In 1948 Lee Motah, "chief of the Commanches," "adopted" Bishop Smith into the Commanche tribe as an honorary "chief." Annual meetings of the Conference were at this time held in the fall. The Conference defeated a motion to meet in June.

Bishop Smith at the 1948 Conference appointed a committee to study a proposal to form a Provisional Conference.

Dewey Etchison made a report that signified the paternalistic attitude cited above. Now serving as a general superintendent in the Oklahoma Indian Mission, he said, "A new experiment was made this year in the Western District for the first time in its history. An Indian was appointed as District Superintendent."[20]

Evelyn Green, a contract worker for the Women's Division, was serving in the Central District (Creek-Seminole-Cherokee) this year. Eventually she would become a deaconess and serve as the Conference youth director. Over a period of several years, she developed a very successful youth program in the Conference. Many contemporary church leaders can trace their early Christian experience to her leadership.

In the 1949 Annual Conference Harry Long was licensed to preach, along with Laura Parker and Joseph Wilkin. Harry Long was appointed as a student at Oklahoma City University and an assistant at the Oklahoma City Mission.

Hunting Horse (103 years of age) was introduced to the Conference.

In 1950 Alfred Harjo and George Kauyedauty were ordained elders. H. W. Anderson and Gabriel John were recommended for elders' orders. In 1953 Robert Pinezaddleby graduated from Perkins School of Theology, the first Native American to earn a degree from a Methodist school of theology.

In 1954 the author of this book, Homer Noley, and Kenneth Deere, and Thomas Roughface were licensed to preach. Noley, a Choctaw, would become the first Native American to hold an executive staff position on a general board (Global Ministries). Deere, a Creek, would be the first Native American to serve on a general commission (Religion and Race). Roughface, a Ponca, would provide top local leadership as a presiding elder in the Oklahoma Indian Mission.

In 1955 Clarks Chapel was organized in Oklahoma City, and Oliver Neal became the first pastor to serve in its original location.

In 1956 Pat Freeman (Creek) was licensed to preach. Homer Noley and Pat Freeman both graduated from Oklahoma City University and became the second and third Native Americans from Oklahoma to earn a seminary degree when they graduated from the first graduating class at Saint Paul School of Theology in Kansas City, Missiouri, in 1962 and 1963, respectively.

A number of significant changes were taking place. The relocation program resulted in many Native American people's moving to designated major cities (relocation centers) with the promise of training and jobs. Many people were stranded but stayed and created new urban communities. Dallas was a relocation center to which the Oklahoma Indian Mission sent a pastor to organize new work. The relocation program, with its false promises, had its impact on local churches as well. As Forbes Durant, district superintendent of the Southeast District, said in 1962, "The relocation program sponsored by the Federal Government has screened the families and moved them to various places for employment. It leaves many of our rural churches with a few potential leaders and financial support is decreasing."[21]

It is necessary at this point to review the first decade of this century in order to give more attention to significant developments in the West and elsewhere, and in particular to Four Corners, Yuma, and Round Valley.

It was noted earlier that the Round Valley Mission in Mendocino County, northern California, was one of the three California reservations that became the permanent site of a Native American local church. This mission was assigned an agent/missionary in 1872 under President Grant's "peace policy." According to Mitzi Frazier's account, "in 1872, under President Grant's Peace Policy, a Methodist Minister John Burchard was appointed Round Valley Indian Agent. The Commissary warehouse became a school and church. It is recorded that in 1874 nearly 870 Indians united with the church, and over 700 were baptized."[22]

Present-day Native American residents in Round Valley represent small tribes who were forced from their homelands by the U.S. government, "some under 'Bataan type death march' conditions by our army."[23] Besides the original inhabitants in Round Valley, the Yuki, there are descendants of several other tribes: the Wailacki, Nomalacki, Maidu, Pomo, Pit River, Wintoon, Little Lake Concow, and Redwood.

> A boarding school was set up in 1893 and all the Indian children over six years of age were required to attend. This was the government's most important tool as they forced upon the Indian culture the ways of the White Man, his language, his dress, his food, and even his Bible. In this manner tribal lore was destroyed in a generation.[24]

Fortunately the resiliency of Native American people in community relations provided the basis for the formation of the present-day community, which in turn is buttressed by a common faith.

In a letter Pastor Foster tells of his work with the Round Valley United Methodist Church:

> I serve the Round Valley Church in addition to my work with the Willets Methodist located 43 miles Southwest of Covelo. I preach

each Sunday in Willets and every other Sunday in Round Valley.
The services are held at 3 pm in the afternoon during the winter
and at 7 pm during the summer. . . . During Advent and Lent we
have services every Sunday.[25]

In September of 1963 Bishop Donald Harvey Tippet visited the
Round Valley Methodist Church.

The congregation expresses considerable pride in their work.
Small in number now, they continue to work against many hardships to keep their church alive and well. Today (1988) the church
is being served by Walter Moffatt, a Native American pastor.

In 1891 the Farmington Mission School among the Navajo was
established. During the years of its services, the school has provided a boarding school that has at some points provided training
for all grade levels. Its high school program is one of the few
among mission schools that are intentional about college prepara-
tory programs. The college prep interest of the Farmington
School Board reflects the Navajo tribe's interest in education.
The tribe itself has developed educational institutions in higher
education and provides encouragement to those who seek college-
level training. In recent years the school has experienced considerable trauma as it has attempted to make adjustments to guarantee the school's continuance, and especially to continue a
spiritually based educational program for Navajo children and
youth.

Many of the graduates from the school sought to find their way
into leadership roles in church and community in the Navajo
Nation. However, a more immediate problem was that upon leaving the school, there were no Methodist churches in the various
Navajo communities to receive them as members.

In 1957 Rev. Robert W. Brooks, Pastor of the Navajo Methodist
Mission School, Farmington conceived the idea of a Methodist
Church in Shiprock for those graduates of the Mission living in the
Shiprock area. The first meeting of these persons for this purpose
was held in the home of Mr. Bennie Gibson. This church was offi-
cially organized on October 8, 1957 with thirty-five members.
Rev. R. L. Willingham, District Superintendent, presented the
Charter to Rev. Brooks.[26]

From this initial outreach, the Four Corners Ministry was launched. This ministry is

> a Native American ministry established by the United Methodist Church as an outreach to the Indian tribes in the four states area [Utah, Arizona, Colorado and New Mexico]. At present its efforts are concentrated on the Navajo Indian Reservation of 25,000 square miles and population of 180,000.
>
> There are 5 established churches within the 4 Corners Native American Ministry. They are Shiprock, N. M. (membership 209), Bistahi, N. M. (membership 32), Window Rock, AZ (membership 25), Do'Wo'Zhiibikooh, UT (membership 30), and Oljato, UT (membership 20).
>
> There are 9 Navajo pastors and preachers under this ministry: Rev. Fred W. Yazzie (fully ordained); Rev. Chee D. Benallie (retired lay pastor); Rev. Henry C. Begay (full time lay pastor); Mr. Raymond Burke and Mr. Eugene Chee (part time lay pastors); Mrs. Lucy Lewis, Mrs. Shirley Montoya, Leonard Begay, and Harry Descheene (lay preachers) also there are 2 missionaries: Rev. Herb Moushon (construction) and Rev. David Warden (pastor.)[27]

An article appearing in *Response Magazine* (June 1985) written by Fred Yazzie, a graduate of Farmington School and of a Methodist school of theology, describes the development of the Four Corners Ministry: "The four Navajo churches are striving to provide a comprehensive ministry in the face of real challenges and needs. . . . People who are confronted with [problems of domestic violence] are finding answers and also a place of safety within the Four Corners Home for women and children."[28]

He states that in two years 325 women and children were helped in the shelter. He also described the leadership training models being developed and implemented in cooperation with the New Mexico Annual Conference Board of Ordained Ministry. Other programs of ministry include an alcoholism counseling center, thriftshops, and tent evangelism. Paul West is the present pastor and director of the Four Corners Ministry. He began his ministry as the pastor of Shiprock United Methodist Church in 1975. Other clergy who have served the Shiprock United Methodist Church are the Reverend Robert Brooks (1957–64), the Reverend V. B. Irby (1964–66), the Reverend Dr. George Ditterline (1966–67), and the Reverend Maurice Haines (1967–75).

Self-Determination and Mission

Changes in the larger national social climate began to affect Native American people as well as other ethnic minorities in the church. While self-determination issues have always been an issue for the Native tribes, the civil rights movement of the late 1950s and 1960s provided a new means of expression. Implementing principles of self-determination in Native American ministries has caused an ideological rift between the national church agencies and Native American leaders in the field that is not yet altogether healed. The National Board staff and apparently the white church interprets mission in terms of self-support. "Mission," in the view of Methodist Church agencies, always has a dollar sign attached to it. An article appearing in the newsletter *Our Brother in Red* discusses the church's mission precisely in those terms.

> Their mission [the Mission Boards] is to assist those who are not able to support themselves—not those who *will not*, but those who *cannot* help themselves. Whenever a people is able to furnish and sustain its own ministers, able to supply means for its moral and religious advancement, then the work of the Mission Board ceases.[29]

It can be seen that "mission," interpreted this way, is not a spiritual mandate but a temporary and practical act of institutional benevolence—a welfare program. The article continues: "A long dependence upon another renders the faculties we have useless."[30]

General Board staff occasionally imply that the funds being spent for missions is their money (that is, the General Board's) instead of the church's money that has been entrusted to the board for administration. An even more devastating aspect of the church's definition of mission is related directly to the issue of self-determination and is of more recent expression. In a letter dated April 8, 1975, Betty Henderson, assistant general secretary of the National Division, attempted to explain why the National Division was not supporting the Indian Missionary Conference's right to vote in the General Conference.

> c. The Missionary Conference [is] defined (and there was consensus among the three conferences on this point) as being "unique" having "limited membership, ministry, financial strength and property." Therefore, a conference so defined is not capable of the responsibility inherent in voting.

Considerable work must be done to reconcile the views of people who believe that "mission" refers to the gospel imperative to carry the good news to the uttermost parts of the earth and that view which sees "mission" as a temporary welfare program that can be withdrawn according to the will of the General Board staff.

The missionary conferences did win the right to vote by a substantial vote of the General Conference. It is necessary, however, that the remaining ideological differences be resolved in the future.

The Development of Grassroots Caucuses

In 1968 (February) a national consultation was called by the General Board of Global Ministries to consider a means of empowerment for Native American Methodists. The outcome of this consultation was the formation of an advisory committee. The steering committee included the Reverend Raymond Baines (Tlingit), Robert Pinezaddleby (Kiowa), and Adolph Dial (Lumbee). Additional persons were named from the General Board staff, and an advisory committee was formed. This was not enough, but it was a beginning. Harry Komuro and General Board of Global Ministries staff whose responsibilities included Native American ministries coordinated the committee for the National Division. From that point on Native American people began a drive for a more self-determined body. As members left the committee for one reason or another, they were replaced by Native American persons.

In 1970, at a meeting of the National Fellowship of Indian Workers, Native Methodists caucused between sessions and decided that it was time for a national all-Indian caucus. The advisory committee, by this time a mostly Native body, became the administrative core of the new national caucus, which retained the name National American Indian Committee. Work groups developed an organizational plan for the national caucus. Members of the caucus came from the Oklahoma Indian Mission Conference and local churches of Native Americans from all over the country.

In 1972 the National American Indian Committee met in Cherokee, North Carolina, and reorganized itself into an all-Native body with thirteen Native voting members, two Native staff (nonvoting), and five jurisdictional consultants. An executive committee was formed, with full powers of the caucus in between full meetings of the caucus, and guidelines were established for the executive committee's administration.

National representation was a problem because of the various locations of the Native Methodist churches. This was resolved by locating the population centers of Native American Methodists and drawing on a chart five eccentric circles so that an equal number of local churches would appear in each circle. This was the origin of the National American Indian Committee regional system. It does not always fit jurisdictional boundaries. Today the regional structure still provides the basis for representation, but the organizational style will continue to be modified to meet changing needs and conditions.

Today the National American Indian Committee is known as the Native American International Caucus (NAIC). It is funded by the General Commission on Religion and Race. The Reverend Kenneth Deere (Creek-Muskogee) is the Native American staff-person on the commission who relates to the caucus on behalf of the commission.

The caucus has forty members at present and a full, functioning executive committee. In 1988 the caucus named an executive director to manage the concerns of the caucus, the Reverend Sam Wynn (Lumbee). His office is in Charlotte, North Carolina.

Current officers on the board of directors are Becky Thompson, chairperson; Barrett Moffatt, vice chairperson; Shirley Montoya, secretary; Debbie Doxtator, treasuruer; and Homer Noley, parliamentarian.

The historic function of the caucus has been to advocate on behalf of Native American local churches and other ministries. That advocacy includes working with the general boards, but in recent years has included significant work at the General Conference level.

One of the first efforts of the caucus was advocating the selection of a Native American for a staff position in the National Division. Harry Komuro, on the staff of the National Division, met with the caucus, and in 1971 the first Native American staffmember was hired, Homer Noley, who held office from 1971 to 1975. Billy Nowabbi (Choctaw) followed, and the last person to hold the original office was Josephine Bigler. An equivalent office is now filled by Cynthia Kent.

At the General Conference of 1976 the NAIC asked the General Conference to authorize the formation of a Native American Study Committee to do a comprehensive on-site study of Native American missions and make recommendations to the 1980 General Conference. A massive amount of research was done under the leadership of Linda Johnson, a Lumbee now living in Phoenix, Arizona. The report was submitted to the General Conference of 1980 meeting in Cincinnati. The primary recommendation was for the formation of a General Commission on Native American Ministries. The General Conference accepted the report but did not accept the recommendation for the commission.

The General Conference of 1984 met in Baltimore, Maryland. At this conference the NAIC worked with an interethnic strategy group to support the continuation of the Ethnic Minority Local Church Fund, a funding program for broadening and strengthening ethnic minority local churches and other ministries. This advocacy succeeded and established a good working relationship between the NAIC and other ethnic caucuses.

Almost immediately after the 1984 General Conference, the NAIC began to think about the 1988 General Conference, scheduled to meet in St. Louis. Working committees formulated ideas and fleshed out a comprehensive plan. Marv Abrams, pastor of

Native American Ministries in Norwalk, California, was the caucus chairperson and provided good leadership.

The comprehensive plan involved some very significant goals. One of these was to double the membership of Native American Methodists by the year 2000. Other goals included establishing a national forum on Native American Theology, hiring more Native American staff in the general boards, protecting and enhancing the land base, confronting issues faced by Native American women, developing health care programs to help Native Americans cope with life-threatening diseases that are under control in the dominant populations, recruiting and training Native American clergy and other full-time workers in the church, and initiating an innovative appointment system for rapid deployment of clergy where they are needed. The comprehensive plan was passed at the General Conference and now awaits implementation.

Chairpersons of the NAIC have been Raymond Baines, Adolph Dial, Thomas Roughface, Diane Moats, Ron Hickman, and Marv Abrams. In the 1989–92 quadrennium, the caucus will be led by Becky Thompson, chairperson, and Sam Wynn, executive director.

Today the results of Native American advocacy are evident in many ways. The metamorphosis of the old Oklahoma Indian Mission Conference into the Oklahoma Indian Missionary Conference in 1972 at the General Conference in Atlanta, Georgia, elevated the legal status of the Conference and provided it the authority to ordain clergy whose credentials would be recognized anywhere in the country. The Conference has churches in Kansas as well as in Dallas, Texas. Becky Thompson of the Oklahoma Indian Missionary Conference became the first Native American to become a diaconal minister. She is presently serving as the Council on Ministries' director. The Conference is also implementing its own comprehensive plan and looks forward to unprecedented growth; it already has churches in Tulsa, Oklahoma City, and other major cities in Oklahoma.

A National United Methodist Native American Center is located in Oklahoma City on the campus of Oklahoma City University. The center is working to open many opportunities for Native church leadership, whether clergy or lay. Mr. Ben Bushyhead is the executive director, and Debbie Doxtator is the chairperson of the board of directors. The center leadership has developed a national youth organization that has high leadership potential. The group meets in connection with the National Family Camp.

New ministries started within the present decade include Urban Ministries in Grand Rapids, Michigan (Joe Sprague, pastor); All Tribes Fellowship in Kansas City, Kansas (Pat Freeman, pastor); Native American ministries, Aberdeen, South Dakota (Joe Dudley); Urban Ministries in Charlotte, North Carolina (Sam Wynn); Urban Ministries in Denver, Colorado; Phoenix Native American Ministries (the Reverend Harry Long, pastor); and new developments in southern California.

The Norwalk United Methodist Church grew out of a ministry that actually began in a series of revival services conducted by Oliver Neal, Woodrow Haney, and Harry Long. In June 1975 Oliver Neal was appointed to a Ministry of Presence. The First United Methodist Church of Huntington Park, California, provided the first meeting place for the new group which first met on Feb. 1, 1976. In a meeting of thirty-two Native Americans, it was decided to proceed with organization of a local church. The first established church site was in the empty facility of the Temple United Methodist Church at 1575 West Fourteenth Street, downtown Los Angeles.

Oliver Neal led the development of the new congregation and established it as a permanent ministry. In 1979 Neal died. He had organized churches in Muskogee, Oklahoma, and in Oklahoma City. He served the new church in Dallas and also in Yuma. His wife, Lois Neal, is presently a pastor in the Angie Smith Memorial United Methodist Church in Oklahoma City. Lois graduated from Saint Paul School of Theology in May 1988 and became one of the first two Native American women to earn a master's degree in theology; the other graduate was Evalene Sombrero graduated from Illif School of Theology in 1988.

The Reverend Marv Abrams succeeded Oliver Neal in Los Angeles. When the congregation's original church building was declared unsafe by the city, the congregation moved into a facility shared with the Norwalk First United Methodist Church. A caring center, to serve American Indians in need of spiritual and physical assistance, using the old facility, remained at the old site.

The Native American United Methodist Church, now at Norwalk, has organized clusters in four areas of Los Angeles as the church has sought to find ways to extend its outreach. Los Angeles is an area of high potential for Native American church development: "The 1980 Census reported 84,000 'American Indian residents living in Los Angeles County, while Orange County reported 18,000, a total of 102,000.' "[31]

It is hoped that areas of high potential such as Los Angeles will be given the opportunity to develop and proliferate the gospel, not to "heathens," as old time missionaries termed Native American people, but to a people whose time has come.

Innovation must be the key word for contemporary Native American ministries. The Norwalk model is an innovation that may help spread the Christian gospel to areas other than Los Angeles. The Ministry of Presence concept must continue to be used, since it was successful in Grand Rapids, Kansas City, Los Angeles, and elsewhere.

Harry Long's ministry in Phoenix is a style of ministry that requires expertise of a special kind. The Phoenix ministry features an outreach program that honors traditional Native American spirituality in its worship style. The ministry is intentional in its programming style so that it appeals to those Native American persons whose spirituality is primarily traditional.

History is being made. Let the record show that it was a faithful effort.

A P P E N D I X A

BOUNDARIES OF INDIAN MISSION ANNUAL CONFERENCE[a]

Year		Annual Conf.	Bishop	Total Members	No. Local Churches[b]	No. of Ministers	Location of Annual Conf. Session
1st	1844 (Oct. 23)	IMC	Thomas A. Morris	85 White 133 "Colored" 2,992 Indian	3 Dist. (18)	27 LP	Riley's Chapel, Tahlequah
2nd	1845 (Oct. 23)	IMC	Joshua Soule				Indian Manual Labor School (Shawnee Mission)
3rd	1846 (Nov. 12)	IMC	Robert Paine				Riley's Chapel
4th	1847 (Nov. 4)	IMC	William Capers				(Choctaw Terr.) Doaksville
5th	1848 (Nov. 1)	IMC	James O. Andrew				(Cherokee Terr.) Muddy Springs
6th	1849 (Oct. 25)	IMC	Robert Paine				Riley's Chapel
7th	1850 (Nov. 7)	IMC	No bishop present				Choctaw Agency
8th	1851 (Nov. 15)	IMC	No bishop present				Muddy Springs
9th	1852 (Oct. 28)	IMC	Robert Paine				Clear Springs Campground
10th	1853 (Oct. 26)	IMC	James O. Andrew				Creek Agency near Muskogee
11th	1854 (Oct. 25)	IMC	H. H. Kavanaugh				Riley's Chapel
12th	1855 (Oct. 10)	IMC	Pierce	4,264	4 Dist. (31)	30	Asbury Man. Labor School, Eufaula
13th	1856	IMC	No bishop present				Chickasaw Academy
14th	1857 (Oct. 29)	IMC	No bishop present				Riley's Chapel
15th	1858 (Oct. 17)	IMC	Early				Between Spiro & Ft. Smith, Skullyville
16th	1859 (Oct. 27)	IMC	Robert Paine				Creek Agency
17th	1860 (Nov. 1)	IMC	H. H. Kavaugh				Riley's Chapel, at or near Cherokee Female Seminary

Appendix A—continued

Year	Annual Conf.	Bishop	Total Members	No. Local Churches[b]	No. of Ministers	Location of Annual Conf. Session
18th 1861 (Oct. 10)	IMC	No bishop present				Chickasaw Man. Labor School
1862		No conference held				
1863		No conference held				
19th 1864 (Sept. 23)	IMC	No bishop present		2 Dist. Army mission	10	Eastman School, near present Colbert
20th 1865 (Sept. 14)	IMC	No bishop present			8	Doaksville
21st 1866 (Sept. 12)	IMC	Enoch M. Marvin			14	Bloomfield Academy
22nd 1867 (Oct. 3)	IMC	Enoch M. Marvin	20 White 22 Negro 1,795 Indian		19LP	Fort Gibson
23rd 1868 (Oct. 15)	IMC	Doggett				Boggy Depot
24th 1869 (Sept. 30)	IMC	Pierce				Okmulgee
25th 1870 (Oct. 26)	IMC	John C. Keener				Fort Gibson
26th 1871 (Oct. 4)	IMC	Holland N. McTyeire	127 White 434 Negro 4,320 Indian		61 LP	Boggy Depot
27th 1872 (Oct. 2)	IMC	William M. Wightman				Creek Co. House
28th 1873 (Oct. 23)	IMC	Pierce				Tahlequah
29th 1874 (Oct. 27)	IMC	Kavanaugh				North Fork, Creek Nation
30th 1875 (Oct. 6)	IMC	Kavanaugh				Atoka
31st 1876 (Oct. 26)	IMC	McTyeire				Vinita
32nd 1877 (Sept. 20)	IMC	Marvin				Stringtown
33rd 1878 (Oct. 17)	IMC	McTyeire				Muskogee
34th 1879 (Sept. 10)	IMC	Pierce				Double Springs
35th 1880 (Sept. 6)	IMC	Pierce				
36th 1881 (Oct. 5)	IMC	Pierce				Caddo
37th 1882 (Sept. 20)	IMC	Pierce				Muskogee

Session	Date	Org	Presiding	Statistics	Location
38th	1883 (Sept. 20)	IMC	Pierce		Webbers Falls
39th	1884 (Sept. 18)	IMC	Robert K. Hargrove		White Bead Hill
40th	1885 (Sept. 17)	IMC	John C. Granbery		Skullyville
41st	1886 (Oct. 20)	IMC	Charles B. Galloway		Eufaula
42nd	1887 (Oct. 12)	IMC	Charles B. Galloway		Vinita
43rd	1888 (Oct. 12)	IMC	Joseph S. Key		White Bead Hill
44th	1889 (Oct. 2)	IMC	Eugene R. Hendrix		Atoka
45th	1890 (Oct. 22)	IMC	Hendrix		Muskogee
46th	1891 (Nov. 4)	IMC	Hendrix		Oklahoma City
47th	1892 (Nov. 16)	IMC	Galloway		(Indian Terr.) Ardmore
48th	1893 (Nov. 1)	IMC	Key		Vinita
49th	1894 (Oct. 31)	IMC	Hargrove		McAlester
50th	1895	IMC	Hargrove	13,999 White / 3,903 Indian / 9 Dist. / 464 (135)	Ardmore
51st	1896 (Oct. 28)	IMC	W. W. Duncan		El Reno
52nd	1897 (Nov. 10)	IMC	Alpheus W. Wilson		Muskogee
53rd	1898 (Nov. 2)	IMC	H. R. Morrison		Norman
54th	1899 (Nov. 1)	IMC	Key		Ardmore
55th	1900 (Oct. 25)	IMC	Key		Vinita
56th	1901 (Oct. 24)	IMC	Key		Chickasha
57th	1902 (Oct. 22)	IMC	E. E. Hoss		Muskogee
58th	1903 (Oct. 21)	IMC	E. E. Hoss		Oklahoma City
59th	1904 (Oct. 26)	IMC	E. E. Hoss		South McAlester
60th	1905 (Nov. 8)	IMC	E. E. Hoss		Lawton
61st[c]	1906 (Nov. 14)	IMC	Key (John J. Tigert)		Tulsa
62nd	1907 (Nov. 13)	OAC	Key		Durant
63rd	1908 (Nov. 6)	OAC	James Atkins		Oklahoma City
64th	1909 (Nov. 3)	OAC	James Atkins		Muskogee
65th	1910 (Nov. 10)	OAC	Collins Denny	49,653 / 15 Dist. / 851 (298)	Ardmore
66th	1911 (Nov. 1)	EOC	Collins Denny		Okmulgee
67th	1912 (Nov. 20)	EOC	Warren A. Candler		Holdenville
68th	1913 (Nov. 5)	EOC	Edwin D. Mouzon,		Norman

Appendix A—*continued*

Year	Annual Conf.	Bishop	Total Members	No. Local Churches[b]	No. of Ministers	Location of Annual Conf. Session
69th 1914 (Nov. 12)	EOC	San Antonio, TX				Ada
70th 1915 (Nov. 10)	EOC	William B. Murrah				Muskogee
71st 1916 (Nov. 22)	EOC	Edwin D. Mouzon				Muskogee
72nd 1917 (Nov. 7)	EOC	Edwin D. Mouzon				Durant
73rd 1918 (Nov. 6)	BIM	Edwin Mouzon		2 Dist. 23 Appt. Min. 20 Circuits		Shawnee
1919	BIM	Edwin D. Mouzon	2,702	82 (18)	8 Licensed 116 LP	Newtown
1920						
1921	BIM	Edwin D. Mouzon	2,683	2 Dist. 84 (31)	10 Licensed 115 LP	Salt Creek
1922 (Sept. 22-24)	IM	John M. Moore, Dallas, TX	2,687	2 Dist. 82 (26)	11 Licensed 96 LP	Seely Chapel
1923 (Sept. 21-23)	IM	John M. Moore	2,642	2 Dist. 81 (22)	10 Licensed 105 LP	(Okemah) Springfield
1924 (Sept. 19-22)	IM	John M. Moore	2,716	2 Dist. 76 (21)	71 Licensed 89 LP	Thloplocco
1925	IM					
1926 (Sept. 17-19)	IM	H. A. Boaz, Little Rock, Ark	2,719	3 Dist. 73 (22)	25 Licensed 120 LP	Seely Chapel
1927	IM	H. A. Boaz	2,594	77 (22)	9 Licensed 121 LP	Thloplocco
1928						
1929	IM	H. A. Boaz	2,679	73 (26)	5 Licensed 112 LP	Picket Chapel
1930						

Year							
1931							
1932	IM	A. Frank Smith	2,675	3 Dist.	78 (27)	9 Licensed 97 LP	Seminole Hitchitee
1933	IM	A. Frank Smith	2,592	3 Dist.	78 (27)	9 Licensed 100 LP	Newtown
1934	IM	A. Frank Smith	2,767	3 Dist.	79 (28)	6 Licensed 104 LP	Middle San Bois
1935	IM	A. Frank Smith	2,878	3 Dist.	82 (30)	15 Licensed 9 Mem. of OAC 111 LP	Big Cussetah
1936	IM	A. Frank Smith	3,067	3 Dist.	80 (30)	10 Licensed 9 Mem. of OAC 113 LP	Salt Creek
1937	IM	A. Frank Smith	3,180	3 Dist.		10 Licensed 8 Mem. of OAC 115 LP	Newtown
1938	IM	A. Frank Smith	3,253		79 (30)	6 Licensed 7 Mem. of OAC 114 LP	Seminole Hitchitee
1939	IM	A. Frank Smith	3,294		78 (30)	7 Licensed 113 LP	Thloplocco
1940	IM	A. Frank Smith	3,410	3 Dist.	78 (30)	13 Licensed 116 LP	Hampton Chapel near Hugo
1941	IM	A. Frank Smith	3,349	3 Dist.	80 (34)	9 Licensed 121 LP	Wares Chapel
1942	IM	A. Frank Smith	3,655	3 Dist.	82 (33)	7 Licensed 123 LP	Seminole Hitchitee
1943	IM	A. Frank Smith	3,937	3 Dist.	84 (35)	14 Licensed 134 LP	Salt Creek
1944	OIM	Angie Smith	4,019	3 Dist.	85 (37)	11 Licensed 144 LP	Salt Creek
1945	OIM	Angie Smith	4,162	3 Dist.	91 (41)	6 Licensed 138 LP	Springfield

Appendix A—*continued*

Year	Annual Conf.	Bishop	Total Members	No. Local Churches[b]	No. of Ministers	Location of Annual Conf. Session
1946	OIM	Angie Smith	4,388	3 Dist. 95 (44)	12 Licensed / 142 LP	Wares Chapel
1947 (Sept. 12-14)	OIM	Angie Smith	4,773	3 Dist. 95 (43)	7 Licensed / 147 LP	Seminole Hitchitee
1948 (Sept. 16-19)	OIM	Angie Smith	4,968	89 (45)	16 Licensed / 155 LP	Kullituklo
1949 (Sept. 9-11)	OIM	Angie Smith	5,224	3 Dist. 91 (42)	11 Licensed / 143 LP	Mt. Scott Commanche
1950 (Sept. 14-17)	OIM	Angie Smith	5,599	3 Dist. 94 (39)	8 Licensed / 135 LP	Seminole Hitchitee
1951 (Sept. 13-16)	OIM	Angie Smith	5,781	3 Dist. 97 (41)	14 Licensed / 69 LP / 27 LE / 47 EL	Boiling Springs
1952 (June 5-7)	OIM	Angie Smith	5,936	3 Dist. 94 (42)	11 Licensed	Jimmy Creek Campground, Lawton
1953 (June 11-14)	OIM	Angie Smith	6,301	3 Dist. 94 (44)	68 LP / 33 LD / 48 LE	Salt Creek
1954 (June 3-6)	OIM	Angie Smith	6,744	3 Dist. 94 (44)	99 LP / 158 Total Min.	Goodland
1955 (June 2-5)	OIM	Angie Smith	7,074	93 (43)	115 LP / 162 Total	W. Dist Cent., Anadarko
1956 (May 31-June 3)	OIM	Angie Smith	7,223	97 (45) / 94 (46)	158 Total / 49 EFF / 163 Total	Newtown
1957	OIM	Angie Smith	7,519	78 (46) (No Rep. W.D.)	122 LP / 47 EFF	Bob-Meyers

Year						Location
1958	OIM	Angie Smith	7,834	99 (51)	169 Total / 52 Appt. / 117 LP	W. Dist. Cent.
1959 (June 6-8)	OIM	Angie Smith	8,151	107 (51)	169 Total / 53 Appt. / 122 LP	Okemah, Springfield
1960	OIM	Angie Smith	8,600	112 (52)	174 Total / 59 Appt. / 124 LP	S.E. Dist., Antlers
1961 (May 25-28)	OIM	Angie Smith	9,031	4 Dist. 111 (59)	183 Total / 61 Appt. / 121 LP	Anadarko
1962	OIM	Angie Smith	9,562	113 (63)	187 Total / 70 Appt. / 122 LP	Preston
1963 (May 30-June 2)	OIM	Angie Smith	10,066	114 (66)	192 Total / 69 Appt. / 116 LP	Antlers
1964 (June 4-7)	OIM	Angie Smith	10,588	120 (67)	192 Total / 131 LP / 74 EFF	Anadarko
1965	OIM	Angie Smith	10,963	118 (66)	205 Total / 202 LP / 74 EFF	Preston
1966 (June 1-5)	OIM	Angie Smith	11,304	115 (67)	207 Total / 200 LP / 75 EFF	Antlers
1967	OIM	Angie Smith	11,455	96 (63)	206 Total / 179 LP / 72 EFF	Anadarko
1968	OIM	Angie Smith			185 Total	
1969	OIM	Angie Smith				

Appendix A—continued

Year	Annual Conf.	Bishop	Total Members	No. Local Churches[b]	No. of Ministers	Location of Annual Conf. Session
1970	OIM	Angie Smith				
1971	OIM	Milhouse				
1972	OIMC	Milhouse				
1973	OIMC	Milhouse				
1974	OIMC	Milhouse	10,341			
1975	OIMC	Milhouse	10,251	115 (59)	22 Assoc. 32 FC 71 Total	Antlers
1976	OIMC	Milhouse	7,752	115 (59)	20 Assoc. 65 EFF 85 Total	Anadarko
1977	OIMC	Milhouse				Preston
1978	OIMC	Milhouse	8,566	118	71	Antlers
1979	OIMC	Milhouse	8,578	118	71	Anadarko
1980	OIMC	John W. Hardt				Preston
1981	OIMC	John W. Hardt				Antlers
1982	OIMC	John W. Hardt				Anadarko

Note: BIM = Brewer Indian Mission; EFF = effective; EL = elder; EOC = Eastern Annual Conference; FC = full connection; IM = Indian Mission; IMC = Indian Missionary Conference; LD = local deacon; LE = local elder; LP = local preacher; OAC = Oklahoma Annual Conference; OIM = Oklahoma Indian Mission; OIMC = Oklahoma Indian Mission Conference.

Source: Conference minutes for years tabulated.

[a] Montana to the north, Rocky Mountains to the west, Arkansas and Missouri to the east, and Texas (or at least some small part of it) to the south.

[b] Charges in parentheses.

[c] From the sixty-first through the seventy-third Conference, neither the Oklahoma Indian Mission nor the Indian Mission Conference was in existence.

Chronology, Indian Mission Conference, Indian Territory, 1844–1935

All information is from Conference Minutes, Babcock and Bryce's *History of Methodism in Oklahoma,* or Mitchell's *Tepees to Towers,* unless otherwise noted.

1844	Charter members are Thomas Ruble, David B. Cummings, J. C. Berryman, Edward T. Perry, N. M. Talbott, William H. Goode, Johnson Fields, Thomas Bertholf, James Essex, Samuel G. Patterson, John M. Steel, Erastus B. Duncan, Isaac F. Collins, William McIntosh, Learner B. Stateler, William W. Okchiah, and John F. Boot.
	Mission Schools opened: Indian Manual Labor School (Shawnee Mission), Fort Coffee Academy.
	John Berry is superintendent of Indian Mission, a post held through 1847. Office of Superintendent is discontinued "as an economy measure."[1]
1845	Note: "A Board of Missions was established and a mission planned for China."[2]
1846	Schools opened: Robertson School at Forst Washita (Chickasaws)
1847	Schools opened: New Hope School (girls), Chickasaw Academy (McKendree Manual Labor School).
1848	Asbury Manual School opened at Eufaula.
1849	Choctaw Academy opened.
1850	Kansas River District placed in the St. Louis Annual Conference, thus reducing size and membership of the Oklahoma Indian Mission.

1851   The year begins with reduced membership due to the loss of Kansas River District and the operations of "other religious bodies, some hostile to Methodism. . . . Great social forces were at work, which were to culminate in the Civil War ten years later. The Church was in a period of decline."[3]

1852   Through Samuel Checote's influence, Creek laws forbidding the teaching of the Christian religion among Creeks are abrogated. The Creek District is formed.[4]

Bloomfield Academy near Durant is opened.

1853   "At the invitation of Samuel Checote, the Conference was held in the territory where not long before the preaching of the Word was forbidden under penalty of at least 39 lashes and perhaps death."[5]

John F. Boot, Conference charter member, dies.

1854   Daniel Asbury dies. He and Samuel Checote present a petition to the 1844 Organizing Conference to have the Scriptures translated into the Creek language. Dixon Lewis is assigned to do the translation but dies before it can be accomplished. "But he failed to accomplish his purpose through lack of support by the leaders of Methodism."[6]

1857   Bishop Pierce is scheduled to preside but is stopped short in Kansas by hostilities related to the impending Civil War.

1858   "Skullyville, located between Spiro and Fort Smith, was the seat of the Choctaw Agency, which disbursed government funds to the Indians through the Indian agent. The money was usually brought to Fort Coffee by steamboat from Fort Smith, then hauled sixteen miles in wagons to the Agency. Often there would be as many as six wagon loads of money in one caravan. There would be one driver and one guard to each wagon, since holdups were unknown in the Indian Territory in that day."[7]

1859   William McIntosh and W. L. McAlester (presiding elder of the Choctaw District) die.

1860   Lincoln is elected president. Southern states secede.

1861   Civil War begins April 11. Choctaws and Chickasaws favor the South. Creeks are divided. Cherokees attempt neutrality.

General Conference schedule for 1862 is postponed until 1866.

Samuel Checote and James McHenry request location to join combat forces on Confederate side, which is granted. Samuel Checote becomes a lieutenant colonel; McHenry, a major.

1862–1863 No Annual Conference sessions are held. No lay representation until 1866. James Essex is captured by Union Army; dies in captivity (1864). Fort Coffee and New Hope schools are closed in

1863 when Union troops invade that part of Choctaw Territory. The Chickasaw Nation, which was never invaded by Union troops, becomes a rendezvous for refugees. Bloomfield Academy remains open during war, no salaries are paid, and people live off the land.

John Page enters the Army and becomes a major. John Harrell is appointed a chaplain in the Confederate Army. He appoints Young Ewing presiding elder of the Cherokee District.

Willis Folsom comes to the Choctaw Nation (Oklahoma) in 1832 and writes a Choctaw dictionary. Acts as interpreter for ministers before being licensed to preach in 1851.

1864	Indian Mission Annual Conference meets. No bishop present.
1865	Civil War ends.
1866	No funds are available for the IMC. Bishop Marvin refuses to consider termination of the work and pledges $5,000 for the work to continue.[8]
1867	Bishop Marvin keeps his pledge. The $5,000 raised is distributed mainly by his personal efforts. No one is admitted on trial; one, Thomas Ruble, is admitted by transfer.
1868	Samuel Checote is appointed presiding elder of the Creek District.
1872	Grant's Peace Policy fails to affect Methodist work in Indian Territory since the territory is located in the jurisdiction of the MEC South
1875	Pauls Valley District is formed.
1877	Bishop Marvin dies on November 26, in St. Louis.
1878	Theodore F. Brewer is received by transfer from the Arkansas Conference; appointed to Muskogee and Eufaula.
1881	Harrell International Institute at Muskogee opens, the first church-funded (Methodist) institute of education.
1882	*Our Brother in Red* Indian Mission newspaper is established. Its Motto is "Christian Education the Hope of the Indian." T. F. Brewer and J. F. Thompson, editors.
1884	Bishop Pierce and Samuel Checote die on the same day, September 3. Bishop Pierce visits the Conference nine times.
1885	J. J. Methvin is admitted on trial; he becomes superintendent of the New Hope Seminary, but that same year the Choctaw National Council withdraws its funds from the school. It closes after forty years of service.

The Asbury Manual Labor School is razed by fire and not rebuilt.

1886   Bishop Galloway meets with the Canadian District Conference (an unprecedented event), which meets from June 2 to June 6.

1887   At this Annual Conference a "missionary" is appointed to the Western tribes. During the summer of 1887, the Reverend J. J. Methvin surveys the territory occupied by the "Western tribes" and finds such "pagan" practices as plurality of wives, the Eagle dance, the Moon dance, the Ghost dance, and the peyote cult, which he termed "indulgence in the harmful peyote bean drug."[9] Methvin is appointed missionary to the Western tribes.

1889   T. F. Brewer and L. W. Rivers are elected clerical delegates to the 1890 General Conference. G. B. Hester and E. H. Culbertson are elected lay delegates to the same Conference.

            Bishop Eugene R. Hendrix, a young man, is appointed to preside over the Indian Mission Conference and arrives in the spring of 1889 to preside over the Pauls Valley District Conference. He appoints the Reverend I. L. Burrow, formerly president of Central Collegiate Institute, Altus, Arkansas (later Hendrix College), presiding elder of the Oklahoma City District, a new District to be organized among the white "settlers" who had made the run on April 22, 1889. For the Methodist Church South (original name of new local church?) that D. R. Burrow organized in Oklahoma City, A. J. Worley is named pastor. (This church was later known as Saint Luke's United Methodist Church.)

1890   *Our Brother in Red* does not mention the massacre of Sioux at Wounded Knee, South Dakota.

1897   Willis Folsom dies at the age of 73 after 55 years of preaching. "Most of that time he was a local preacher, but in his old age the Conference admitted him into full connection as a mark of love and recognition of his long and efficient service."[10]

1901   At this Conference Bishop Key announces that new churches will be built in Okmulgee, Lawton, Hobart, and Anadarko. The latter fails to be built at this time.

1902   General Conference is held in Dallas, Texas. J. M. Gross, S. G. Thompson, T. F. Brewer, C. F. Roberts are elected clerical delegates, N. B. Ainsworth, J. F. Quillian, J. M. Doss, and N. R. Dinsdale are elected lay delegates.

1904   The Reverend N. E. Waters (?) dies this year. He had concluded a revival, and after a baptismal service by immersion died of a cold.

1905   W. J. Sims, J. S. Lamar, T. F. Brewer, N. L. Linebaugh, and C. M. Coppedge are elected clerical delegates to the General Conference (1906) to be held in Birmingham. A. S. McKennon, J. W. Jackson, J. M. Doss, D. R. Rankin, and W. G. Ditzler are elected lay delegates.

1906   Bishop John J. Tigert, elected bishop in May, was to hold the
              Conference. While visiting in Atoka, Indian Territory, a few days
              before the opening of the Conference, a chicken bone lodged in
              his throat and started a local infection. He attempted to preside
              but, being unable to continue, asked Bishop Joseph Key to finish
              the Conference. Bishop Tigert then died.

              Samuel N. Jones and William Jimboy die. The last hours of Jim-
              boy, a full blooded Creek, are full of pain, but he dies singing
              "What wondrous love is this, oh my soul."

              The third morning of the Conference a change in name was voted. It was
              pointed out that the Indian and missionary character of the Conference
              had changed, and a committee was asked to consider whatever names
              might be suggested. This committee composed of N. L. Linebaugh, T. F.
              Brewer, P. R. Faglebarger, J. F. Thompson and J. J. Methvin, recom-
              mended that the name be changed to "Oklahoma Annual Conference."
              This motion was adopted. Thus after sixty-two years of missionary work
              among the Indians prior to being organized as a Conference, the work of
              the Indian Mission Conference came to a close and that of Oklahoma
              Annual Conference began, at the same time the two territories became a
              state.[11]

1907   Oklahoma attains statehood.

1910   There are fifteen Districts in the Oklahoma Conference at this
              time. Included among the presiding elders are W. U. Witt (Ard-
              more District), Alexander S. Williams (Choctaw-Chickasaw Indi-
              an District), and Orlando Shay (Creek-Cherokee District).

              It was voted to divide this Conference into the East and West Oklahoma
              Conferences, the line of division being a north-to-south line in the mid-
              dle of the state, running along the eastern boundary of Love, Carter,
              Murray, Garvin, McClain, Cleveland, Oklahoma, Logan, Noble and Kay
              counties. All full-blood Indian work among the Five Civilized tribes was
              placed in the East Oklahoma Conference, giving that conference eight dis-
              tricts, six white and two Indian districts. The West Oklahoma Conference
              was given seven districts, the Ardmore, Chickasha, Clinton, Guymon,
              Lawton, Mangum, and Oklahoma City districts.[12]

1913   The Reverend Milton E. Clark dies. "Brother Clark pioneered
              work among the wild tribes in 1887 and served as teacher, pastor
              and presiding elder."[13]

1918   Brewer Indian Mission (Oklahoma Indian Mission) organized by
              Bishop Mouzon.

1924   A. S. Williams dies (reported in minutes of East Oklahoma Annu-
              al Conference 1925), "a Choctaw minister and a brilliant inter-
              preter." He became the second Native American clergyman to be
              appointed as a district superintendent (the first was Samuel
              Checote).

1930   East and West Oklahoma Conferences are reunited. The first ses-
              sion of the reunited Oklahoma Conference meets in Boston

Avenue Methodist Church (October 29). This would have been the 85th session of the original Conference. A. Frank Smith presides.

1935   Johnson E. Tiger dies. Son of Moty Tiger, supreme judge of the Creek Nation, he had entered the ministry in 1903. He was a leader of the Indian Mission, which he represented in the 1930 General Conference.

Notes

1. Paul D. Mitchell, *From Tepees to Towers* (Oklahoma City, OK: Oklahoma Annual Conference, 1947), p. 24.
2. Ibid., p. 23.
3. Ibid., p. 25.
4. Ibid., p. 25.
5. Ibid., p. 26.
6. Ibid., p. 28.
7. Ibid., p. 29.
8. Ibid., p. 33.
9. Ibid., p. 42.
10. Ibid., p. 46.
11. Ibid., p. 47.
12. Ibid., p. 50.
13. Ibid., p. 50.

A P P E N D I X C
CONFERENCE–RELATED CHURCHES

Year Established	State	Church	First Pastor
ND	Wisconsin	Odanah	
1832	Wisconsin	Oneida	Daniel Adams
1867	Wisconsin	De Pere	
1832	Michigan	Zeba	
1845?	Michigan	Athens	
1861	Michigan	Greensky Hill Mission	
ND	Michigan	Mt. Pleasant	
1871	Michigan	Kewadin	
1839	Michigan	Bradley	
1916	Michigan	Salem	
1860	Michigan	Pinconing	Simon Greensky
	Michigan	Brethren (preaching point for pastor at Manstee)	
1875	Michigan	Saganing	Simon Greensky (beginning 1896)
1856	Michigan	North Port (not on Mikado Circuit)	Davis Thomas
1860	Michigan	Oscodo	John Tad-Gwo-Sune
			Simon Greensky (1st ordained pastor)
1850	Michigan	Hermansville	
1931	Michigan	Bay Mills	
1919	Michigan	Hubbard Lake	
1854	New York	Four Corners (Cattarougus Reservation)	Simon Greensky
1850	New York	Onondaga	John Timmerman
1847	New York	St. Regis (Hogansburg)	Founded by William Woodman (Oneida)
1844	New York	Cherokee Mission (East)	Rev. Wing

Appendix C—*continued*

Year Established	State	Church	First Pastor
1865	Washington	White Swan (Church built 1879)	James A. Wilbur
1875	Nevada	Walker River/Schurz Mission	
1872	Oregon	Siletz (abandoned 1966)	
1868	Oregon	Williamson River (Modoc Point)	John Howard
1908	Oregon	Beatty (Klamath, Modoc, Paiutte 1908 mission activity)	T. F. Royal / Mr. and Mrs. Peffley
1873	Oregon	Yainax (evolved into Beatty Mission)	James Harrar
1930	Oregon	Sprague River	
1872	California	Round Valley	John Burchard
1929	California	Garcia River Indian Mission (Pomo Tribe)	Ella Brown
1917	Minnesota	Nett Lake Mission (Chippewa)	Edwin E. Beach
ND	Minnesota	Sawyer Mission	
ND	Minnesota	White Earth (Pine Bend)	
ND	Minnesota	Isle (Preaching point)	
1930?	Minnesota	Leech Lake (preaching point: Sugar Point)	
1930	Minnesota	Red Lake (preaching point: Ponemah)	
1930	Washington	Del Norte Parish, Smith River, Washington (Tolowas tribe)	Miss Charlotte Hickman
1930		Gushchu Church	Miss Charlotte Hickman
1875	Washington	Nooksac	
ND	Washington	Nespelem	
1872	Idaho	Lapwai (Nez Perce Indian Mission)	
1876	Montana	Blackfeet Methodist Parish	John Young
1888		Browning United Methodist Church	
1960		Christ United Meth. Church, Babb	
ND		Heart Butte (under development)	
ND	Arizona	Phoenix Native American Ministries	Harry Long

1975	California	Los Angeles Native American Ministries	Oliver Neal
ND	Arizona	Yuma Mission	
1977	New Mexico	Four Corners Ministries	Brooks
		Shiprock (founded 1957)	
		Bisti (founded 1958)	
		Window Rock (founded 1983)	David Tutt
		Do'Wo'zhiibikooh United Methodist Church, Utah (founded 1983)	Raymond Burk, lay pastor
ND	New Mexico	Farmington	
1988	North Carolina	Charlotte	Sam Wynn
ND	Washington	Traceyton	Roy Wilson
1987	Michigan	Grand Rapids	Joe Sprague
1988	South Dakota	Sioux Ministries	Joe Dudley
1886	Alaska	Unalaska (the Jesse Lee Home)	John Carr
1897	Alaska	Alaska Mission	C. J. Larsen
1936	Alabama	Aldersgate	W.P. Patillo
1985	Kansas-Missouri	Greater Kansas All Tribes Fellowship	Patrick Freeman
1986	Colorado	Denver Native American Ministries	

Note: ND = no date.

A P P E N D I X D

Indian Methodist Churches in and near
Robeson County, North Carolina

		Date Est.
Pembroke	1 acre brick, 5 rooms	1906
Prospect	¼ acre frame, 1 room	1874
Sandy Plain	¼ acre frame, 1 room	1908
Pleasant Grove	6 acres	1912
Bethel	¼ acre	*
Thessalonia	¼ acre	*
Hopewell (S.C.)	¼ acre	*
New Dee Dee	¼ acre	*
Latta (S.C.)		
Hopewell (N.C.)	¼ acre	*
Collins Chapel		1960
Branch St.		1962
Fairview		1912
Hickory Grove		1910
Philadelphus		1958
Ashpole Center		1906
Coharrie		1963

Note: * = date unknown.

N O T E S

Chapter 1

1. Jerome O. Steffen, ed., *The American West: New Perspectives, New Dimensions* (Norman, Okla.: University of Oklahoma Press, 1969), p. 124.
2. Norris Handley, ed., *The American Indian: Essays from Pacific Historical Review* (Santa Barbara: Clio Press, 1974), p. 101.
3. Ibid., foreword.
4. Virgil Vogel, *This Country Was Ours* (Evanston, Ill.: Harper & Row, Harper Torchbooks, 1974), p. 94.
5. Barry Fell, *America B. C.: Ancient Settlers in the New World* (New York: Pocket Books, 1976), p. 15.
6. Ibid.
7. Ibid., p. 17.
8. Alvin Josephy, *The Indian Heritage of America* (New York: Bantam Books, 1969), p. 37.
9. Charles Panati, *Brower's Book of Beginnings* (Burlington, Mass.: Houghton Mifflin, 1984), pp. 151-52.
10. *World Book Eycyclopedia,* 1977, Vol. 4, p. 496.
11. Ibid.
12. William Cronon and Richard White, "Indians in the Land," *American Heritage Magazine* 37, no. 5 (Aug–Sept. 1986): 22.
13. Robert E. Spencer et al., *The Native Americans,* 2nd ed. (New York: Harper & Row, 1977), p. 132.
14. Charles W. Eliot, ed., *The Harvard Classics: American Historical Documents* (New York: P. F. Collier & Son, 1938), p. 51.
15. *Chronicles of American Indian Protest* (Greenwich, Conn.: Fawcett, 1971), p. 7.
16. Ibid.
17. Ibid., p. 8.
18. Eliot, *Harvard Classics,* p. 141.
19. William Warren Sweet, *The Story of Religion in America* (New York: Harper & Brothers, 1950), p. 156.
20. Ibid.
21. Eliot, *Harvard Classics;* p. 140.

22. David R. Wrone and Russell S. Nelson, Jr., *Who's the Savage?* (Greenwich, Conn.: Fawcett, 1973), p. 60.
23. Ibid.
24. Ibid., p. 61.
25. *Chronicles of American Indian Protest,* p. 10.
26. W. Crawford Barclay, *Early American Methodism: Missionary Motivation and Expansion, 1796–1844* (New York: Board of Missions and Home Extension, 1949), p. 231.
27. Sweet, *The Story of Religion,* p. 28.
28. Ibid., p. 34.
29. Ibid., p. 35.
30. Ibid.
31. Ibid., p. 38.
32. Ibid.
33. Ibid., p. 160.
34. Ibid., p. 35.
35. George C. Bedell, Leo Sandon, Jr., and Charles T. Wellborn, *Religion in America* (New York: Macmillan, 1975), p. 35.
36. Ibid.
37. Sweet, *The Story of Religion,* p. 162.
38. Ibid., p. 163.
39. Ibid.
40. Ibid., p. 164.
41. Sweet, *The Story of Religion,* p. 171.
42. *The New Encyclopaedia Britannica,* 15th ed., 1980, Micropaedia vol. 5, p. 128.
43. Sweet, *The Story of Religion,* p. 171.

Chapter 2

1. William Warren Sweet, *Methodism in American History* (Nashville: Abingdon Press, 1954), p. 33.
2. Josephy, *Indian Heritage,* p. 320.
3. Sweet, *Methodism in American History,* p. 41.
4. Gary B. Nash, *Red, White and Black: The Peoples of Early America* (Englewood Cliffs, N.J.: Prentice-Hall, 1974), pp. 349-50.
5. Ibid., p. 269.
6. Ibid.
7. Ibid., p. 243.
8. *The New Encyclopaedia Britannica,* Micropaedia vol. 10, p. 90.
9. Samuel Sewall, "On Accommodating the Indians," in *The Annals of America* (Chicago: Encyclopedia Britannica, 1976), vol. 1, p. 315.
10. Ibid.
11. Edward H. Spicer, *The American Indians: Dimensions of Ethnicity* (Cambridge: Harvard University Press, Belknap Press, 1982), p. 37.
12. Barclay, *Early American Methodism: Missionary Motivation and Expansion, 1796–1844,* p. 200.
13. Ibid., p. 201-202.
14. Sweet, *Methodism in American History,* p. 84.
15. Ibid., p. 89.
16. Ibid., p. 92.
17. Ross Phares, *Bible in Pocket, Gun in Hand: The Story of Frontier Religion* (Lincoln, Neb.: University of Nebraska Press, 1971), p. 2 (also see note 2 on p. 167).
18. Barclay, *Early American Methodism: Missionary Motivation and Expansion, 1796–1844,* p. 92.
19. Ibid., p. 85.

20. Phares, *Bible in Pocket,* p. 8.
21. Barclay, *Early American Methodism: Missionary Motivation and Expansion, 1796–1844,* p. 91.
22. Wrone and Nelson, *Who's the Savage?* p. 170.
23. Ibid., p. 199.
24. Phares, *Bible in Pocket,* p. 26.
25. Ibid., p. 76.

Chapter 3

1. Vogel, *This Country Was Ours,* p. 66.
2. Francis Paul Prucha, ed., *Documents of United States Indian Policy* (Lincoln, Neb.: University of Nebraska Press, 1975), p. 11.
3. Ibid., p. 12.
4. Ibid.
5. Ibid., p. 13.
6. Ibid., pp. 12-13.
7. Ibid., p. 13.
8. Moses Austin; "Exploring the Ohio Valley," in *Annals of America,* vol. 4, p. 3.
9. Sweet, *Methodism in American History,* p. 121.
10. Barclay, *Early American Methodism: Missionary Motivation and Expansion 1796–1844,* p. 201.
11. Ibid., p. 202.
12. Ibid.
13. Barclay, *Early American Methodism: Missionary Motivation and Expansion 1796–1844,* p. 202.
14. Richard A. Humphrey, "Cherokee Religious Experience in Southern Appalachia," 1984, unpublished manuscript, p. 19.
15. Anson West, *History of Methodism in Alabama* (Spartanburg, S.C.: The Reprint Company, in association with Commission on Archives and History, Alabama-West Florida Conference of The United Methodist Church, 1983), pp. 15-16.
16. Ibid., p. 26.
17. Ibid., p. 27.
18. Vine Deloria, Jr., ed., *Of Utmost Good Faith* (New York: Bantam Books, 1972), p. 11.
19. Ibid., p. 13.
20. Sweet, *The Story of Religion,* p. 68.
21. *Chronicles of Indian Protest,* pp. 4-5.
22. Ibid., pp. 61-62.
23. Deloria, *Of Utmost Good Faith,* p. 22.
24. Arthur H. DeRosier, Jr., *The Removal of the Choctaw Indians* (Evanston Ill.: Harper & Row, Harper Torchbooks, 1972), p. 10.
25. Sweet, *Methodism in American History,* p. 100.
26. Ibid., pp. 144-45.
27. Ibid., p. 143.
28. Josephy, *Indian Heritage,* p. 80.
29. Vogel, *This Country Was Ours,* p. 67.
30. Walter Jarrett, "Tecumseh," in Raymond Friday Locke, ed., *The American Indian* (Los Angeles: Mankind Publishing, 1976), p. 208.
31. E. O. Randall, "Tecumseh, the Shawnee Chief," *Ohio Archaeological and Historical Society Publications* 15 (1906): 429.
32. Locke, *The American Indian,* p. 208.
33. Ibid., p. 208.
34. Randall, "Tecumseh," p. 430.
35. Ibid., pp. 430-431.

36. Ibid., p. 431.
37. Ibid., p. 432.
38. Jarrett, "Tecumseh," p. 210.
39. Ibid.
40. Randell, "Tecumseh," p. 440.
41. Ibid., p. 441.
42. Ibid., p. 443.
43. *World Book Encyclopedia,* vol. 17, p. 30.
44. Jarrett, "Tecumseh," p. 215.
45. Ibid., p. 216.
46. Randall, "Tecumseh," p. 469.
47. Jarrett, "Tecumseh," p. 215.
48. Ibid., p. 222.
49. Ibid., p. 223.
50. Randall, "Tecumseh," p. 479.
51. *Chronicles of American Indian Protest,* pp. 77-78.
52. Dan Georgakas, *The Broken Hoop: The History of Native Americans from 1600 to 1890, from the Atlantic Coast to the Plains* (Garden City, N.Y.: Doubleday, Company, 1973), p. 33.
53. Randall, "Tecumseh," p. 487.
54. Ibid., p. 490.
55. Ibid., p. 492.

Chapter 4

1. Calvin D. Linton, ed., *The American Almanac* (Nashville: Thomas Nelson, 1977), p. 57.
2. Barclay, *Early American Methodism: Missionary Motivation and Expansion, 1796–1844,* p. 268.
3. Ibid., pp. 165-66.
4. John Randolph, "Against War with England," in *Annals of America,* vol. 4, p. 294.
5. Ibid., p. 294.
6. Ibid., p. 295.
7. Barclay, *Early American Methodism: Missionary Motivation and Expansion, 1796–1844,* pp. 186-87.
8. Ibid., p. 187.
9. Ibid., p. 162.
10. Ibid., p. 265.
11. Grant Foreman, *Indian Removal: The Emigration of the Five Civilized Tribes of Indians* (Norman, Okla.: University of Oklahoma Press, 1976), p. 19.
12. DeRosier, *Removal of the Choctaw Indians,* p. 28.
13. Ibid., p. 41.
14. Ibid., p. 40.
15. Almer Pennevell, *A Voice in the Wilderness* (Nashville: Parthenon Press, n.d.), p. 130.
16. Barclay, *Early American Methodism: Missionary Motivation and Expansion, 1796–1844,* p. 205.
17. Ibid., p. 101.
18. Ibid., p. 206.
19. Ibid., p. 209.
20. Ibid.
21. Barclay, *Early American Methodism: To Reform the Nation, 1796–1844,* p. 115.
22. Barclay, *Early American Methodism: Missionary Motivation and Expansion, 1796–1844,* pp. 2056.
23. Barclay, *Early American Methodism: To Reform the Nation, 1796–1844,* p. 112.

24. Don W. Holter, *Fire on the Prairie: Methodism in the History of Kansas* (Nashville: Parthenon Press, 1969), p. 38.
25. Methodist Episcopal Church, *Missionary Society Report,* 1824, appendix 30.
26. Barclay, *Early American Methodism: To Reform the Nation, 1976–1844,* p. 118.
27. Ibid., p. 119.
28. Ibid., p. 119.
29. Ibid., p. 122.
30. Ibid., p. 122.
31. Methodist Episcopal Church, *Missionary Society Report,* 1824, pp. 28-29.
32. Barclay, *Early American Methodism: To Reform the Nation, 1796–1844,* p. 123.
33. Methodist Episcopal Church, *Missionary Society Report,* 1825, p. 24.
34. Ibid.
35. Ibid., p. 26.
36. Ibid., p. 30.
37. Ibid.
38. Ibid.
39. Barclay, *Early American Methodism: To Reform the Nation, 1796–1844,* p. 124.
40. Ibid., p. 125.
41. Ibid.
42. Holter, *Fire on the Prairie,* p. 40.
43. Pennevell, *A Voice in the Wilderness,* p. 132.
44. Ibid., p. 135.
45. Ibid., p. 138.
46. Annual Conference of Southern Illinois, unpublished minutes, 1929.
47. Albert Pennevell, *A Voice in the Wilderness* (Nashville: Parthenon Press, n.d.), p. 140.
48. Barclay, *Early American Methodism: To Reform the Nation, 1796–1844,* p. 145.
49. Peter Jones, *Autobiography of Peter Jones,* n.p., n.d., p. 8.
50. Barclay, *Early American Methodism: To Reform the Nation, 1796–1844,* p. 165.
51. Methodist Episcopal Church, *Missionary Society Report,* 1824, p. 18, citing a letter from the Rev. William Case dated Oct. 7, 1823.
52. Methodist Episcopal Church, *Missionary Society Report,* 1825, p. 20.
53. Jones, *Autobiography,* p. 7.
54. Ibid.
55. Ibid., p. 8.
56. Ibid., p. 9.
57. Ibid., pp. 9-10.
58. Ibid., p. 11.
59. Ibid., p. 13.
60. Ibid., p. 14.
61. Barclay, Vol. 2, p. 155.
62. Ibid., p. 158.
63. Ibid., pp. 159-60.
64. Ibid., p. 160.
65. Ibid., p. 161.
66. Ibid., p. 146.
67. Ibid.
68. Ibid.
69. Ibid., p. 148.
70. [Black Hawk], *"Autobiography of Black Hawk, Life of Ma-ka-tai-me-she-kia-kiak or Black Hawk,"* in *Chronicles of American Indian Protest,* p. 102. (Originally published in 1834.)
71. Josephy, *Indian Heritage,* p. 318.
72. Barclay, *Early American Methodism: To Reform the Nation, 1796–1844,* pp. 171-72.

Chapter 5

1. Angie Debo, *The Rise and Fall of the Choctaw Republic* (Norman, Okla.: University of Oklahoma Press, 1972), p. 32.
2. DeRosier, *Removal of the Choctaw Indians,* p. 35.
3. Ibid.
4. Ibid., pp. 36-37.
5. Linton, *The American Almanac,* pp. 79-80.
6. Althea Bass, *Cherokee Messenger* (Norman, Okla.: University of Oklahoma Press, 1968), p. 31.
7. Debo, *Rise and Fall,* p. 43.
8. Ibid., p. 45.
9. Ibid.
10. Barclay, Vol. 2, p. 136.
11. DeRosier, *Removal of the Choctaw Indians,* p. 61.
12. Ibid., p. 64.
13. Ibid.
14. Ibid.
15. Ibid., p. 11.
16. Ibid., p. 81.
17. Ibid., p. 82.
18. Ibid., pp. 106-7.
19. Barclay, *Early American Methodism: To Reform the Nation, 1796–1844,* pp. 136-37.
20. Barclay, *Early American Methodism: To Reform the Nation, 1796–1844,* p. 137.
21. Foreman, *Indian Removal,* p. 23.
22. Prucha, *Documents,* p. 53.
23. Foreman, *Indian Removal,* pp. 39-40.
24. Ibid., p. 56.
25. John B. Davis, "The Life and Work of Sequoyah," *The Chronicles of Oklahoma* (1930): 169.
26. Barclay, *Early American Methodism: To Reform the Nation, 1796–1844,* p. 129.
27. DeRosier, *Removal of the Choctaw Indians,* p. 93.
28. *Chronicles of American Indian Protest,* p. 112.
29. Bass, *Cherokee Messenger,* pp. 100-101.
30. Ibid., p. 102.
31. Barclay, *Early American Methodism: To Reform the Nation, 1796–1844,* p. 131.
32. Ibid.
33. Ibid.
34. *Chronicles of American Indian Protest,* p. 126.
35. Barclay, *Early American Methodism: To Reform the Nation, 1796–1844,* p. 133.
36. Ibid., p. 138.
37. William T. Hagan, *American Indians* (Chicago: University of Chicago Press, 1961), p. 46.
38. Jesse Burt and Robert B. Ferguson, *Indians of the Southeast: Then and Now* (Nashville: Abingdon Press, 1973), p. 177.
39. Foreman, *Indian Removal,* p. 150.
40. Ibid., p. 153.
41. Sidney Henry Babcock and John Y. Bryce, *History of Methodism in Oklahoma* (Oklahoma City, Okla.: 1937) vol. 1, p. 119.
42. Foreman, *Indian Removal,* p. 187.
43. Ibid., p. 180.
44. Ibid., p. 181.
45. Ibid., p. 190.
46. Barclay, *Early American Methodism: To Reform the Nation, 1796–1844,* pp. 168-69.

Chapter 6

1. Nancie Peacocke Fadeley, *Mission to Oregon* (Eugene, Ore.: 1976), p. 8.
2. Ibid.
3. Barclay, *Early American Methodism: To Reform the Nation, 1796–1844*, p. 207.
4. Thomas D. Yarnes, *A History of Oregon Methodism* (Nashville: Parthenon Press, for the Oregon Methodist Conference Historical Society), p. 24.
5. Ibid.
6. Barclay, *Early American Methodism: To Reform the Nation, 1796–1844*, p. 207.
7. Yarnes, *History of Oregon Methodism*, p. 26.
8. Fadeley, *Mission to Oregon*, p. 1.
9. Barbara Leitch, *A Concise Dictionary of the Indian Tribes of North America* (Newport Beach, Calif.: Reference Publishers, 1979), p. 83.
10. Ibid., p. 84.
11. Barclay, *Early American Methodism: To Reform the Nation, 1796–1844*, p. 208.
12. James Daughtery, *Marcus and Narcissa Whitman: Pioneers of Oregon* (New York: Viking Press, 1961), p. 100.
13. Barclay, *Early American Methodism: To Reform the Nation, 1796–1844*, p. 223.
14. Daugherty, *Marcus and Narcissa Whitman*, p. 96.
15. Ibid., p. 127.
16. Ibid.
17. Ibid., p. 132.
18. J. Gaston, *The Centennial History of Oregon* (Chicago: S. J. Clark Publishing Co., n.d.), p. 59.
19. Ibid.
20. Barclay, *Early American Methodism: To Reform the Nation, 1796–1844*, pp. 262-63.
21. Adolph L. Dial and David K. Eliades, *The Only Land I Know: A History of the Lumbee Indians* (San Francisco: The Indian Historian Press, 1975), p. 44.
22. *Minutes of the General Conference of the Methodist Episcopal Church*, May 15, 1844.
23. Babcock and Bryce, *History of Methodism in Oklahoma*, p. 51.
24. Ibid., p. 171.
25. Ibid., p. 67.
26. Ibid., p. 66.
27. John W. Mitchell, *From Teepees to Towers* (Oklahoma City, Okla.: Oklahoma Annual Conference, 1947), p. 30.
28. Babcock and Bryce, *History of Methodism in Oklahoma*, p. 126.
29. Ibid., p. 91.
30. Holter, *Fire on the Prairie*, p. 41.
31. Babcock and Bryce, *History of Methodism in Oklahoma*, p. 90.
32. Ibid., p. 107.
33. Ibid., p. 109.
34. Ibid., p. 123.
35. Ibid., p. 125.
36. Ibid., p. 128.
37. Ibid., p. 129.
38. Ibid., p. 130.
39. John W. Morris, *Ghost Towns of Oklahoma* (Norman, Okla.: University of Oklahoma Press, 1986), p. 177.
40. Henry David Thoreau, "A Plea for Captain John Brown," in *Annals of America*, vol. 9, p. 140.
41. David Wallechinsky and Irving Wallace, *The People's Almanac* (Garden City, N.Y.: Doubleday, 1975), p. 180.
42. Babcock and Bryce, *History of Methodism in Oklahoma*, p. 132.
43. Dial and Eliades, *The Only Land I Know*, p. 46.
44. Babcock and Bryce, *The History of Methodism in Oklahoma*, p. 137.

45. Stan Hoig, *The Sand Creek Massacre* (Norman, Okla.: University of Oklahoma Press, 1982), pp. 19-20.
46. Holter, *Fire on the Prairie*, p. 43.
47. Hoig, *Sand Creek Massacre*, p. 24.
48. Ibid., p. 35.
49. Ibid., pp. 46-47.
50. Ibid., p. 51.
51. Ibid., pp. 52-53.
52. Ibid., p. 62.
53. Ibid., pp. 150-51.
54. Ibid., p. 158.
55. Ibid., p. 176.
56. Ibid.
57. *Chronicles of American Indian Protest*, p. 302.
58. Ibid., p. 305.
59. Ibid.
60. Ibid., p. 307.
61. Ibid., p. 308.
62. Babcock and Bryce, *History of Methodism in Oklahoma*, p. 145.
63. Ibid., p. 146.
64. Ibid., p. 339.

Chapter 7

1. Debo, *Rise and Fall*, p. 89.
2. Prucha, *Documents*, p. 102.
3. U.S. Bureau of Indian Affairs, *Commissioner of Indian Affairs Report*, 1889.
4. Ibid., p. 104.
5. Ibid., p. 108.
6. Ibid.
7. Ibid., p. 109.
8. Dial and Eliades, *The Only Land I Know*, p. 48.
9. Ibid., p. 87.
10. Ibid., p. 200.
11. Wallechinsky and Wallace, *The People's Almanac*, p. 194.
12. "On Permitting Women to Preach," in *Annals of America*, vol. 10, p. 375.
13. Ibid., p. 375.
14. Wallechinsky and Wallace, *The People's Almanac*, p. 195.
15. Red Cloud; "Indian Rights," in *Annals of America*, p. 243.
16. Robert M. Utley and Wilcomb E. Washburn, *The American Heritage History of the Indian Wars* (New York: American Heritage/Bonanza Books, 1982), p. 289.
17. Prucha, *Documents*, p. 95.
18. Ibid., p. 112.
19. Ibid., p. 144.
20. Ibid., p. 145.
21. Ibid., p. 149.
22. *Chronicles of American Indian Protest*, p. 258.
23. Ibid.
24. Prucha, *Documents*, p. 152.
25. Ibid., p. 153.
26. Ibid.
27. Ibid., p. 152.
28. Ibid., p. 157.
29. Ibid., p. 155.

30. Ibid., p. 156.
31. Ibid., p. 157.
32. Ibid.
33. Helen Hunt Jackson, *A Century of Dishonor* (New York: Harper & Row, Harper Torchbooks, 1965), p. vii.
34. *Chronicles of American Indian Protest*, p. 159.
35. Ibid., p. 167.
36. Ibid., p. 163.
37. Ibid.
38. Wrone and Nelson, *Who's the Savage?* p. 526.
39. Board of Home Missions, unpublished Board of Ministries report, 1931.
40. Lumbee River Legal Services, Inc. *The Lumbee Petition* (Pembroke, N.C.: Lumbee River Legal Services, Inc., 1986), vol. 1, 83.7 HN, p. 39.
41. Board of Home Missions, unpublished Board of Ministries report, 1931.
42. *Chronicles of American Indian Protest*, p. 163.
43. Yarnes, *History of Oregon Methodism*, p. 139.
44. Ibid., p. 140.
45. Ibid., p. 143.
46. Ibid., p. 144.
47. Board of Home Missions, unpublished Board of Ministries report, 1931, pp. 128-29.
48. W. Crawford Barclay, *The Methodist Episcopal Church: Widening Horizons, 1845–1895* (New York: Board of Missions and Home Extension, 1957), p. 357.
49. Ibid.
50. Ibid., p. 359.
51. Ibid.
52. Ibid., p. 342.
53. Duane Porter, *Autobiography of Duane Porter* [1934], p. 3.
54. Ibid., p. 4.
55. Ibid.
56. Ibid., p. 9.
57. Charles Purdham, *Fragile Starts: A History of United Methodist Ministries Among the Native People of Minnesota* (Bloomington, Minn.: 1985), p. 12.
58. Ibid., p. 15.
59. Barclay, *The Methodist Episcopal Church: Widening Horizons, 1845–1895,* p. 347.
60. Ibid., p. 351.
61. Ibid., p. 351.
62. Ibid.
63. "*Blackfeet Mission History* 1874 to 1949" (Browning, Mont.: Blackfoot Mission, 1949).
64. Babcock and Bryce, *History of Methodism in Oklahoma*, pp. 147-48.
65. Ibid., p. 149.
66. Ibid., p. 153.
67. John Y. Bryce, "Some Notes of Interest Concerning Early Day Operation in Indian Territory by the Methodist Church South," *Chronicles of Oklahoma* 4 (Mar.-Dec. 1926); pp. 233-241.
68. *Our Brother in Red* 1, no. 10, June 1883, p. 1.
69. Babcock and Bryce, *History of Methodism in Oklahoma*, p. 211.
70. Ibid.
71. Mitchell, From Teepees to Towers, p. 40.
72. *The Cherokee Advocate*, Nov. 17, 1882.
73. Ibid., p. 172.
74. Ibid., p. 182.
75. *Our Brother in Red* 1, no. 10, June 1883, p. 4.
76. Babcock and Bryce, *History of Methodism in Oklahoma*, p. 382.
77. Mitchell, *From Tepees to Towers*, p. 47.

Chapter 8

1. J. Tremayne Copplestone, *Twentieth-Century Perspectives: The Methodist Episcopal Church, 1896–1939* (New York: The Board of Global Ministries of The United Methodist Church, 1973), p. 871.
2. Ibid., p. 877.
3. Ibid., p. 882.
4. Ibid., p. 883.
5. Ibid., p. 863.
6. Ibid., p. 864.
7. R. Pierce Beaver, ed., *The Native American Christian Community: A Directory of Indian, Aleut, and Eskimo Churches* (Monrovia, Calif.: Missions Advanced Research and Communication Center, 1979), pp. 241-42.
8. Lumbee River Legal Services, *The Lumbee Petition,* p. 42.
9. Jerry Lowry, "A Brief History of Native American Methodist Missions," n.d., unpublished manuscript, p. 31.
10. Board of Home Missions, unpublished Board of Missions report, 1931.
11. Purdham, *Fragile Starts,* p. 16.
12. Board of Home Missions, unpublished Board of Missions report, 1931.
13. John Collier, *Indians of the Americas* (New York: The New American Library, 1947), p. 143.
14. Ibid.
15. Wrone and Nelson, *Who's the Savage?* pp. 484-87.
16. *Our Brother in Red,* vol. 1, no. 10, June 1883, p. 4.
17. Mitchell, *From Teepees to Towers,* p. 47.
18. *The Fulsom Forum,* July 15, 1923, letter from Johnson Bobb.
19. Oklahoma Indian Mission Conference, "Report of District Superintendent Byars Columbus," in *Oklahoma Indian Missions Conference Minutes,* 1946.
20. Oklahoma Indian Mission Conference, "Report of General Superintendent Dewey D. Etchison," in *Oklahoma Indian Missions Conference Minutes,* 1948.
21. Oklahoma Indian Mission Conference, "Report of District Superintendent Forbes Durant," in *Oklahoma Indian Missions Conference Minutes,* 1962.
22. Mitzi Frazier, "History, Religion Come Together," *Newsletter of the Round Valley United Methodist Church,* 1984.
23. *The Round Valley Circle,* Nov. 2, 1963, letter from the Rev. John M. Foster. Letter in the custody of the General Commission of Archives and History Madison, N. J.
24. Ibid.
25. "History of Round Valley Indian Mission," n.d., unpublished manuscript, p. 1.
26. *Shiprock First United Methodist Church,* n.d., pamphlet.
27. Paul West, "Navajo Find Christ Through 4 Corners Native American Ministry," n.d., unpublished manuscript.
28. *Response Magazine,* June 1985.
29. *Our Brother in Red,* vol. 1, no. 5, Jan. 1883, p. 6.
30. Ibid.
31. *Report to the Annual Charge Conference of the Norwalk First United Methodist Church,* Feb. 8, 1986.

BIBLIOGRAPHY

Alexander, Hartley Burr. *The World's Rim*. Lincoln, Neb.: University of Nebraska Press, 1967.

American Friends Service Committee. *Uncommon Controversy: Fishing Rights of the Muckleshoot, Puyallup,and Nisqually Indians*. Seattle, Wash.: University of Washington Press, 1970.

Annual Conference of Southern Illinois Conference of the Methodist Church. Unpublished minutes. 1929. Southern Illinois Conference of The United Methodist Church, Mt. Vernon, Ill.

The Annals of America. 20 vols. Chicago: Encyclopaedia Britannica, 1976.

Babcock, Sidney Henry, and John Y. Bryce. *History of Methodism in Oklahoma*. Vol. 1. Oklahoma City, Okla.: 1937.

Bahr, Howard M., Bruce A. Chadwick, and Robert C. Day, eds. *Native Americans Today, Sociological Perspectives*. Evanston, Ill.: Harper & Row, 1972.

Baird, W. David. *Peter Pitchlynn, Chief of the Choctaws*. Norman, Okla.: University of Oklahoma Press, 1972.

Barclay, W. Crawford. *Early American Methodism: Missionary Motivation and Expansion, 1769-1844*. Vol. 1 of *History of Methodist Missions*. New York: Board of Missions and Home Extension, 1949.

———. *Early American Methodism: To Reform the Nation, 1769-1844*. Vol. 2 of *History of Methodist Missions*. Vol. 1 of *History of Methodist Missions*. New York: Board of Missions and Home Extension, 1950.

———. *The Methodist Episcopal Church: Widening Horizons, 1845-1895*. Vol. 3 of *History of Methodist Missions*. New York: Board of Missions and Home Extension, 1957.

Barton, Garry Lewis. *The Life and Times of Henry Berry Lowry*. Pembroke, N.C. The Lumbee Publishing Co., 1979.

Bass, Althea. *Cherokee Messenger*. Norman, Okla.: University of Oklahoma Press, 1968.

Beaver, R. Pierce, ed. *The Native American Christian Community: A Directory of Indian, Aleut and Eskimo Churches*. Monrovia, Calif.: Missions Advanced Research and Communication Center, 1979.

Bedell, George C., Leo Sandon, Jr., and Charles T. Wellborn. *Religion in America*. New York: Macmillan, 1975.

Berkhofer, Robert. *Salvation and the Savage*. New York: Atheneum, 1972.

Oklahoma Historical Society. *Between Two Worlds, The Survival of Twentieth Century Indians*. Oklahoma City, Okla.: Oklahoma Historical Society, 1986.

"Blackfeet Mission History 1874 to 1949." Browning, Mont.: Blackfoot Mission, 1949. Photocopy.

Blue, Karen I. *The Lumbee Problem*. New York: Cambridge University Press, 1980.

Board of Home Missions and Church Extension of the Methodist Episcopal Church. *Unpublished Board of Ministries report*. 1931. The Board of Missions of The United Methodist Church, New York, N.Y. Board of Global Ministries, 475 Riverside Drive.

Bowle John. *Western Political Thought*. New York: Methuen University Paperbacks, 1961.

Bryce, John Y. "Some Notes of Interest Concerning Early Day Operation in Indian Territory by the Methodist Church South." *Chronicles of Oklahoma* 4 (Mar.-Dec. 1926): 233-241.

Burt, Jesse, and Robert B. Ferguson. *Indians of the Southeast: Then and Now*. Nashville: Abingdon Press, 1973.

Cahn, Edgar S. *Our Brother's Keeper: The Indian in White America*. Washington, D. C.: New Community Press, 1969.

Cartwright, Peter. *Autobiography of Peter Cartwright*. Nashville, Abingdon Press, 1984. (Originally published 1856.)

Ceram, C. W. *The First American: A Story of North American Archaeology*. New York: The New American Library, 1972.

The Cherokee Methodist Church. The Cherokee United Methodist Church, 1952. Pamphlet.

Chronicles of American Indian Protest. Greenwich, Conn.: Fawcett, 1971.

Clausen, Carl E., ed. *A Brief History of the Pine Bend Indian Mission*. [1970]. Available from Clavin Clark, Pine Bend Indian Mission, Rt. 1, Lengby, MN 56651.

Collier, John. *Indians of the Americas*. New York: The New American Library, 1947.

Collier, Peter. *When Shall They Rest?* New York: Holt, Rinehart, & Winston, 1973.

"Conference Colleges Part III: Ebenezer Manual Labor School." *The Central Illinois Historical Messenger* 10 (April-May-June 1978): 2.

Copplestone, J. Tremayne. *The Methodist Episcopal Church: Twentieth Century Perspectives, 1896-1939*. Vol. 4 of *History of Methodist Missions*. New York: The Board of Global Ministries, 1957.

Cronon, William, and Richard White. "Indians in the Land." *American Heritage Magazine* 37, No. 5 (Aug.-Sept. 1986): 18-25.

Cummings, Simeon, ed. *Summary Report, Southeastern Jurisdictional Association for Native American Ministries*. Pembroke, N.C.: Simeon Cummings, 1986.

Dale, Edward Everett. *The Indians of the Southwest*. Norman, Okla.: University of Oklahoma Press, 1976.

Daugherty, James. *Marcus and Narcissa Whitman: Pioneers of Oregon*. New York: Viking Press, 1961.

Davis, John B. "The Life and Work of Sequoyah." *Chronicles of Oklahoma* 8 (1930): 149-80.

Debo, Angie. *The Rise and Fall of the Choctaw Republic*. Norman, Okla.: University of Oklahoma Press, 1972.

Deloria, Vine, Jr., ed. *Of Utmost Good Faith*. New York: Bantam Books, 1972.

DeRosier, Arthur H., Jr. *The Removal of the Choctaw Indians*. Evanston, Ill.: Harper & Row, Harper Torchbooks, 1972.

Dial, Adolph L., and David K. Eliades. *The Only Land I Know: A History of the Lumbee Indians*. San Francisco: The Indian Historian Press, 1975.

Eliot, Charles W., ed. *The Harvard Classics: American Historical Documents*. New York: P. F. Collier & Son, 1938.

Fadeley, Nancie Peacocke. *Mission to Oregon*. Eugene, Ore.: 1976.

Fell, Barry. *America B. C.: Ancient Settlers in the New World*. New York: Pocket Books, 1976.

Forbes, Jack D., ed. *The Indian in America's Past*. Englewood Cliffs, N.J.: Prentice-Hall, 1964.

Foreman, Grant. *Indian Removal: The Emigration of the Five Civilized Tribes of Indians*. Norman, Okla.: University of Oklahoma Press, 1976.

Frazier, Mitzi: "History, Religion Come Together." *Newsletter of Round Valley United Methodist Church,* 1984. Available at P.O. Box 187, Colvelo, CA 95428.

Friends Committee on National Legislation. "Senator John McCain Speaks on Economic Development, Indian Policy." *Indian Report* I-29 (Spring 1988): 1-2.

Gaston, J. *The Centennial History of Oregon.* 4 vols. Chicago: S. J. Clark Publishing Co., n.d. Oregon Annual Conference Archives. Microfilm.

Georgakas, Dan. *The Broken Hoop: The History of Native Americans from 1600 to 1890, from the Atlantic Coast to the Plains.* Garden City, N.Y.: Doubleday, 1973.

Gordon, Milton M. *Assimilation in American Life.* New York: Oxford University Press, 1964.

Hagan, William T. *American Indians.* Chicago: University of Chicago Press, 1961.

Handley, Norris, ed. *The American Indian: Essays from Pacific Historical Review.* Santa Barbara: Clio Press, 1974.

Hendrickson, Kenneth D., Jr., ed. *Hard Times in Oklahoma: The Depression Years.* Oklahoma City, Okla.: Oklahoma Historical Society, 1983.

"History of Round Valley Indian Mission." N.d. Unpublished manuscript. Available from Round Valley United Methodist Church, P.O. Box 187, covels, CA 95428.

Hoig, Stan. *The Sand Creek Massacre.* Norman, Okla.: University of Oklahoma Press, 1982.

Holter, Don W. *Fire on the Prairie: Methodism in the History of Kansas.* Nashville: Parthenon Press, 1969.

Humphrey, Richard A. "Cherokee Religious Experience in Southern Appalachia." 1984. Unpublished manuscript. Available from the Rev. Richard A. Humphrey, Box 158, Lebanon, VA 24266.

Jackson, Helen Hunt. *A Century of Dishonor.* New York: Harper & Row, Harper Torchbooks, 1965.

———. *Ramona.* New York: Avon Books, 1970.

Jacobs, Wilbur R. *Dispossessing the American Indian.* New York: Charles Scribner & Sons, 1972.

Jennings, Francis. *The Invasion of America.* New York: W. W. Norton, 1975.

Jordan, H. Glenn, and Thomas M. Holm, eds. *Indian Leaders Oklahoma's First Statesmen.* Oklahoma City, Okla.: Oklahoma Historical Society, 1983.

Jones, Peter. *Autobiography of Peter Jones.* N.p., n.d. Microfilm. General Commission on Archives and History, The United Methodist Church, Madison, N.J.

Josephy, Alvin. *The Indian Heritage of America.* New York: Bantam Books, 1969.

———. *Red Power: The American Indian's Fight for Freedom.* New York: McGraw-Hill Paperbacks, 1971.

Katz, Jane, ed. *I Am the Fire of Time: The Voices of Native American Women.* New York: E. P. Dutton, 1977.

Kickingbird, Kirke, and Karen Ducheneaux. *One Hundred Million Acres.* New York: Macmillan, 1973.

Leckie, William H. *The Buffalo Soldiers.* Norman, Okla.: University of Oklahoma Press, 1967.

Leitch, Barbara. *A Concise Dictionary of the Indian Tribes of North America.* Newport Beach, Calif.: Reference Publishers, 1979.

Linton, Calvin D., ed. *The American Almanac.* Nashville: Thomas Nelson, 1977.

Locke, Raymond Friday, ed. *The American Indian.* Los Angeles: Mankind Publishing, 1976.

Lowry, Jerry. "A Brief History of Native American Methodist Missions." N.d. Unpublished Manuscript. Available from P.O. Box 1707, Pembroke, NC 28372.

Lumbee River Legal Services, Inc. *The Lumbee Petition.* Vol. 1. Pembroke, N.C.: Lumbee River Legal Services, Inc., 1986.

McNickle, D'arcy. *Native American Tribalism.* New York: Oxford University Press, 1973.

Marriott, Alice, and Carol K. Rachlin. *American Epic: The Story of the American Indian.* New York: The New American Library, 1969.

———. *American Indian Mythology.* New York: The New American Library, 1968.

Marshall, Peter, and David Manuel. *The Light and the Glory.* Old Tappan, N. J.: Fleming H. Revell, 1977.

Marty, Martin E. *Pilgrims in Their Own Land: 500 Years of Religion in America.* Little, Brown & Co., 1984.

Maxwell, James A., ed. *America's Fascinating Indian Heritage.* New York: Reader's Digest Association, 1978.

Methodist Episcopal Church. *Missionary Society Report.* 1824. General Commission on Archives and History, The United Methodist Church, Madison, N.J.

————. *Missionary Society Report.* 1825. General Commission on Archives and History, The United Methodist Church, Madison, N. J.

The Minutes of the General Conference of the Methodist Episcopal Church. May 15, 1844. General Commission on Archives and History, The United Methodist Church, Madison, N.J.

Milner, Clyde A. II, and Floyd A. O'neil, eds. *Churchmen and the Western Indians 1820–1920.* Norman, Okla.: University of Oklahoma Press, 1985.

Mitchell, Paul D. *From Tepees to Towers: A History of the Methodist Church in Oklahoma.* Oklahoma City, Okla.: Oklahoma Annual Conference, 1947.

Morris, John W. *Ghost Towns of Oklahoma.* Norman, Okla.: University of Oklahoma Press, 1986.

Nash, Gary B. *Red, White and Black: The Peoples of Early America.* Englewood Cliffs, N. J.: Prentice-Hall, 1974.

Native American International Caucus. *The Comprehensive Plan for Native American Ministries.* New York: The Board of Global Ministries of The United Methodist Church, 1988.

————. *The Sacred Circle of Life: A Native American Vision.* New York: The Board of Global Ministries of The United Methodist Church, 1988.

Oklahoma Indian Missions Conference. "Report of District Superintendent Byars Columbus." In *Oklahoma Indian Missions Conference Minutes.* 1946. Oklahoma City University Library Archives, Oklahoma City, Okla.

————. "Report of General Superintendent Dewey D. Etchison." In *Oklahoma Indian Missions Conference Minutes.* 1948. Oklahoma City University Library Archives, Oklahoma City, Okla.

————. "Report of District Superintendent Forbes Durant." In *Oklahoma Indian Missions Conference Minutes.* 1962. Oklahoma City University Library Archives, Oklahoma City, Okla.

"Oregon Mission: Dalls Station Journal." N.p., n.d. Report. General Commission on Archives and History, The United Methodist Church, Madison, N.J.

Panati, Charles. *Browser's Book of Beginnings.* Burlington, Mass.: Houghton Mifflin, 1984.

Pennevell, Almer. *A Voice in the Wilderness.* Nashville: Parthenon Press, n.d.

Phares, Ross. *Bible in Pocket, Gun in Hand: The Story of Frontier Religion.* Lincoln, Neb.: University of Nebraska Press, 1971.

Phillips, John Franklin. *The American Indian in Alabama and the Southeast.* 1987. Available from Frances Phillips, 412 N. Temple Ave., Fayette, AL 35555.

Porter, Duane. *Autobiography of Duane Porter.* [1934]. Minnesota Annual Conference Archives of the United Methodist Church. Minneapolis, Minnesota.

Prucha, Francis Paul, ed. *Documents of United States Indian Policy.* Lincoln, Neb.: University of Nebraska Press, 1975.

Purdham, Charles. *Fragile Starts: A History of United Methodist Ministries Among Native American People.* Bloomington, Minn., 1985.

Randell, E.O. "Tecumseh, the Shawnee Chief." *Ohio Archaeological and Historical Publications* 15 (1906): 418-97.

Reeves, Carolyn Keller, ed. *The Choctaw Before Removal.* Jackson, Miss.: University Press of Mississippi and Choctaw Heritage Press, 1985.

Reitman, Alan, ed. *The Pulse of Freedom.* New York: W. W. Norton, Mentor Books, 1975.

Report to the Annual Charge Conference of the Norwalk First United Methodist Church. Feb. 8, 1986. Available from Norwalk United Methodist Church, Norwalk, Calif.

Reuter, Mrs. Floyd. *Methodist Missions to Indians of Michigan.* N.d. Booklet. Available from West Michigan Conference Office of Advance Specials, West Michigan Conference, Grand Rapids, Mich.

Self, Huber, and Melvin Self. *Growing up in Indian Territory.* Manhattan, Kans.: AAG Press, 1932.

Skipworth, Walton. *Oregon Mission and Methodism in the Klamath Country.* Portland, Ore.: Oregon Historical Society, 1937.

Shiprock First United Methodist Church. N.d. Pamphlet. Available from The First United Methodist Church, Shiprock, NM 87420.

Smith, Robert E., ed. *Oklahoma's Forgotten Indians.* Oklahoma City, Okla.: Oklahoma Historical Society, 1981.

Spencer, Robert F., Jesse D. Jennings, Elden Johnson, Arden R. King, Theodore Stern, Kenneth M. Stewart, William J. Wallace. *The Native Americans.* 2nd ed. New York: Harper & Row, 1977.

Spicer, Edward H. *The American Indians: Dimensions of Ethnicity.* Cambridge: Harvard University Press, Belknap Press, 1982.

Steffen, Jerome O., ed. *The American West: New Perspectives, New Dimensions.* Norman, Okla.: University of Oklahoma Press, 1969.

Steiner, Stan. *The New Indians.* New York: Dell, 1968.

Sweet, William Warren. *Methodism in American History.* Nashville: Abingdon Press, 1954.

———. *The Story of Religion in America.* New York: Harper & Brothers, 1950.

Thurman, Melvena, ed. *Women in Oklahoma, A Century of Change.* Oklahoma City, Okla.: Oklahoma Historical Society, 1982.

Tibbles, Thomas Henry. *The Ponca Chiefs: An Account of the Trial of Standing Bear.* Lincoln, Neb.: University of Nebraska Press, 1972.

U.S. Bureau of Indian Affairs. *Commissioner of Indian Affairs Report.* 1889.

Utley, Robert M., and Wilcomb E. Washburn. *The American Heritage History of the Indian Wars.* New York: American Heritage/Bonanza Books, 1982.

Vogel, Virgil. *This Country Was Ours.* Evanston, Ill.: Harper & Row, Harper Torchbooks, 1974.

Wallechinsky, David, and Irving Wallace. *The People's Almanac.* Garden City, N.Y.: Doubleday, 1975.

West, Anson. *History of Methodism in Alabama.* Spartanburg, S.C.: The Reprint Company, in association with the Commission on Archives and History, Alabama-West Florida Conference of The United Methodist Church, 1983.

West, Paul. "Navajo Find Christ Through 4 Corners Native American Ministry." N.d. Unpublished manuscript. Available from Paul West, P.O. Box 657, Shiprock, NM 87420.

Wisler, Clark. *Red Man Reservations.* New York: Macmillan, Collier Books, 1971.

National Geographic Society. *The World of the American Indian.* Washington, D.C.: National Geographic Society, 1974.

Wrone, David R., and Russell S. Nelson, Jr. *Who's the Savage?* Greenwich, Conn.: Fawcett, 1973.

Yarnes, Thomas D. *A History of Oregon Methodism.* Nashville: Parthenon Press, for the Oregon Methodist Conference Historical Society, n.d.

Yazzie, Fred. "Navaho Churches Minister at Four Corners." *Response Magazine* (June 1985): 18, 19, 36.

I N D E X